SITTING DUCKS!

A few determined men pushed on until they reached midstream, but the panic-stricken screams of those drowning in the river had alerted the enemy. A single rifle shot rang out. It seemed to act as a signal. Suddenly the whole eastern bank burst into hectic activity. The star shells burst above the Americans trapped in the middle of the river. The slaughter had commenced. . . .

Jove Books by Charles Whiting

48 HOURS TO HAMMELBURG
PATTON'S LAST BATTLE

PATTON'S LAST BATTLE

CHARLES WHITING

JOVE BOOKS, NEW YORK

PATTON'S LAST BATTLE

A Jove Book / published by arrangement with
Stein and Day, Incorporated

PRINTING HISTORY
Stein and Day edition published 1987
Jove edition / December 1990

ISBN: 0-515-10477-9

Jove Books are published by the Berkley Publishing Group,
200 Madison Avenue, New York, New York 10016.
The name ''JOVE'' and the ''J'' logo
are trademarks belonging to Jove Publications, Inc.

PRINTED IN THE UNITED STATES OF AMERICA

10   9   8   7   6   5   4   3   2   1

ACKNOWLEDGMENTS

For assistance with this book, I should like to thank M. Jean Milmeister, Luxembourg, Mr. Tom Stubbs, Bitburg Air Base, Germany, *Stadtarchiv* Bitburg, Prum, Bad Toelz, Sir Kenneth Strong (deceased), Mr. Hy Schorr, New York.

I should also like to thank that large number of humble Luxembourg and German citizens, all old people now, living with their memories, who related their experiences of those far-off days when General Patton's Third Army burst into their humdrum lives with such startling suddenness . . .

C.W.
Wittlich, West Germany
January 1986

Contents

ILLUSTRATIONS

Patton and other generals in Luxembourg
Patton and Bradley with their staffs
Working on a frozen machine gun
American tanks cross the Our River
Barrage commences on the Our-Sauer river line
Terrified German villagers
Wittlich's main street
Suspected snipers
Bitburg after its capture
Women raped by Red Army
Occupied Mainz
Making ready for a Rhine crossing
Crossing the Rhine under fire
Mauldin's lampoon of Patton's Third Army
German toddler rebuilding
Civilians unload supplies
Surrendering weapons
Standing in line in Frankfurt
Patton as newly appointed governor of Bavaria
Patton with female admirers
Army hospital in Heidelberg
Patton is carried to the grave
Patton's grave site
Inscription on Patton's grave

PATTON'S
LAST BATTLE

INTRODUCTION

If I were fierce, and bald, and short of breath
I'd live with scarlet Majors at the Base,
And speed glum heroes up the line to death . . .
And when the war is done and youth stone dead,
I'd toddle safely home and die—in bed.
— SIEGFRIED SASSOON

It was exactly *five minutes after midnight!* On the morning of
Monday, January 1, 1945, the year in which the greatest war
ever fought would come to an end and a new age commence.

On the minute, after a bombastic trumpet fanfare so typical
of that vulgar, cruel, jackbooted empire, whose master
boasted it would last a thousand years, he began to shout
shrilly but confidently into the microphone, "Our people are
resolved to fight this war to victory under any and all circumstances . . . We are going to destroy everybody who does not
take part in the common effort . . .

"The world must know that this State will, therefore, never
capitulate . . . Germany will rise like a phoenix from its ruined cities and this will go down in history as the miracle of
the twentieth century!"

Adolf Hitler, who had exactly five more months to live,
paused and then roared, "I want, therefore, as spokesman of
Greater Germany to promise solemnly to the Almighty that
we shall fulfill our duty faithfully and unshakably in the New
Year, too, in the firm belief that the hour will strike when
victory will ultimately come to him who is most worthy of
it—the Greater German Reich!"

As that coarse, guttural Austrian voice died away in Berlin,
far away in snowbound, embattled Belgium, every gun of the
U.S. Third Army burst into angry life. For twenty crazy,
earsplitting minutes, the American gunners plastered the German positions with rapid fire. It was the Third Army's flamboyant commander's unique way of wishing the enemy an

unhappy New Year. Fire, steel, and sudden death—it was typical of him.

As the unhappy Germans, crouched in their freezing foxholes and fortified barns, received this lethal salute "in sullen silence," the dogfaces, bearded, hollow-eyed, weary from the weeklong battle, were assembled. Their commanders had been ordered by headquarters to read out his New Year's greeting to his men. With the explosions echoing and re-echoing angrily among the low hills that fringed the Bastogne front, these men, many of whom were fated to die this 1945, listened in the snow, as that flowing, flowery message flowed on and on.

"From the bloody corridor at Avranches, to Brest, thence across France to the Saar. . . . Over the Saar into Germany, and now on to Bastogne, your record has been one of continuous victory. . . . Not only have you defeated a cunning and ruthless enemy. . . . But also you . . . have overcome by your indomitable fortitude every aspect of terrain and weather. Neither heat nor dust nor floods and snow have stayed your progress. The speed and brilliancy of your achievements is unsurpassed in military history . . . My New Year wish and sure conviction for you is that . . . you will continue your victorious course to the end, that tyranny and vice shall be eliminated, our dead comrades avenged and peace restored to a war-weary world . . ."

Then the whistles shrilled and that old, old cry sounded once again, "Okay, men, let's go!" and they were slogging forward through the snow once more, each man wrapped in a cocoon of his own thoughts, bodies tensed for what must soon come . . .

Fifty miles behind the front, as it grew lighter and one thousand German planes swooped in to celebrate the New Year by shooting up Allied airfields throughout the Low Countries and France, and yet another German counterattack, eight divisions strong, was launched against the U.S. Seventh Army in Alsace,* the staff worried about casualties. The Third Army had already lost thousands of men killed, wounded, and captured—three thousand in one day alone

---

*See C. Whiting, *Operation Northwind: The Unknown Battle of the Bulge* for further details.

since Dec. 22, 1944—their highest losses since they had first gone into action five months before.

That morning General John Millikin, commander of the U.S. III Corps, called Third Army headquarters to inquire about reinforcements for his badly depleted divisions. The savage fighting of the last week had consumed riflemen faster than they could be replaced. The combat divisions were 12,000 men—the equivalent of a whole division—under-strength; and there were no more replacements in the pipeline until January 10.

Anxiously, Millikin explained to the deputy chief-of-staff, Colonel Paul Harkins, that he had only two battalions of infantry left in reserve. Harkins laughed. "General," he said, "you had better not let the Commanding General know you have two battalions. They are not only *your* reserve, but that's all the *Army* has in reserve. If the general hears you've got them, he'll commit them, sure as hell!"

Two battalions in reserve in an Army that numbered that day 353,655 men!

But that Commanding General, as he faced the press for his first conference in 1945 at his headquarters in Luxembourg City's *Fondation Pescatore,** exuded confidence. Tall and immaculate, with a brick-red face, imposing forehead, and silver-gray hair, he fixed the correspondents with his shrewd, expressive blue eyes and began to lecture them in that incongruously high-pitched voice of his. The elegantly tailored, imperious figure was unmistakably Caesar, but the voice was strictly Caspar Milquetoast! In spite of the fact that he would confide to his diary in three days' time that "we can still lose this war," his every word proclaimed victory. "The purpose of this operation, as far as Third Army is concerned," he squeaked, "is to hit this son-of-a-bitch—pardon me," he grinned, showing his dingy, ground-down teeth, "in the flank. And we did it, with the result that he is damned well stopped and going back."

Furiously the correspondents scribbled, while the German guns boomed in the distance, for now they were shelling Luxembourg City itself. The speech was a patent lie, for at that very moment the first of seven strong German counterattacks

*The Pescatore Foundation, today an old folks' home.

against his Army had commenced. The general was whistling in the dark.

"To me," he continued, "it is a never-ending marvel what our soldiers can do. . . . The people who actually did it were the youngest officers and soldiers. . . . Marching all night in the cold, over roads they had never seen, and nobody getting lost, and everybody getting to the place on time—it is a very marvelous feat. I know of no equal to it in military history. . . . I take my hat off to them!" The tall, imposing, general, minus his usual gleaming, lacquered helmet with its outsize three stars, made a symbolic gesture.

The correspondents, huddled in their coats, for coal was in short supply in the Pescatore Foundation, laughed. The commanding general was always good for a laugh. Invariably he provided good copy. The editors back home in the States loved it.

"The only way you can win a war is to attack—and keep on attacking," he continued, "and after you have done that, keep attacking some more." He concluded with, "We have to push people beyond endurance in order to bring this war to its end. . . . Thank you, gentlemen." Courteously, he dismissed the newspapermen, whom he knew were his lifeline to the Great American Public and the headlines he craved like a drug; although he disliked many of the journalists and felt, with that persecution complex of his, that they were out to "get" him. A year ago he had been in disgrace. He had slapped a private soldier suffering from "combat fatigue," and the papers had gotten hold of the story. Eisenhower, his boss, had taken his army away from him and his onetime subordinate, Gen. Omar Bradley, who was five years younger and had never seen any action in his whole career, had been given the plum job of commanding all American forces in the invasion of Europe.

To bolster up his spirits, then, he had written on New Year's Eve 1943, "My destiny is sure and I am a fool and a coward even to have doubted it. I don't any more. Some people are needed to do things and they have to be tempered by adversity as well as thrilled by success. I have had both. Now for some more success . . . Destiny will keep me floating down the stream of fate."

Destiny had. Now he commanded a great American army,

fighting to save a general whom he had characterized that miserable New Year of a year before, thus, "At Benning . . . he failed to get discipline. At Gafsa . . . he suggested we withdraw . . . In Sicily . . . he bolted . . . in fear."

Now, once again, this fiery, romantic, and unique commander was in charge. Given easily to tears and emotional outbreaks, unsure of himself, given to attacks of near hysteria, sensitive in spite of his customary vulgar profanity, he had taught himself by sheer, naked willpower to become a military leader. "The leader," he had once written, "must be an actor" and have "the fixed determination to acquire the warrior soul" and "is unconvincing unless he lives his part."

But where does the real man cease and the "actor" commence? By 1945, the commanding general, or so it seemed, could no longer distinguish between the two personalities; between the real man and the swashbuckling, flamboyant actor.

Only a week before he had addressed an extraordinary "prayer" to God, talking to Him as an equal, *demanding* that God take sides. "Damn it, Sir, I can't fight a shadow," he had complained. "Without Your cooperation from a weather standpoint, I am deprived of an accurate disposition of the German armies and how in the hell can I be intelligent in my attack? All this probably sounds unreasonable to You, but I have lost all patience with Your chaplains who insist this is typical Ardennes winter, and I must have faith. Faith and patience be damned! You have got to make up Your mind whose side You're on. You must come to my assistance so that I may dispatch the entire German Army as a birthday present to Your Prince of Peace. . . ."* What does one make of a soldier who promises God's Son, "The Prince of Peace," dead Germans by the thousands as a "Christmas present"? Where does the playacting end and the dementia begin?

What does one make of a three-star general who addresses his young soldiers going into battle for the first time with a speech like this, his standard one for giving to enlisted men: "We'll win this war, but we'll win it only by fighting and showing the Germans that we've got more guts than they

*M. Blumenson, *Patton Papers*

have—or ever will have. We're not going to shoot the sons-of-bitches, we're going to rip out their living goddam guts and use them to grease the treads of our tanks! We're going to murder those lousy Nazi cocksuckers by the bushel-fucking-basket! War is a bloody, killing business. You've got to spill their blood, or they will spill yours. Rip them up the belly! Shoot them in the guts! When shells are hitting all around you and you wipe the dirt off your face and realize that instead of dirt it's the blood and guts of what was your best friend beside you, you'll know what to do . . . We are going to go through him like crap through a goose! Like shit through a tin horn!''

Addressing a rally in Boston, his adopted hometown, he strutted to the platform, impeccably groomed as ever, and declared, ''It is foolish and wrong to mourn the men who died. Rather we should thank God that such men lived.'' Pointing to four hundred wounded soldiers of his own Army, seated in a special section, he said, ''These men are the heroes.'' Drawing himself up to his full height, the general saluted them dramatically. Was it surprising that the many mothers and widows of his soldiers wrote in protest to the President and that one of the Commanding General's most articulate critics commented, ''These utterances are atrocities of the mind; atrocities in being communicated *not* to a psychoanalyst but to great numbers of soldiers, civilians, and school children; and atrocious as reflections of what war-making has done to the personality of Patton himself.''*

Naturally, we are talking about General George S. Patton, the most flamboyant American soldier of World War II, perhaps of the whole of the twentieth century: a man who became a legend in his own time and, since the appearance of the movie *Patton: Lust for Glory*, in which that fine actor George C. Scott portrayed him, larger than life, something of an American folk hero.

His men, as one of them wrote much later, ''usually started by loathing their overpublicized, overdressed, ostentatious general, and ended by respecting him for the very good military reason that his rough disciplinary methods and skillful

*Dwight Macdonald in C. Whiting, *Patton*.

tactics saved many of their lives. They almost always, I think, disliked Ol' Blood and Guts—*his guts, our blood!*"*

Now in this last year of his life, General Patton had over a third of a million (in April 1945 nearly half a million) young American soldiers under his autocratic command. These men he would command as if they were a private army, almost like a personal chattel; for by the start of 1945, Eisenhower, the Supreme Commander, had virtually lost control of his field armies. With some *eight million* soldiers of a dozen varying nationalities, ranging from Algerians to New Zealanders, at his orders, it had become virtually impossible for "Ike" to retain control. In the case of Patton, Eisenhower visited his Army in the fall of 1944 and not again for another six months, by which time the war was virtually over.

In essence, Eisenhower relied on Bradley, his army group commander, to keep control of the headstrong, moody commander of the Third Army. But the Bradley-Patton relationship was so badly flawed that the former, too, was unable to exercise any real authority over his onetime chief, Patton. After a two year love-hate relationship between the two generals, Bradley, by the start of 1945, now found himself in a position where he was indebted to Patton, owing him favors. Patton had saved his bacon during the Battle of the Bulge and had stuck by him in the subsequent after-battle recriminations, accusations, and counteraccusations.

Although a subordinate role was envisaged for Patton's Third Army in the coming Battle for Germany, Patton would consistently involve his Third in what he would term "an armored reconnaissance" and then, when his young soldiers were committed, turn the "reconnaissance" into a full-scale campaign. Bradley, for his part, would stand by impotently, knowing that these battles had not been authorized by Eisenhower, and, in the end, would acquiesce tamely when they seemed to be going successfully. Thus it would appear that Patton was fighting a private war, of which Eisenhower and Washington knew little or nothing until they were faced with a typical Patton *fait accompli*: a war conducted for Patton's personal amusement and advancement.

Patton, it seems, was motivated by the almost pathological

*Constantine FitzGibbon in C. Whiting, *Patton*.

feeling that he was being passed over in favor of younger and less worthy American commanders. Men who had graduated from the Point years later than he, men of much less talent and experience, were receiving those precious silver stars, on which he doted, earlier than he.

Of his hated rival Gen. Mark Clark, who received his fourth star before he did, Patton wrote bitterly, "I wish something would happen to Clark." To his fellow Gen. William Simpson, he complained, "Isn't it peculiar that three old farts like us [Simpson, Courtney Hodges, and Patton] should be carrying the ball for those sons-of-bitches!" He meant his two much younger bosses, Eisenhower and Bradley. But in this last year of his life General Patton seemed to be motivated by a much more deep-seated malaise than envy. A psychoanalyst peering into his mind would surely have been fascinated by his obsession with killing—and being killed. For as his Army crossed into Hitler's Reich and began that last campaign, Patton frequently uttered the fervent desire to be killed "by the last bullet of the last battle." On the last evening of his last leave in the U.S.A., he told his children, "I have not been a good enough man in my life to be killed by a bullet like General Bee at Manassas. I don't know how it is going to happen, but I'm going to die over there!"

That was exactly what happened. After his tragic automobile accident, Patton died—ironically enough—not on the battlefield, *but in bed*! But why this strange death wish in a fit-enough man of fifty-nine, who well might have lived on to a great old age?

Was it connected with a personality conflict, an inner feeling that life and time were passing him by? We know that his sexual prowess and reputation as "a cocksman" were very much on his mind throughout that last year. At fifty-nine, commanding the destinies of nearly half a million young men and involved in a major war, Patton was greatly concerned with his sex life. While Eisenhower, who was five years younger, had already been rendered impotent (if we are to believe the indiscretions of Kay Summersby*), by the awe-

---

*His English *chauffeuse*, or driver, and, according to some authorities, his lover.

some burdens of command, Patton was involved with at least two women.

One was an unknown Englishwoman who lived near his former headquarters in Knutsford. She had taken the place of a Mary June Cooper, who had been his mistress in Africa. When Patton went to visit the unknown Englishwoman at Knutsford just after the war, he told his crony Gen. Everett Hughes that he was taking nine condoms with him. Afterward he boasted to Hughes that he had used four of them in three days.

The other was his niece, Jean Gordon, of whom he confided to Hughes in a strangely old-fashioned manner that "she has been mine" for twelve years. Jean Gordon, in the guise of a Red Cross doughnut girl, would appear periodically at Patton's various headquarters throughout the campaign—Nancy, Luxembourg, Regensburg—acting as hostess to "visiting firemen" and *more*. Two weeks after Patton died, she would put her head in the gas oven of her New York apartment and commit suicide. According to some sources, she left behind her a note stating, "I will be with Uncle Georgie in heaven and have him all to myself before Beatrice arrives."*

Patton's sexual peccadilloes, whatever may be thought of them, were the least of his problems at this time. Ever since his fall from grace in Sicily, he had developed what can only be described as severe paranoia. He felt that somehow he was above the law, the normal code of conduct of a general officer, on whom the lives of nearly half a million young soldiers depended. He felt, too, that he was justified in indulging himself in flashes of euphoria, alternating with moods of black despair. In his opinion, he could afford to be backbiting, petulant, even downright childish—that is if he were ever aware that he was being these things.

Eisenhower, for instance ("the best general the British have") would be addressed as "Sir Dwight" or "Divine Destiny"—a play on his initials, "D.D." He would write Eisenhower wounding letters, such as the one in which he

*Beatrice Patton, the general's long suffering wife, the woman Patton feared more than the German Army. Source: D. Irving. *The War Between the Generals*.

complained about the behavior of Captain Butcher, Eisenhower's aide and PR man—"Harry Butcher, KC, CT, SS, SOB etc"—stating, "I would further call your attention to the fact that he referred to you as a three-inch man (a three-bottle man would have been all right) and cast some doubts as to your ability of becoming the First Father of the Country at your present age." In what he apparently supposed was a humorous manner, Patton concluded, "While not wishing to push myself, I should be very happy to fulfill the duties of president of the courtmartial court before which you will indubitably send him, or as his defense counsel. In either position, I can assure you of a conviction!"

Lieutenant General Bernard Montgomery was a "little fart" who he could "outfight anytime." General Bedell Smith, Eisenhower's Chief-of-Staff: "the son-of-a-bitch" was "selfish, dishonest, and very swell-headed." Hodges, the U.S. First Army commander, was "dumb. He is also very jealous of me." Eisenhower was "bitten by the Presidential Bug and he is yellow." On and on this litany of childish, self-indulgent peevishness went, without any restraint, expressed in front of the most junior officers, with no concern that these wounding insults might one day reach the persons they referred to.

After the war ended, Patton seemed to throw all restraint to the wind. He acquired another—and very dangerous—pet hate, the Russians. Since he had first landed in Africa in November 1942, he had grown to hate one nation after the other. First he had come to loathe the Arabs. Then it was the Sicilians. He told his staff he could not understand how Arabs could share their tumbledown hovels with their animals. Arriving in Sicily, he added that now he couldn't understand how the *animals* could live with the Sicilians in their yards! Thereafter had come the British and, to some extent the French, followed by Polish Jews who made him "physically sick." Indeed, it almost seemed that the only nation that he admired without reservation was the erstwhile enemy, the Germans!

By June 1945, Patton was writing to his wife that "we have destroyed what could have been a good race and we [are] about to replace them with Mongolian savages." Two months later he would note in his diary, "I have no particular desire to understand them [the Russians], except to ascertain how much lead or iron it takes to kill them.''

Steadily his phobia mounted until he could snort to a superior over an unsecured telephone line, ''In ten days I can have enough incidents happen to have us at war with those sons-of-bitches [the Russians] and make it look like their fault. So much so that we will be completely justified in attacking them and running them out!''

The mind boggles. Whatever one might think of the correctness of Patton's point of view forty-odd years later, there is something bordering on the insane in Patton's suggesting this in August 1945. Weeks after the ending of that horrific, catastrophic conflict known as World War II, Patton was advocating attacking a former ally and starting World War III! The very thought takes one's breath away. How could any responsible person, with great power at his disposal, even begin to think that way?

Perhaps the title of Christopher Leopold's outrageous *M.A.S.H.*-type novel aptly sums up what seemed to be happening to General Patton that summer? It was: *Blood and Guts Is Going Nuts.**

Fortunately for General Patton—and perhaps for many of his young soldiers—that eventuality did not take place. That strange, so opportune accident of December 1945, which brought the general's life to an abrupt end, ensured that there would be no more brash loose talk—and no ''incidents.'' It also ensured that the general's wartime reputation remained unmarred. Although his staff was already beginning to worry about the state of his mental health, General Patton died a sane and rational man. At least, it was impossible to prove otherwise.

Now the general, with his flamboyant and eccentric style, could enter the simplistic, popular, folk mythology as a genuine folk hero: an uncomplicated black-and-white figure, untroubled by dark thoughts and contradictions of character.

---

*Published in 1976, the novel depicts General Patton involving his Third Army in a shooting war with the Russians. As the *London Sunday Times* commented on it: ''This book is not history; but it just could have been.''

Hereafter, the Great American Public would see General Patton through the eyes of his latter-day hagiographers, who knew all too well what an excellent money-spinner their larger than life subject was.

The movie of 1970—*Patton: Lust for Glory*—helped to rekindle the flagging legend of the profane, vulgar, aggressive, but war-winning Great Captain, who had lived in a time that now seemed as remote to the great majority of ordinary Americans as the Middle Ages. In short, Patton was a great soldier and a great man in the best American tradition.

But, in essence, Patton was neither a great man nor a great soldier. If he had not lived, it would not have mattered one little bit. His existence did not change the course of human events one iota. He made no contribution to the betterment of man. Nor was he a dreamer of some vast scheme that lived on after his death. Alive or dead, the world would not have missed him greatly.

Nor was he a Great Captain. He initiated no new tactics, such as Guderian's and von Manstein's concept of the *Blitzkrieg*. He made no awesome, overwhelming, irrevocable military decision, such as the one Eisenhower made when he decided to go ahead with D-Day, which could decisively affect the course of the war. He fought no decisive battle such as Montgomery did at El Alamein, or the unknown General Alexander Patch in Alsace. If his Third Army had been defeated during the Battle of the Bulge, it would have been a serious blow for the Allies. But it would not have had a serious influence on the outcome of World War II. If Patch, fighting in the same battle further south, had been defeated, however, de Gaulle's government might well have been overthrown and France flung into chaos. That would have been a near mortal blow for the Western Coalition.

Never once did he fight a set-piece battle successfully. He had neither the patience nor the organizational talent for such a task. Once his armor had ceased rolling in Lorraine in the fall of 1944 and he was committed to a slogging match outside the fortress of Metz, his dash and verve turned into impotent rage. It would take him three months of quite uncoordinated attacks before he finally overcame the last fort at Metz. Patton's real strength lay in the ability to maneuver, motivate, and move large masses of armor swiftly against relatively light opposition. He had no talent for an infantry slogging match, which was what the war in Europe became in 1944/45 once the Allies reached the frontiers of that vaunted ''One Thousand Year Reich.'' In essence, Patton was an old-school cavalry general who had moved from the real thing to the iron steeds of the twentieth century.

If he was not a great man, he *was* a strange, unique person, plagued by inner fears and doubts, a cut above his *petite bourgeois* fellow commanders, who had been plucked from middle-aged obscurity at the beginning of the war and had become national—international—figures. Patton, as erratic and as irrational as he was, had grown into his role; for if he was not a great man, he did have the vision of greatness. Most of his fellow American generals did not. To the end of their days, they remained what they had always been, average hidebound, Regular Army field-grade officers, who by a tremendous stroke of luck found themselves catapulted from commanding companies and battalions into the command of corps and armies, three times, four times as big as the whole of the prewar U.S. Army!

It was because Patton had this vision of greatness, although he was not a great man himself, that he has been ill-served by sycophantic hagiographers. He deserved better than to be portrayed as ''Ol' Blood and Guts,'' that flamboyant, supremely confident, war-winning commander who never really existed. For Patton was a very special man, the product of a culture, outlook and privileged background that has long vanished, placed in a position in which he could wield almost unlimited power, unfettered by the restraints of society and military law.

By January 1945, Patton had become a law unto himself. It is the purpose of this book to depict how, in the last year of his life, Patton, plagued as he was by his inner fears and doubts, perhaps even neuroses, exercised that virtually unlimited power. Perhaps never again will an American soldier be able to fight such a battle, unrestrained by Congress, unexposed to the merciless scrutiny of the media mulling the results of his every decision over on the television screen in each household in the land.

If it does not make an altogether pleasant story—for it is Patton "warts and all"—let it be remembered that there were few pleasant stories in that lethal spring of '45 when so many of Patton's young men died—*violently*.

PART I

INTO THE REICH

One

Now it snowed.

Thick, heavy, wet flakes streamed down from the leaden sky to cover the pine forests, the mountains, and the line of the two rivers in the deep gorge below. It was as if God Himself wished to blot out that miserable, war-torn winter landscape, as the infinitely weary, pathetic remnants of the beaten German Army struggled across the rivers back into the Reich. Six weeks before, on December 16, 1944, they had advanced confidently across that same frontier—a quarter of a million of them—to deal the surprised, hopelessly outnumbered Americans in the Ardennes a staggering blow. But after the initial gains and victories, the "Battle of the Bulge," as it was named by British Prime Minister Winston Churchill, had become a murderous battle of attrition.

Since January 1, 1945, the survivors of the beaten *Wehrmacht* had been forced back relentlessly by the victorious Americans. But they had fought doggedly for every yard of that murderous, snowbound terrain, their passing marked by abandoned vehicles, bloodstained feces in the snow (for most of them had dysentery now), and purple-faced, stiffened bundles of rags, which were their dead. Hitler's armies in the West were in retreat. They would never attack again . . .

Remorselessly, the American guns pounded them as they straggled over the makeshift bridges of the Our and Sauer* rivers, which marked Germany's frontier with Belgium and Luxembourg, desperately trying to reach the safety of the bunkers and pillboxes on the heights above. For here, running like a gray, concrete dragon's spine the length of the frontier, lay Hitler's *Westwall*, the Siegfried Line, Germany's

*Known also as the *Sûre* in French-speaking countries.

last man-made defensive line. But the gunners were determined not to let them escape and fight again.

Clambering up the western heights, the weary dogfaces of the U.S. 5th Infantry Division cheered at the rich gunnery targets seen below on the Sauer River. Packed columns of tanks, trucks, and horse-drawn artillery waited to cross in the freezing cold, all of them, man and beast, mantled in snow. "Let her go, boys!" the artillery observer jubilantly radioed to his gunners. "You can't miss a Jerry—wherever you land one!"[1]

Once again the guns spoke, and with a shrill scream the great 105mm shells fell out of the sky, tearing huge holes in the suddenly panicked columns, slaughtering man and animal indiscriminately.

Despite the weather, the pilots of the U.S. 9th Tactical Air Force, in their Thunderbolts and Lightnings, risked death themselves to come zooming in at treetop height, seeming to skim over the snowfield at 400 mph, to strafe and slaughter the retreating German field-grays. For the pilots, it was August 1944 all over again, when they had slaughtered the Krauts trapped at Falaise. They simply couldn't miss!

Excited and still flushed with success that January day, Capt. Wilfred Crutchfield of the USAF told a BBC war reporter, "We'd come in on the road that leads northeast out to Prüm. To our surprise this road, and the others we could see, were jammed with German vehicles of all kinds. Double columns, bumper-to-bumper . . . stretched as far as the eye could see. In my 118 missions I've never seen so much enemy equipment!

"As I led the squadron down, I found myself headed straight for a flak-gun. I gave it a burst, and knocked it out. . . . I dropped my two wing bombs on the curve, tore big holes in the road, and knocked out six trucks. This stopped the whole column deader than a duck. Then we really went to work: bombed and strafed the column of tanks, half-tracks, cargo trucks and horse-drawn vehicles over an area of about five miles.

"Hundreds of Jerries jumped from their vehicles and ran for cover. Others started pulling their vehicles off the road in an attempt to hide them in the trees. But the ground was all snow-covered so it didn't do them any good. We followed the tracks and bombed and strafed them in their hideouts. After our bombs were all gone, we worked back and forth on the column—and all hell broke loose, as we'd knocked out all the flak and they were helpless. I've never seen so much confusion. The Jerries would run into the woods and then out again. They were like chickens with their heads cut off!"[2]

As a helpless, sickened Gen. Erich Brandenberger, commanding the retreating German Seventh Army, commented, "For the first time [in the Ardennes], the situation in the air was similar to that which prevailed in Normandy. . . . The enemy *jabos** were everywhere. My poor soldiers didn't have a damned chance. . . ."[3]

But it was not only the pathetic, lice-ridden frightened field-grays who suffered at the hands of these confident, well-fed, young pilots. Now the Americans were out for blood. The suffering in the December battle had been too great; in the last two weeks of that terrible month, the U.S. Army had suffered 41,000 battle casualties, the population of a medium-sized American town vanishing in fourteen short days! The Krauts, soldier and civilian, would have to suffer for what they had done to the dogfaces.

Now those men, women, and children of the "Red Zone," the border area, who had not fled with the Party bosses and the rest of the Nazi *Prominennz*, cowered in their cellars or in the caves dug into the sides of the mountains as the mighty four-engined bombers from England and the much more feared Allied *jabos* attacked their remote snowbound villages and small country towns, hour after hour, day after day. The whole of that long freezing January the Air Force flew mission after mission (in one day alone, January 22, 1945, *25 TAC squadrons flew no less than 627 sorties*) against the virtually defenseless civilian populace.

And they weren't particularly choosy about their targets. Hospitals, schools, churches, even single civilians foolish enough to wander into the open during daylight, were all attacked with equal impunity. At the beginning of January, the hospital at Stadtkyll, just across the frontier, clearly marked with a huge red cross on its roof, was hit. One hun-

---

*Jagdbomber, i.e., fighter-bomber.

dred and fifty persons, including 135 wounded American and German soldiers, were killed outright. A day later it was the hilltop township of Kyllburg. The medieval church there was destroyed. Soldiers and civilians were killed at the railway station. The local cemetery was hit. Skeletons were uprooted and strewn across the shattered, smoking streets. Bits and pieces of recently interred bodies were piled high in ghastly disarray like offal behind a butcher's shop. The village of Speicher was wiped out. The monastery being used as a military hospital at Daleiden, again clearly marked, was hit; seven wounded soldiers died. Prüm was attacked. The jabos came racing down the main street just in front of the Abbey church, machine guns blazing. Again civilians were killed and wounded, and ten American prisoners being led off into the local cage were killed among them, another tragic irony of the bitter war being waged on that snowbound frontier as the Germans were "softened" up for what was soon to come.

But on the western bank of the river line, the young men of General Patton's Third Army, preparing for the attack, cared little for the suffering of the Krauts. The hard slog to the Our and Sauer rivers had been too bitter and costly. From January 3–28, they and their comrades of the First Army had suffered another 39,673 battle casualties.

The losses, the strain, the sheer physical effort of reaching the river line had been tremendous. It was the worst winter in living memory in Europe, and the young GIs of General Patton's infantry divisions had fought up and down snowbound mountainsides in such bitter cold that frostbite had been epidemic, with quite a few cases needing amputation. Apart from the cold, the snow had worn down men just *advancing* to the attack, laden down as they were like pack animals, with weapons and ammunition, shovels and extra rations. Men who led these weary columns, breaking a path through the knee-deep fresh snow, had to be relieved every hundred yards or they simply broke down like overstrained machinery.

Marching up with the infantry, this time through a rainstorm, medic Lester Atwell recalled after the war the sheer strain of that advance into the unknown. "The night was pitch-black with a high, veering wind. The rain beat against us, noisy on helmets and raincoats. A constant spray bounced off the rim of the helmets, and in the back, rivulets poured down inside one's collar. Trying to rush, the men slipped and skidded in the sucking, ankle-deep mud. As the night progressed and the rain continued to smash down in sheets, the dirt roads grew softer and softer, deeper and deeper. Sometimes against the rainy sky and flailing trees you caught a dim silhouette of the men. It looked like a scene from the First World War, showing the doughboys slogging through the mud."[4]

Next to Private Atwell, his undersized commander, Lieutenant Serletis, kept moaning, "Oh, Jesus, I can't . . . I can't," as he tried to drag his skinny little legs out of the clinging mud. But he had to. For suddenly to their front, "there was a sudden, blinding flash," and then very loud, very close in the darkness, came the cry, "Medics! medics!"

"Everyone was shouting, screaming, scattering, as if we had been exploded apart. Men hurled themselves past me down into the ditchful of water."[5] And the screams continued. "Mother! Mother! Legs . . . My legs. My le-e-egs!" A second voice was crying. "Help . . . help. I'm blind. God, I'm blind!"[6]

Oh, yes, the survivors, who had reached this far and who now huddled around the purple-glowing stoves in stout Luxembourg cellars or froze and trembled in their icy foxholes on the heights, felt little sympathy for the Krauts on the other side of the two rivers. They had suffered too much in the past three weeks!

Coming back to his old outfit after two months in hospital, Staff Sergeant Henry Giles, a combat engineer, thought his old comrades who had fought throughout December and January looked "ten years older and ten years dirtier and ten years tireder. . . . Riding down here yesterday gave me some idea of what it's been like. The whole countryside is frozen, drifts two and three feet deep, but burned out tanks, half-tracks, jeeps, every kind of vehicle are everywhere and most of the villages are nothing but rubble." Giles concluded, "One thing—this offensive has been expensive to us, but I hope it has been the ruin of the Krauts."[7]

It hadn't, as many of the anxious young men waiting for

the order to attack would learn to their great regret, as the great gaps in their ranks were filled up with fresh-faced replacements: eighteen year olds, some straight from the States after three months' training; or older men culled from the military police, coastal artillery, or the Army Air Corps. So desperate was General Eisenhower, the Supreme Commander, for replacements to make up his infantry losses that he offered men serving seven-year sentences, or even longer ones, in the military stockades spread throughout his command the chance of freedom if they would volunteer for the infantry. But in the end only a mere 105 GIs volunteered for combat duty from the thousands of men behind bars. (This, at a time when virtually the total personnel of two whole railway-operating battalions had gone behind bars for black-market activities in France!)

Life was short in the infantry that month. Indeed many of those already at the front were making attempts to get out of their combat outfits before the new battle commenced. As Medic Lester Atwell noted that last week of January 1945, "A wave of self-inflicted wounds broke out. Time after time men were carried into the aid station from nearby houses, wincing with pain, shot through the foot. Each swore it had been an accident, 'I was cleaning my rifle,' sometimes the wounded man would say, pointing to a friend. 'He can tell you. He was in the room with me.' And often on the face of the friend there would be a look of duplicity as he backed up the story."[8]

That month, Commanding General Patton, visiting the hospitals under his command, to his surprise found even an officer with a self-inflicted wound! Patton had suffered bitterly on account of his treatment of "combat fatigue victims" in Sicily. Indeed, his shocking treatment of one of them had cost him his command of the U.S. Seventh Army. So this time, instead of ranting at the unfortunate men who would "soldier" no more, or striking them, as he had done in 1943, "I got out an order, that from now on so wounded would be tried, first for carelessness, and then for self-inflicted wounds. It is almost impossible to convict a man for self-inflicted wounds, but it is easy to convict him for carelessness, for which he can get up to six months."[9]

Tongue in cheek, Patton considered, however, the effect of

his new order on "carelessness." "After the soldiers had thought this over for about two months, they began to get their friends to shoot them; however, since the friends were frequently inaccurate and took off too many toes, the practice was never highly developed!"[10]

But in spite of freezing weather, the impossible terrain of the river-line front, the looming danger of impending combat, there was one major group of *volunteers* for Patton's Army that January—the non-persons of American society of forty-odd years ago: third-class citizens who called themselves with wry cynicism tinged with sadness, the "invisible men."

Back in December '44, Gen. John Lee, commander of all rear-line U.S. troops in Europe, many of whom were black, "offered Negro troops of the Com Z," as the *Stars and Stripes* put it "the *privilege* [my italics] of joining veteran front-line divisions as reinforcements."

"It is planned to assign you without regard to color or race to the units where assistance is most needed," the general told Negro soldiers. "Your comrades at the front are anxious to share the glory of victory with you. Your relatives and friends everywhere have been urging that you be granted the privilege. The Supreme Commander, your Commander General, and other veteran officers who have served with you, are confident that many of you will take advantage of this opportunity and carry on in keeping with the glorious record of our colored troops in former wars."[11]

Surprisingly enough, in spite of the shameful treatment most blacks had received in a segregated U.S. Army (where in both World Wars I and II black combat soldiers had almost invariably become supply and labor troops once they reached the war zone, although twenty black soldiers had won the Medal of Honor for heroism in the Civil War and eight the same award in the Spanish-American War), they volunteered in the thousands.

In one black engineer company, 171 men out of 186 volunteered to fight as infantrymen! Four first sergeants in that same outfit accepted reductions to private to qualify for the training plan. In a black laundry company, 100 men out of the 260 wanted to fight, though, in the end, only 36 were allowed "the privilege" of being transferred to the infantry.

So it was that by January 1945, 2,500 black infantrymen were being assigned to the assault divisions after a two-week infantry refresher course. "We're all in this thing together, now, white and Negro Americans in the same companies," a Pfc Leroy W. Kemp of Atlantic City—"now a BAR man and proud of it"—reportedly told the *Stars and Stripes* correspondent that month.[12] "And that's how it should be. That's why I volunteered. Most Negro troops are in service outfits. We've been giving a lot of sweat. . . . Now, I think we'll mix some blood with it!"

It was a noble sentiment.

Despite his many prejudices—he hated Arabs, Jews, Englishmen, Frenchmen, and quite a number of his fellow Americans—the commander of the Third Army, General Patton, did not seem to share the color prejudice of many of his fellow generals (as late as 1945 General Eisenhower was talking of his black servants as "darkies"). Indeed he had personally gone out of his way to welcome the two black tank battalions already under his command.

As one veteran of the black 761st Tank Battalion recalls, "Upon our arrival in France we were addressed by General Patton. . . . He told us: 'Men, you are the first Negro tankers ever to fight in the American Army. I would never have asked for you if you were no good. I have nothing but the best in my army. I don't care what color you are as long as you go up there and kill those Kraut sons-of-bitches! Everyone has their eyes on you and are expecting great things from you. Most of all, your race is looking forward to your success. Don't let them down and, damn you, don't let me down! They say it is patriotic to die for your country, well let's see how many patriots we can make out of the German motherfuckers!' "[13] To another black outfit, the 614th Tank Destroyer Battalion, Patton was more succinct: "There is one thing you men will be able to say when you go home. You may all thank God that thirty years from now when you are sitting with your grandson upon you knees and he asks, 'Grandfather, what did you do in World War II?' you won't have to say, 'I shoveled shit in Louisiana!' "[14]

Now the newest of his thirteen assault divisions assembling for the attack into the Reich, the 76th Infantry Division (which three months before had been still training in the States), contained the first integrated black and white companies. Not only would the 76th be expected to make an assault crossing of the swollen Sauer River, near the border township of Echternach, it would also go into action for the first time with the highly suspect black soldier in its ranks. For already rumors were beginning to circulate in the line about the questionable conduct and steadfastness of the first all-black division—the 92nd Infantry Division. It had gone into action in Italy at Christmas 1944 and, according to one source, "broke and fled the field."[15] Would these new "nigger" companies do the same?

But if the "old men" were weary of combat, the young "wet-noses," scared of what was soon to come, and their field commanders anxious about the quality and courage of the replacements, both white and black, their commander General Patton radiated confidence. In spite of the fact that he was the oldest U.S. Army commander in Europe, now nearing his sixtieth year, he was still fighting fit, after six months of campaigning and having seen virtually every member of his staff (including the army surgeon) fall sick.

In that last week of January before the attack was due to kick off, he was here, there, and everywhere, "peeping"* from one outfit to another, trying to pep up his fading commanders, threatening, cajoling, praising . . .

Visiting Gen. Manton S. Eddy, who had long concealed his high blood pressure from the Army commander in order not to be sent home, he told the portly XII Corps commander to start his attack two days earlier than planned.

Eddy flushed and snorted. "Goddammit, General, you never give me time to get ready. . . . The trouble is you have no appreciation of the time and space factor in this war!"

An impatient Patton was in no mood for arguments. He snapped back at Eddy, a general he had already threatened to sack when he had hesitated to attack at Metz, France, "Is that so? Well, if I *had* any appreciation of it, we'd still be sitting on the Seine!"[16]

Reluctantly Eddy agreed to carry out Patton's order.

---

*A peep, closed-in version of the jeep.

The commanding general was equally tough on Gen. Harry J. Malony, who led the 94th Infantry Division. His division had done less than well in the Saar area. Now Patton went into a blind rage when he discovered the 94th's ratio of combat to non-combat casualties was the worst in the whole of the Third Army. In addition, Malony's division was losing more prisoners to the enemy than any other, a sure sign of poor morale. "If you don't do something to improve this situation," Patton thundered, "you'll be a non-combat casualty yourself—and pretty soon!"[17]

Later he assembled as many officers and men of the division as could be found and gave them a thorough tongue-lashing, full of typical Patton invective, stomping up and down as he spoke, as if he could hardly contain his rage. "He told us we were a bunch of yellow-bellies and no-goods," one senior noncom recalled many years later. "Did he hate us that day! And we sure as hell hated him!"[18]

Afterward, having blown off steam, Patton relented a little. He told a crestfallen Malony: "You're doing fine otherwise—but Goddamnit, do something about those slackers!"[19]

For in this last week of January 1945, George S. Patton, Jr., was a man in a hurry. Time was running out fast for him and his beloved Third Army. He felt he had bailed Eisenhower and his Army Commander General Bradley out of the mess they had gotten themselves into during the Battle of the Bulge. True or otherwise, he believed that the decisive intervention of his Third Army on the southern flank of the Bulge had saved Bradley from defeat and Eisenhower from disgrace.

Now the two of them were strangely—ominously—silent about the future of the Third. But he *did* have a sneaking suspicion that his "armored reconnaissance" into Germany (as Patton delicately phrased the full-scale attack he planned with *six* whole divisions) would soon be brought to a halt. The rugged terrain of the German Eifel-Moselle area offered, so the top brass thought, little chance of armored exploitation. Nor was there any strategic value to be gained by conquering the area. Patton guessed—correctly—that the running in the coming battle of Germany would be made by his hated rival "the Field Marshal" (as he had always called the British commander Sir Bernard Law Montgomery since his promotion to that rank in September 1944). Soon, he believed, his attack would be brought to a halt, while Montgomery's armies and the attached U.S. Ninth Army assaulted to the north, driving for the last, great, natural barrier, the Rhine River. In due course the detested, cocky little Britisher would gain the kudos of having been first to cross the Rhine, while he and his Third marked time.

And that was something that George S. Patton could not—*would not*—tolerate. From now onward, "those gentlemen up north," as he called Montgomery, Eisenhower, and anyone else who he thought was getting in his way, would learn what he, Patton, had done *after* he had done it. From this January till hostilities ceased, General Patton, the commander of over one-third of a million American soldiers, would conduct his last campaign as if it were a private war.

Two

☆

"My favorite general is George S. Patton. Some of our generals like Stilwell have developed a sly ability to simulate human beings. But Patton always behaves as a general should. His side arms (a brace of pearl-handled revolvers) are as clean as his tongue is foul. He wears special uniforms which, like Goering, he designs himself and which are calculated like the ox-horns worn by ancient Gothic chieftains to strike terror into the enemy (and any rational person for that matter)."[1] Thus wrote New York columnist Dwight MacDonald in a bitter and bold (for Patton was the darling of the great American public by this time) attack on Patton in 1944. It was a portrait of Patton favored by the liberal establishment of the time: the commander of the Third Army as a foul-mouthed American Goering!

It was nothing new for Patton to be called names. Throughout his career, he had attracted derogatory, malicious nicknames. Before the war, as one of the best-hated men in the U.S. Regular Army, he had been known as the "Madman of Fort Clark." Later, with the coming of the war, he had been baptized "the Green Hornet." This nickname was gained on account of his self-designed tanker's uniform, with its bright green color and strange futuristic helmet, oddly similar to those worn by the astronauts four decades later. After the notorious slapping incident in Sicily in 1943, many another epithet was applied to him by an outraged American press: "that monster Patton," "Patton the Ogre," and so on.

But the name that finally stuck to him for the rest of his short career and the one that is usually associated with him to this very day, seemed to characterize him for the mass of the American people. It appeared to sum up his most outstanding characteristics: his love of war and everything that

28

went with it—boldness, courage, glory. It was simply "Ol' Blood and Guts."

For the great American public, "Ol' Blood and Guts" Patton was—and is—the epitome of the American frontier tradition. His nickname itself was sufficient to indicate the tough, rough, brawling, masculine figure he was. He was violent and vulgar. He was concerned with getting just the right sneer on his face and practiced doing so in front of a mirror in his quarters to perfect what he called his "war face."

His image as a pistol-packing general who pulled no punches and knew how to talk the language of the ordinary soldier was very important to him (it also made good newspaper copy). In public, his language was always replete with "SOBs" and "goddamns" and worse.

Greeting a new division going into combat for the first time, he told them, "The way most new soldiers use their rifles, they are no more use than a pecker is to the Pope!"[2]

Another division was told, "All this bull about thinking of your mother and your sweetheart and your wives is emphasized by writers who have never heard a hostile shot or missed a meal." His staff was told, "The second reason we are fighting [the war] is to defeat and wipe out the Nazis who started all this goddamned son-of-bitchery."[3]

Captain Abraham Baum, one of his most decorated soldiers and one who in March would risk his life for Patton, was shocked when he first heard the commanding general speak to his outfit. The vulgarity and obscenity was just too much for a nicely brought up Jewish boy whose religion forbade him even to use the name of God. "Did I turn red when he kept on cursing and cussing, like that? I'd never heard anyone speak in that manner before!"[4]

Once, in a moment of disgust, Patton told his intimate, General Hughes, "As you know, at the close of the war I intend to remove my insignia and wristwatch, but will continue to wear my short coat so that everyone can kiss my ass!"[5]

He also cultivated the image of a womanizer and, in the parlance of the time, that he was a great "swordsman," despite the fact that he had celebrated his fifty-ninth birthday on November 12, 1944 (reputedly in the company of a young woman in his Nancy headquarters).

On leave in Paris, he went to visit the Folies Bergeres with his friend General Hughes. The latter, based in the French capital, had seen the show many times and noted in his diary later, "A man can get accustomed to naked women if he sees enough naked women. But George has his mind mostly on. . . . He can't talk about anything except that. He must be getting impotent!"[6]

Hughes need not have worried. A little later, when Patton was about to go on leave to London, he told Hughes unblushingly that he had ordered nine condoms for his trip.

And there was no doubt that Patton was attractive to a certain type of woman who admired power and military bearing. That spring he gave a luncheon at his Luxembourg headquarters for his boss, Eisenhower. Acting as hostess was his niece, Jean Gordon. Off and on she played the same role for her uncle as Kay Summersby, Eisenhower's personal assistant and *chauffeuse*, did for the Supreme Commander, and both were reputed to be the mistresses of their respective bosses. Also present at the luncheon were four Red Cross Clubmobile girls who had primped themselves up in their best uniforms, complete with white gloves, white scarves—and expensive perfume. The leader of the team, which really should have been up the line serving coffee to the front-line troops, a Capt. Betty Smith, made no secret of her admiration for Patton's magnificent tall figure. "There was arrogance unspeakable there," she recalled afterward, "authority unrelinquished, even to his superior officer, the Supreme Allied Commander, whom he was toasting."[7]

But the tough-talking, very masculine general also bewildered her a little. "I was not altogether successful," she admitted later, "in keeping my pose as I watched the general's gentle, twinkling eyes full of infectious humor when something amused him, change abruptly to flashing, angry blazes at something else which displeased him and back again as quickly to frank, guileless, simple honesty. His agility in leaping back and forth between vulgar and shocking profanity and cultured, gentlemanly speech bewildered me. I was particularly hard-pressed to know what to do or say when he turned tearful eyes to me and spoke about God and prayer."[8]

• • •

Captain Betty Smith was not the only one to be bewildered by the contradictions in Patton's career, once they came to know him. The tough, pistol-packing, coarse, fighting-man image might be all right for the Great American Public and his soldiers. It was part of the "act." As Captain Baum explained it many years later, "Patton was an egomaniac, who believed in ninety percent psychology—and ten percent killing!"⁹ But there was a completely different side to him that remained completely unknown to those who admired him for those red-blooded, down-to-earth qualities that they thought of as typically American.

There was something arrogant, aristocratic, and definitely un-American about George S. Patton. He had been born independently wealthy, and he had married into the family of a Boston textile tycoon who was so grand that even his own children called him "Sir Frederick." At the start of his career as a humble second lieutenant, he and his wife always dressed for dinner in the bare rooms assigned to them as quarters. Almost at once, the Pattons gained for themselves the envious, malicious title of "the Duke and Duchess."

After World War I, when most of his fellow officers could hardly afford a Model T Ford, Patton always lived in the finest accommodation available in the town nearest to his base, traveling back and forth to duty in the latest and most expensive automobile available.

During the Depression of the '30s, Patton could afford to keep a string of polo ponies and was one of the American team that won the Argentinian Polo Trophy. Invariably these ponies aroused the ire of his much poorer commanding officers, who frequently ordered Patton to take the ponies off post. This he would do, housing them at the nearest civilian stable at his own expense.

In short, Patton was *not* an average American. His life was aristocratic, upper class, a black-tie affair, quite out of step with the humdrum, lower-middle-class existence of fellow officers of field grade such as Eisenhower, Bradley, Hodges, and the like. Indeed Patton's style of life up to World War II had more in common with that of those languid, titled, English cavalry officers whom he affected to detest.

It was not surprising in the light of this kind of moneyed

background that when Patton was finally given the command of the U.S. Third (after his year's exile in Sicily on account of the notorious slapping incident there), he seemed to want to turn that army into a private force: one that he would try to command without any restraint from above and thus, incidentally, gain the maximum amount of personal publicity for General George S. Patton, Jr.

Addressing his new staff at Peover Hall, England, that raw spring day, Patton, superbly tailored as always, told them: "I am here because I have the confidence of two men: the President of the United States and the Theater commander. They had confidence in me because they don't believe a lot of goddamned lies that have been printed about me!''[10]

His staff fell in love with him immediately. From then onward and, for the most part, for the rest of their lives, his officers were Patton's greatest fans, indulging him in his whims, lavishing fulsome praise, sycophants to a man. Patton possessed no fiery-tempered Bedell Smith, as Eisenhower did, who stated bluntly, that if "Ike" always played the role of the "good guy," somebody "around here has to be a son-of-a-bitch!" At Patton's HQ there were none of "Monty's young men," who although they were only lowly captains and majors (both British and American), were allowed to criticize the "master's" decisions to his face every evening after work.

On the contrary, Patton's staff vied with each other to heap praise on their boss. His chief-of-staff, one-eyed Gen. Hobart Gay, thought of Patton as "the bravest man I know.''[11] Another staff member and intimate, Col. Robert Allen, wrote of his commander, "Very few of Patton's superiors liked him. . . . They had good reason for that. He was a far abler battle commander than they.''[12] His personal aide, Col. Charles Codman wrote: "He [Patton] has contributed to the science of warfare professional proficiency of the highest modern order. More significantly, however, and it is this that sets him apart, he brings to the art of command in this day and age, the norms and antique virtues of the classic warrior. In the time of Roger the Norman or in ancient Rome, General Patton would have felt completely at home.''[13]

Very heady stuff indeed.

• • •

Of course, Patton, egomaniac that he was, was also a shrewd judge of character. He knew just how mediocre and sycophantic his staff was. Yet in view of his background and the flatteries of the men all around him, it was difficult for him *not* to believe that he was a really great man. One of the first commanders to fight a war against the background of "instant communication," his name was in the headlines back in the States every day. His face had become famous to movie audiences throughout the free world. It was "Patton," and not his soldiers, who had made the bold dash from the Normandy bridgehead to the Breton ports—over two hundred kilometers. "Patton" had relieved Bastogne. "Patton" had pushed the Germans back to the Reich's frontier. By January 1945, Patton had become as much a cult figure as any modern pop star. Back in 1940, an obscure colonel in spite of his wealth, he had been thinking in terms of retirement, slippers, and a nice, gentle game of golf. Suddenly, startlingly, he had been propelled into the limelight, commanding a force that was twice as big as the *whole* of the prewar U.S. Army. Within four short years he had made a career like some twentieth-century Grant, save that the decisions he made were not taken in some obscure backwoods of the Republic, but before the eyes of the world—in Africa, Sicily, England, France, and Germany—and affecting the future of national states for decades to come.

Now nearing sixty and his career virtually over, there was only one more battle left for him, a commander who loved war. "Compared with war, all other forms of human endeavor shrink to insignificance," hadn't he told Codman, after viewing a Normandy battlefield littered with German corpses? "God, how I love it."[14] That last battle was the battle for Germany. Thereafter retirement and obscurity loomed for a commander who would soon declare, "the best end for an old campaigner is a bullet at the last minute of the last battle."[15]

Could he, then, accept a secondary and unimportant role in the coming battle for the Reich? Could he be content to let the "gentlemen up north" gain the glory and the headlines of reaching—and crossing—the Rhine River, while his Third Army played flank guard for them? Of course not!

Already he had made it quite clear to his superior, General

Bradley, whom he despised, that "I was the oldest leader in age and combat experience in the United States Army in Europe and that if I had to go on the defensive, I wanted to be relieved."[16]

Bradley had given in, in spite of the fact that he knew Eisenhower planned that the main attack into the Reich would take place in the north. Eisenhower had ordered that Patton should merely conduct an "aggressive defense" along the river line. On January 23, however, Bradley told Patton he could conduct his "defense" any way he saw it. Patton was not slow to seize the opportunity offered him. He told his amused staff that they would carry out an "armored reconaissance" of the West Wall *with six divisions*, with their objectives the capture of the road and rail centers of Prüm and Bitburg and, later, the seizure of the area's major city, the ancient Roman provincial capital of Trier on the Moselle. The method he would use to fool Eisenhower to his real intentions would be his famed "rock soup" tactic.

He had explained the tactic to his staff back in 1944: "A tramp once went to a house and asked for some boiling water to make 'rock soup.' The lady was interested and gave him the water in which he placed two polished stones. He asked then if he might have some potatoes and carrots to flavor it a little, and finally ended up with some meat!

"In other words," Patton went on, "in order to attack, we'll have to pretend to reconnoiter, then reinforce the reconnaissance, and finally put on the attack."[17] Patton had beamed at them, obviously pleased with his ingenuity and ability to thumb his nose at the top brass. Now he intended to use the method again in the German Eifel. First he would commit Gen. Troy Middleton's VIII Corps on his left flank. Middleton's 4th and 90th Infantry Divisions would attack through the West Wall over the mountains and into Prüm, while Middleton's 87th Division would guard the corps' northern flank.

In the center of Patton's line, General Millikin's III Corps would remain temporarily on the defensive, but on its right flank, General Eddy's XII Corps would begin its assault crossing of the Sauer River with the 5th and 76th Infantry Divisions and commence the drive for Bitburg. Meanwhile

Gen. Walton Walker, commanding Patton's fourth corps, the XX Corps, would continue his nibbling way at the West Wall defenses on the Saar River. In essence, Patton hoped that the Germans caught between the two prongs—Middleton's drive on Prüm and Eddy's on Bitburg—would not chance being outflanked. They would withdraw, leaving the Eifel wide open and for the taking. Millikin's corps would then be able to advance virtually unopposed.

Attacks on both Prüm and Bitburg had been tried before, in September 1944. Both had failed, and the American outfits that had done the attacking had been forced to retreat back across the river line. Such considerations played no role in Patton's planning. He wanted his Third Army so deeply committed that, by the time Eisenhower had become aware of what he was doing, there would be no turning back. Carried on by the relentless terrible momentum of battle, the Third would *have* to advance until it reached the last natural barrier—the Rhine. The plan was brash and bold. It was typical of Patton who, isolated in his headquarters, surrounded by admiring yes-men, had lost contact with reality, running the war as if it were a private matter, independent of overall strategy and political considerations.

For if Patton's ruse succeeded—and it was little better than that—he would drag the whole Allied battlefront further south than was intended. If Patton's young soldiers managed to reach the Rhine in the Koblenz-Mainz area and crossed there, the whole remaining strategy of the war in Europe would have to be changed. Patton's army and the others under the command of General Bradley's Twelfth Army Group might well end World War II fighting for the scenery of rural Bavaria, while the Red Army aimed for the glittering political prizes of Berlin, Prague, and Vienna.

What was being planned this snowy January in that shabby HQ—Pescatore Foundation—in the provincial Ruritanian atmosphere of the Grand Duchy of Luxembourg could well decide the fate of Central Europe for the rest of the twentieth century.

Three

It began to snow again in that remote border country. With the stark, black tree boughs heavy with new snow, the young men of the assault force across the Our and Sauer rivers crowded the cobbled, potholed roads and the half-wrecked hamlets of the front-line area. Everywhere there were the signs of the new offensive. Great dumps of ammunition in the fields, piles of filled jerricans (5-gallon gas cans) along the roadsides. Signal Corps men were out stringing up cables and telephone wires. Engineers fought desperately to keep the road system from collapsing, repairing the existing roads to prevent them from disappearing into the mud and slush, cutting new ones through the forests. On all sides tanks, half-tracks, great 8-inch howitzers and 105mm cannon—the long Toms—trucks, bridging equipment, a great mass of olive-painted equipment clogging every track, every little farmyard, every field—and all pointing one way: *toward Germany!*

At the village of Lanzerath, just on the Belgo-German frontier, engineer Sergeant Giles worked all out with his company, laboring hard to build a Bailey bridge across the Our for the infantry to attack over. And it was "a bitch. The river is 189-feet wide here, and the chasm is 100-feet deep. The weather is lousy—snowing and blowing. And we had plenty of artillery fire. That's my idea of real T.S.* It's round the clock, boys, and don't spare the horses!"[1] Not far away in the village of Kobscheid in Germany itself, Medic Atwell waited for the order to advance. "The captain paced up and down in silence, impatiently awaiting the word to move up further. Attacking the Siegfried Line, I thought, and prayed

*Tough shit.

36

suddenly. God, don't let this be a slaughter. Help them. End this!"[2]

Atwell knew that already trouble had broken out among the ranks of the young men waiting to attack. For the first time in months, the infantry was up to strength, but as the day of the great attack neared, the riflemen were falling sick by the hundred, the thousand. Severe respiratory infection was decimating whole companies. Already the medical brass was setting up special hospitals behind the front to deal with only respiratory cases. By the time the offensive got underway they would have dealt with the equivalent of a whole infantry division—14,000 sick riflemen! And still it continued to snow, as if it would never stop.

Tension began to mount.

The first flares sailed effortlessly into the gray, dawn air. For a while they hung there, coloring the upturned faces of the waiting infantry a ghastly, unreal hue. As they dropped like fallen angels, the barrage commenced. In an instant the frozen Our River lit up a startling orange, as the bombardment descended upon the German positions on the heights beyond. A fantastic pattern of myriad stabs and flashes of orange flame took shape and died an instant later. In an urgent, lethal Morse, tracer zipped back and forth. Rockets hissed into the lowering sky, trailing fiery spluttering sparks behind them, like man-made forked lightning. Here and there a maverick shell exploded and tossed up a ball of fire like a Roman candle. "Shorts" fell into the water, breaking the ice, sending it up in angry, white spurts. Awed and gaping like village yokels at some monstrous carnival, the waiting infantry watched and waited for what had to come.

It did. Whistles shrilled. Red-faced noncoms bellowed orders. Officers rose to their feet, waved their carbines, and yelled the old command, "Let's go, men!" Like weary old men, the infantry rose from their freezing holes and began to plod across the snow toward the river. Now the killing would start once again.

The 4th Infantry Division, which would spearhead Middleton's drive for Prüm, had been this way once before. In September 1944, they had crossed the German frontier full of

confidence. They had passed through these same hills, knowing that the "Kraut" was beaten; that the end of the war was
only a matter of weeks away. But they had been disappointed.
The Germans had rallied and the "Ivy League" men, as the
division was nicknamed, had been thrown back. Then had
come the ordeal of the fighting in the *Hürtgenwald*. In that
"green hell," the 4th had about fallen apart, suffering hor-
rendous casualties, with companies breaking and running and
even battalion commanders refusing to take their men into
action. Now the 4th Infantry Division, going into the attack
against Prüm for a second time, was virtually a new forma-
tion, with only a few veterans of the Normandy landings left,
its ranks filled out with thousands of replacements. Like the
old 4th back in September 1944, it felt the Krauts were about
beaten. This time the enemy would crack!

The Ivy League men had not reckoned with their opponent, Major-General Ludwig Heilmann, commanding the 5th
German Parachute Division. The hard-faced German general
was "an old hare," as veterans were called in the *Wehrmacht*. He had been fighting since 1940, when most of the
4th's men had still been in high school, seeing action on
virtually every front. Back in early 1944 he had stopped the
Allies dead at Monte Cassino and later in that same year he
had almost prevented Patton from reaching Bastogne.

Now his division was decimated—a mere 1,500 men
against nearly 15,000 Americans—and his men were para-
chutists in name only. But they had inherited the tradition of
that elite corps and were prepared to make the *Amis*, as they
called the Americans contemptuously, fight—and bleed—for
whatever gains they made.

Soon the new boys of the 4th Infantry Division would have
a bitter fight on their hands.

At first everything went well. On January 31, the 4th captured
the first German settlement to fall into American hands since
the Battle of the Bulge. The village of Elcherrath was taken
without too much trouble. Thereafter, a series of villages and
hamlets were captured by the Ivy League men as they plodded steadily eastward through the knee-deep snow in the direction of Prüm.

Bleialf, where the ill-fated U.S. 106th Infantry Division

had fought, bled, and surrendered en masse the previous December, became American once again. Now the Americans had again reached the site of their deepest penetration into Hitler's vaunted "1,000 Year Reich." For a day they paused on the heights outside the ruined village, surveying the dead-straight road that led to the hamlet of Brandscheid.

Brandscheid was a dreary, gray sort of a place: a post office, a couple of run-down farms, a straggle of white-painted houses to left and right of the onion-roofed church next to the crossroads. An unimportant sort of a place, not marked on small-scale maps; unimportant save for one thing—Brandscheid had been integrated into the Siegfried Line!

The officer who was to lead the Ivy League's attack on Brandscheid, Colonel "Buck" Lanham, was not only a professional soldier who had fought with his 22nd Infantry Regiment right through from Normandy; he was also something of an intellectual, who numbered among his friends "Ole Ernie Hemorrhoid, the Poor Man's Pyle."* Indeed "Ernie Hemorrhoid," alias Ernest Hemingway, had attached himself to Lanham's regiment during that first advance into Germany in what seemed now another age. But in the fighting in the *Hürtgenwald*, Lanham's regiment had suffered 2,678 casualties and the colonel had agonized that "my magnificent command had virtually ceased to exist."[3]

Now the thin, wiry, bespectacled colonel determined there would be no new slaughter of his 22nd at Brandscheid. Once his men had cleared the eleven pillboxes guarding the approach to the hamlet, his assault companies would attack, well supported by armor. Let the tankers earn their pay for a change.

On February 5, Lanham attacked. Under heavy mortar and artillery fire one of his battalions spent the morning clearing the pillboxes. Now ten Sherman tanks and seven tank destroyers, armed with huge 90mm guns, rumbled up. At midday precisely they opened fire at all visible pillboxes guarding the road into Brandscheid itself. From the woods heavy machine guns and mortars joined in. Tracer whizzed back and forth a dazzling white. Shells bounced off the thick, steel hide of the tank destroyers like glowing Ping-Pong balls. Mortar

---

*A pun on the name of the GIs' favorite reporter, Ernie Pyle.

shells howled obscenely. Great steaming brown holes like the work of gigantic moles appeared suddenly on the glittering white surface of the snowfield.

Now it was the turn of Lanham's infantry. They burst from the cover of the fir trees shouting and yelling like men demented. As they ran and stumbled through the snow, they fired from the hip, lobbing white phosphorus grenades in front of them. Rapidly they closed on the burning village.

At first the poor quality "people's grenadiers" holding the ring of pillboxes around Brandscheid returned their fire. But they were not of the caliber of Heilmann's paratroopers waiting in reserve. The fire began to slacken. More and more of the dirty, lice-ridden defenders began to emerge from their pillboxes crying *"Kamerad!"* knowing that if they waited until the *Amis* stormed the place it would be too late. Then they would be slaughtered where they stood; the Americans were taking no prisoners.

In three short hours it was all over. Lanham's men had taken the Siegfried Line position with its formidable ring of pillboxes at a surprisingly light cost—forty-three casualties.

But the Germans would be back.

Now the weary but triumphant infantry rested while the guns thundered on both sides, and the engineers braved the fire from another huge Siegfried Line fortification that barred the road ahead while they attempted to lift the mines that seemed to have been planted everywhere.

Behind them more and more troops of Middleton's VIII Corps poured over the frontier, desperately trying to find cover for the night, turning the few remaining villagers out of their houses that stank of boiled cabbage and animal droppings, locking them into churches and barns and threatening them with death if they attempted to escape.

For these were not the happy-go-lucky, likable, young men who had come this same way the previous September. This time there were no Hershey bars and chewing gum for the kids, no coffee and canned rations for the women, or Camels for the remaining old men. This time there were blows and kicks and threats, backed up by leveled rifles.

In Auw, the advancing infantrymen forced the local civilians to cover them as they cleared the village. More than one terrified civilian was killed in the process. In Winterspelt, where an American headquarters was set up, 180 civilians, many of them sick, were locked up for two weeks in two small houses. There were the first cases of rape. Soon they would be numbering five hundred, actually brought to trial, a month!

Everywhere the soldiers threw out of the windows the things they didn't need, littering the village streets with the civilians' pathetic possessions. Sometimes the soldiers seemed to take a perverse delight in destroying and burning these bits and pieces in front of the horrified villagers. But the war had brutalized these young men. Their lives were short and violent. Maybe they would be killed on the morrow. What did they care about the weeping women and whining old men? They lived in a different world from the "civvies." The civvies would live to grow old. More than likely they wouldn't.

Young Johannes Nobusch of Elcherrath, the first village to be captured by the 4th, who would one day become a professor of philosophy, could not understand these cruel, young Americans. Perhaps they had seen too much destruction caused by the Germans during the Battle of the Bulge; or perhaps it was Goebbels' propaganda that was at fault, making the Americans believe that all Germans were fanatics? But they were wrong. "How tired and weary of war the people really were! They longed for peace! Now one thing and one thing only occupied the civilians' every thought. When in God's name would this terrible war be over?"[4]

The German counterattack came at four A.M.

It was a miserable February night. The rain came down in sheets, intermingled with sleet that cut the faces of the men slogging up the slushy road from Bleialf to Brandscheid like a myriad of sharp knives. For one of the most dangerous of all military exercises was taking place, one that gave every advantage to any attacker; the 22nd Infantry at Brandscheid was being relieved by the 358th Infantry of the U.S. 90th Infantry Division.

Now the soaked, frozen, new boys began to assemble in the village, with the rain still beating down furiously, while to the north the sky flushed pink with the rumble of the permanent barrage. As always, there was the usual controlled chaos: officers consulting maps with the aid of torches; guides trying to find the companies allotted to them; jeeps splashing back and forth in the mud; harassed staff officers attempting to discover the location of the German positions; soldiers wandering off to "take a crap," "find a cupa Java," "somewhere where I can get my frigging blisters treated . . ."

Startlingly, it happened. Without even a preliminary barrage, the Germans attacked from the south. Over four hundred of them. They came running out of the night, firing from the hips, the officers urging them on with sharp, controlled bursts from their Schmeissers. Lanham's Company K was shattered immediately. The panicked survivors fled into the village itself, yelling, "The Krauts are coming. . . . The Krauts are behind us!"

And they were. As usual, the Germans were lightning-quick, eager to take advantage of the new situation. They flooded into the center of the village, right behind the survivors of Company K. Here and there a rifleman of Lanham's 3rd Battalion, to which K belonged, tried to hold them up. A couple of tank destroyer crews joined in. But the German dash was too strong. The Ivy League men started to pull out of Brandscheid.

But Lanham, the veteran, was equal to the situation. Hastily he rallied his Company L, the only unit in the 22nd that had completed the handover. Company L went into the attack. Fierce hand-to-hand fighting developed in the center of the village, with men pelting from doorway to doorway firing as they ran, grenades being tossed through shattered doors, snipers dropping from upper-floor windows like sacks of wet cement.

In the end the Germans gave in. More than 150 of them surrendered as a gray ugly dawn broke, as if God were reluctant to illuminate that scene of sudden death and destruction. But the cost had been high. The men of the 90th Infantry Division had suffered only nine fatalities, but the 22nd's 3rd Battalion had lost one-fifth of its effective strength in two short hours. That grim dawn "Buck" Lanham must have wondered whether luck had run out yet again for his beloved regiment. Was the tragedy of *Hürtgenwald* going to be repeated here on the 22nd's second foray into this awful country?

• • •

A score of miles away that same February 6, General Eddy's three infantry divisions, the veteran 80th and 5th, plus the totally inexperienced 76th Infantry, prepared to assault the Sauer River between Echternacherbruck and Bollendorf. Launching their attack from the Luxembourg side of the river, the 5th and the 76th would not only have to contend with the Sauer, flooded and running a ten-knot current, but then would have to fight up the clifflike hills beyond, which had been integrated into the Siegfried Line. Indeed Patton's greenest division, with its newly integrated black soldiers, had been given one of the toughest assignments of the whole campaign. As one of the greenhorns would remark after the killing was over, "So help me, the job at first seemed just too much for human beings to accomplish!"[5]

To the north, the veterans of the 80th were the first to jump off. They attacked at one in the morning under light snow. Almost immediately they ran into trouble with the river, swollen to twice its normal size. The small, rubber dinghies, captured from the *Luftwaffe*, hadn't a chance in the fast, wild water. Some capsized immediately, throwing the heavily laden infantrymen into the icy water. Others careened crazily back to the western bank.

A few determined men pushed on until they reached midstream, but the panic-stricken screams of those drowning in the river had alerted the enemy. A single rifle shot rang out. It seemed to act as a signal. Suddenly the whole eastern bank burst into hectic activity. The star shells burst above the Americans trapped in the middle of the river. The slaughter had commenced.

It was no different in the 5th Division sector. The veterans of a dozen river crossings had already run straight into massed German fire from the heights above. The enemy couldn't miss. The infantrymen in their frail boats were sitting ducks. Mortar shells burst among them, sending great spurts of crazy, white water upward. Angry, killing tracer sped low across the river's surface. Numbly the trapped infantrymen accepted their fate, being slaughtered like dumb animals.

Organization fell apart. Now it was every man for himself. A house on the Luxembourg side went up in flames. It turned night into day, outlining men struggling for their lives in the water against a lurid backdrop of scarlet flame. Private Harold Garman, a medic, was one of those trapped.

Moments before as a German machine gun had zeroed in on them, wounding four of Garman's companions, the rest of the crew had dived overboard, leaving Garman and the wounded to their fate. Now Garman acted. He slipped overboard. With German slugs plucking the icy water all around him, he began to push the boat with its cargo of moaning, frightened men back to the American side—and he made it.

Later in March when Patton came up to award him the Medal of Honor, even the Commanding General was astonished at such bravery on the part of a man whose comrades had deserted him. He asked the young medic why he had done it. Garman (in Patton's words) "looked surprised and said, 'Well, someone had to do it, sir.' "[6] So the slaughter of the 80th and 5th Divisions continued, and soon it would be the turn of the greenhorns of the 76th Infantry Division.

Four

Exactly ninety days before, the men of the 76th Infantry had been attacking a simulated foe in the peaceful hills of Wisconsin. Now they were going to attack the real thing.

All night long, tank destroyers and "Long Toms" had been pounding the opposite bank of the Sauer River, where it rose steeply to the fortified heights of the Ferschweiler Plateau, trying to knock out the enemy pillboxes overlooking the site where Companies A and B of the 471st Infantry Regiment would cross. Already their commanders knew that their neighbor the 5th had virtually failed at Bollendorf. Only one boatload from each of the division's two assault regiments had reached the opposite shore, sixteen very frightened men in all. Now it was their turn.

Coincidentally, it was from Echternach that St. Willibrod, an English monk, had sallied forth across the river to convert the heathen German back in the ninth century. Now, as the nervous young men of the 76th crept by the ruins of his abbey toward the river, they were going to do the same—*with bayonet and rifle!*

The lead company pushed off, praying that the rumble of their own artillery would drown any noise they might make, each man wrapped up in a cocoon of his own thoughts. The minutes ticked by in nerve-tingling, electric apprehension, as they plied their paddles against the fast-flowing current. Above them on the glowing heights, the German defenders remained strangely silent. *Were they going to make it?*

A sudden whoosh. A sharp crack. Above them the flare exploded, coloring the night sky a harsh, unreal silver. They had been spotted!

Almost immediately the massed German machine guns on the opposite side opened up on the men in the frail little rubber boats. Red, green, and white tracer zipped toward them like a flight of angry hornets. Desperately they crouched low and paddled with all their might. An obscene howl, and the first mortar bomb came falling out of the sky right into their midst.

Craft after craft was hit. Behind the boat carrying Private Harry Goedde and some of his platoon, the nearest dinghy received a direct hit. It went under, carrying its cargo of dead and dying men with it. Goedde gasped in shocked horror in the very same instant that his own craft came under heavy machine-gun fire. Frantically, Goedde and the rest directed the craft away from it. But in their panic, they swamped the boat and they tumbled overboard in a mass of flailing arms and legs, fumbling madly to rip off their heavy equipment.

Most of them were swept away almost immediately, being taken by the fast-running current, past the ruins of the little bridge to their right, on and on, until they drowned. But Goedde was a strong swimmer. He struck out for the bank. As he swam he spotted a medic screaming for help. He took him in tow and together they managed to reach the shelter of some frozen reeds. Weaponless and helpless, shivering with the cold, the two survivors watched as the second company went in, to be slaughtered just as the first one had been.

In the end, fifty-six men and three officers of Company A and fifty-two men and two officers of Company B made it. In their first combat action, the 76th Division had suffered 50 percent casualties. Thus it was that as dawn approached, it appeared that Patton's first venture into the Reich had failed. Nowhere it seemed had he secured even a toehold on German soil.

Four days before Middleton's and Eddy's attacks stalled on that disastrous night of February 6/7, 1945, Patton had been called to attend a top-level conference at Spa, Belgium. The brass met in the watering place's Hotel Britannique, which had been the Imperial German Army headquarters in World War I. Here, from the windows of the office where they met, Patton could see the lake around which the German kaiser had walked impatiently in November 1918, waiting for Supreme Commander Hindenburg to decide whether the war against the Western Allies should be continued or not. That freezing day Patton must have sensed a fellow feeling for the crippled monarch, while *he* waited to hear what his supreme commander, Eisenhower, had dreamed up for his Third Army.

The news was bad. The Third could continue its "armored reconnaissance" for eight more days until February 10, when the "Field Marshal," i.e., Montgomery, would begin his full-scale offensive. Then the Third would be forced to stop offensive operations, as SHAEF* claimed that there was only sufficient ammunition and replacements for one major thrust. In addition, the Third would be required to transfer several infantry divisions to General Simpson's Ninth U.S. Army, which would be fighting under Montgomery's command.

Immediately after he had returned to his HQ, Patton had summoned his corps commanders to tell them the bad news. But at the same time he revealed to his generals that he was going to have his own way, even if it meant disobeying Eisenhower. "Personally," he said slowly in that squeaky voice of his, "I think that it would be a foolish and ignoble way for the Americans to end the war by sitting on our butts. And, gentlemen, we are not going to do anything foolish or ignoble. . . . Let the gentlemen up north learn what we are doing when they see it on their maps!"[1]

Now, five days later and with only three days to go before the "Field Marshal's" great offensive in the north started, which well could mean the end of his own attack, he found his two corps stalled and, in the case of Eddy's XII Corps, in a really desperate position on the Sauer.

Patton reacted immediately. He set off to visit all the units involved, rallying their commanders, urging them to throw in new attacks; and above all, he insisted that Gen. LeRoy "Red" Irwin commanding the 5th Division should get a bridge across the Sauer at once.

Tired, cold, and weary, he returned to his HQ that night in Luxembourg, only a dozen miles as the crow flies from the scene of the desperate struggle, to be told by one of his staff, "The Fifth doesn't seem to be doing so good. Wonder what's wrong? It's taking them a long time to put a bridgehead across the river."

As angry as he was himself with the 5th, Patton rounded on the officer. "It would take you a hell of a long time, too!"

*Supreme Headquarters Allied European Forces.

Patton snapped. "That river is one mean son-of-a-bitch, and the whole hillside is covered with pillboxes, mines, and barbed wire. The Fifth is doing all right. Let it alone. It's making a great fight and it *will* get over." He forced a grin, showing his dingy teeth, though he must have felt very low this gray, freezing February afternoon, with the guns rumbling ominously in the distance. "And once it does, it'll go like a bat out of hell!"[2]

Now the three attack divisions went all out. The 80th managed to get a battalion across. Eddy drove down personally to the site of the 5th's attack and directed tank destroyers to go to the very edge of the water and pound the German positions in order to cover the sixteen GIs on the other side, the total number of 5th Division's soldiers who had made it across.

Then he ordered Irwin to start passing his division through the bridgehead opened up by the 80th. By nightfall the move was in process, and the unfortunate sixteen soldiers were left to fend for themselves, the only men of the 5th on the German side.

A little further downstream, however, small, disorganized groups of the 76th Division were also across, fighting in platoons, even ones and twos, trying to fight their way up the steep hillside, meeting withering fire from concealed German posts.

Private Ulrich found himself completely alone on the German side of the river. His whole platoon had been wiped out just after they had left the boats. Ulrich, temporarily blinded by shell flashes, his rifle wrenched from his hand by the blast, wandered about the thickly wooded slope that led up to the Siegfried Line positions, being fired upon all the time. Later he reported: "I couldn't see anyone else from my outfit. I felt all alone . . . It seemed to me that I was the only Yank in Germany and the whole *Wehrmacht* was zeroing in on me!"[3]

Sergeant Bliss and Private Meyer, attacking and then being cut off from their platoon, went to ground in what they thought was a "cave." Later they discovered they had hidden themselves "on a seven-room pillbox full of Jerries."[4]

But not all the greenhorns went to ground. As Pfc. Lyle Corcoran's platoon left their boats and began to plod across the road that ran parallel with the river, they heard the first frightening rumble of tanks and faint cries in German. New boys they were all right, but they knew what that meant. The Krauts were counterattacking. They prepared for the assault to come.

They didn't have long to wait. Suddenly three tanks came rumbling toward their positions, small groups of German infantrymen perched on their decks or grouped carefully behind them in what the *Wehrmacht* called a "grape." Hugging the protection of the steel monsters, they came closer and closer, confident that the *Amis* would break and run soon. They were mistaken. Pfc. Corcoran's Irish temper was roused. Jamming his bazooka on his shoulder, he aimed and fired. Once . . . twice.

There was the hollow boom of steel striking steel. A bright, glistening silver scar suddenly appeared on a tank turret. It shuddered to a stop and began to burn fiercely. This David had won his lone battle against the metallic Goliath.

Not all of the greenhorns were so lucky. A horrified Guida Fenice watched as the second tank "ran over one of our men in a foxhole. There were about seven German soldiers riding on the outside and I saw a buddy of mine running alongside the tank firing at them with a pistol. They shot him down so I grabbed his gun and continued to fire."[5]

But in the hectic panic, the German tank driver made a mistake. Pursued by the lone sergeant, he drove straight into a patch of marshy ground. Desperately he gunned his huge engine. To no avail! The tracks flailed, showering mud everywhere. But that only succeeded in bogging the tank down even further.

The jubilant GIs were not slow to take advantage of the situation. A sergeant and a private pelted forward under fire. They tossed grenades into the tank's open turret. The deadly little eggs exploded with terrible effect in the confined space of the tank's interior. Its occupants were churned to a pulp, and almost immediately the tank burst into flames.

That was the end of the German attack. The remaining tank and the surviving infantry fled back to the cover of the woods. The scattered bands of greenhorns were safe for this day. But it would be another five days before they finally got out of the trap they found themselves in.

• • •

The problem, of course, was the river. Even now, two days after the initial assault, there was not one single bridge across the Sauer in the 5th and 76th Divisions' sector. Even a telephone link was lacking between the two banks. Two volunteers swam the first line across, but were stopped by mines on the other side. Someone came up with the ingenious idea of firing a rope across by means of a bazooka. But German artillery knocked out that particular rope. More volunteers swam another rope across under the cover of a smoke screen, this time weighting the cable so that it remained below the surface. The Germans spotted them, and, trying an old trick of theirs, they floated mines down the Sauer to destroy the cable. One exploded directly above it, but this time the line held and now the hard-pressed soldiers on both sides of the Sauer River were linked at last.

It was high time. The situation of the men on the German side was perilous. Food, ammunition, and oil to clean waterlogged weapons were needed urgently. Casualties—and there were many of them—needed evacuating at once. Some of the seriously wounded men had been lying in the snow and mud for over thirty-six hours. Dog teams were rushed up, but they couldn't make it across the river.

General Hans Schmidt, commanding the 76th, ordered all divisional artillery spotter planes into action. The Piper Cubs would ferry the desperately needed supplies across the Sauer. The wounded would have to look after themselves.

Now the Piper Cubs winged their way across the river through a lethal barrage of German machine-gun fire, with the pilots dropping the precious supplies out of the door like old-time World War I fliers. "We were getting pretty short of ammunition and food when the Piper Cubs started dropping stuff to us," Sgt. Joseph E. Williams of the 76th recalled after the war. "The first bundles landed out in the open fields under snipers' fire, but later they hit the edge of the woods where we were."[6]

In spite of the sleet and the rain, water was desperately needed, too. Later, Lieutenant Robert Seiter would tell a relief party, "Here's some water in my canteen, that drained through the blanket over my foxhole. Tastes a little like dye, but it's not bad. Our Halazone tablets purified it."[7] Some men risked their lives to bring in the supplies, which lay so tantalizingly close, but might well have been on the other side of the moon. One such man was Private Lowell of the 76th who rushed into no-man's-land under heavy fire to bring in food for his trapped platoon, which had been without rations for thirty-six hours.

Desperately the hard-pressed engineers, working under fire and fighting the fierce current, threw bridge after bridge across the Sauer only to have it destroyed by German artillery or swept away by the sheer force of the flooded river. At least twelve bridges were carried away by the water. Then, at last, the 5th got lucky. It managed to throw a bridge across that held. Immediately, a permanent smoke screen was thrown over it to blind the German gunners.

Patton was informed. Together with Eddy, he drove across and then "peeped" along the German side. For the first time in World War II, George S. Patton had crossed into Germany. Finally, after three years of combat in two continents and in six different countries, he had arrived at his objective, the country of his enemy. There he would die before this year was out.

On that cold February day, Patton was all conqueror. Spick and span in his lacquered helmet with its outsize three stars and his custom-tailored uniform, complete with the famed pistols, there was no mistaking the general with the imperious bearing. It was "Ol' Blood and Guts" himself!

The dirty, mud-splattered GIs lining the road that ran from Echternacherbruck to Bollendorf could hardly believe the evidence of their own eyes. How had Patton gotten across? (They knew nothing of the new bridge as yet.) Almost immediately, wild rumors began to circulate—*Patton had swum the Sauer single-handed!*

Patton, when informed of the rumor, grinned and let it go. "Crossing the assault bridge in the smoke," as he wrote later, "where we could not see more than a foot ahead and there were no guard rails, was a very interesting operation."[8] Perhaps he felt that he deserved the awed adulation of his men this day. So on that gray February afternoon a new legend about Patton was born.

As the *Stars and Stripes* recorded: "A fighting front is the breeding place for wild stories. Here is one from this sector. Out of the misty night appeared General George S. Patton, Jr. 'Call back the boats!' he screamed. 'They make too high a silhouette. *We will swim!*' The boats turned in mid-stream. The GIs climbed onto the west bank. They hesitated. The general acted. He waded deep into the river and struck out with a powerful crawl. Halfway to the other side, he turned his head and waved. The inspired troops dove in and swam across."[9] Patton must have loved it!

Prüm fell on February 12, with Heilmann's paratroopers— what was left of them—fading away into the steep hills above the town, leaving a handful of snipers to hold the men of Lanham's 22nd Regiment up as best they could. The cost had been high. Leading his first-ever attack, Company Commander Tom Reid found himself losing twenty men and one officer just to capture a handful of miserable run-down cottages. One fifth of his company gone in a single morning— and it was no different in Lanham's other companies. But at least he was established in the key objective and one of his forward observers watching the Germans from a wrecked department store in the center of the ruined town could radio his commander jokingly, "88mm shell just gone straight through ladies' underwear!"[10]

Lanham told him to get on with war. The little colonel was in no mood for jokes.

Neither was Corps Commander Middleton. He had been called to a corps commander conference at Patton's HQ. Here Patton, who knew that time was running out for the Third Army, with only one objective, Prüm, captured, said to Middleton, "Troy, don't you think you could *maneuver* about eight kilometers and take Gerolstein?"* Middleton told Patton he thought he could. "But when I did, I would have no artillery ammunition left. And knowing George as I did, I reminded him how emphatic Bradley was when he told Patton to remain in place." Middleton warned his Army Commander, "If you should fail in this endeavor, there might be serious consequences as far as *you're* concerned."

Patton grinned and said, "I'll take the risk."[11]

*The next town to Prüm.

Patton then urged Eddy, "Manton, what's to keep you from *edging* forward and capturing Bitburg?"[12]

Finally he turned to portly Gen. Walton H. Walker, commanding the XX Corps on the Moselle River, "Can't you, Walton, with all the strength you have, sort of *sidle* ahead about ten kilometers and capture Trier?"[13]

In the end all three corps commanders agreed to "sidle, edge, maneuver"—straight ahead, although they knew that Bradley had ordered the "armored reconnaissance" to halt.

For now that his troops had finally overcome the Our-Sauer obstacle, had captured Prüm, and were poised to do the same at Bitburg, Patton was consumed with the burning desire to achieve that glittering objective that had tempted him since the previous September.

Before him now lay one more river line, that of the Kyll River, three to ten miles east of Prüm-Bitburg, a stream that Col. Robert S. Allen of Patton's staff characterized as "one mean son-of-a-bitch!"

Patton didn't think so. Besides, beyond it there was a mere fifty miles to the Rhine. He assembled his staff and told them that he estimated it could be assaulted and bridged in a mere twenty-four hours. "This river is out in the open," he lectured his officers, "and it will be easier to cross than the Sauer. There is no Siegfried Line there in which the Hun can hole up and shoot at us. Also after crossing the Moselle and Sauer in full flood, our men can cross any goddamned river. This is certainly the river-crossingest Army there ever was."

He let his words sink in, then he chuckled and added, "You know it's got so that the Third Army's theme song has become 'One More River to Cross.' " He paused. "I hope that one isn't the Jordon."[14]

Five

Now while the 4th Infantry Division consolidated its position at Prüm and the 5th Infantry, with the assistance of Patton's favorite armored division, the 4th Armored, "edged" their way closer to Bitburg, the bulk of the Third Army rested. After a week of bitter combat, the survivors of the 76th Infantry's attack on the Sauer were brought back across the river to be fed and cleaned up.

As the divisional history of the 76th recorded: "All that could be seen in those dirty whiskered faces, in the sag of wet shoulders, in the shuffle of mudcaked feet, was the weariness of men who had lived in continuous danger, little food and less sleep for nearly a week—complete utter fatigue."[1]

Several hundred of them trekked to an open field next to a little Luxembourg village where a quartermaster shower unit had been set up. Stripping naked, unconcerned by the fact that they were being watched by the local women and children, they dropped their uniforms in the mud (they'd get clean, deloused ones at the end of the shower line) and shuffled along the wooden skids in their flapping boots into the tents to surrender their skinny, dirty bodies to the benison of hot water and soap. As one of them sighed happily, "I had to travel through France, Belgium, and most of Luxembourg to get a chance of hot water and soap, but boy, it was worth it!"[2] Others settled down where they had fought. Sergeant Giles found himself in a desolate stretch of the battlefield— "nothing but stumps of pine trees, limbs all blown off, upper halves splintered"—and found it "weird and spooky and gave you the creeps."[3] But what was to come worried him more. "This is the part of the war I have dreaded the most—being in Germany. I even dreaded crossing the border and knowing I was in Germany . . . I have always thought the Krauts would fight like devils for every inch of German soil—and in a way they are. I dreaded this Siegfried Line. I still dread the Rhine. It stands to reason they have their backs to the wall and that lunatic Hitler will fight till the last German is dead before he gives up."[4]

Veterans, such as Atwell and his fellow medics, no longer cared where they were and what was to come. In the shell-shattered, local Catholic church, they watched Abbott and Costello in *Lost in a Harem* and Rita Hayworth in *Cover Girl* four times over on the same day until the Catholic chaplain complained. "At that time," wrote Atwell after the war, "no one seemed to care about anything. Sentences went unfinished, listening faces were loose and vacant; everyone yawned, sprawled, wrote letters in a desultory way, waiting for one tiresome, not quite sufficient, meal to follow the other. The men hung around the sacristy, crawling over each other like puppies. "Go wan, ya f——." "Aaah, ya f——." "Git ya feet off me, ya greasy bastard." "Ah'm telling you, boy, if Ah ever gits back home for a furlough, they're gonna have to burn the woods and sif' the ashes to find *me* again!"[5]

It was the familiar, drained mood of men after any combat. And often there was no real letup for them, especially if they were still in the line. Daytime was all right: just the long, boring routine of strengthening freezing foxholes, filling sandbags, stringing new wire, and waiting for the next meal—more than likely hash or fried Spam, washed down with GI coffee, usually instant.

But nighttime was different, even in a quiet sector. Night was silence, isolation, fear. Time crept by with leaden feet, while the men isolated in their foxholes were prey to all kinds of unreasoning fancies. A shell-shattered tree stump, a hummock of earth, a coil of rusting barbed wire all took on new and menacing forms in the eerie half-light of the exploding flares and flashes of artillery fire.

It was not surprising that the men were jaded, apathetic, easy victims of nervous disorders and chest troubles. They were a sharp contrast to the keen, smart, well-fed "feather merchants" who served behind the lines—six of them to keep one rifleman in combat. "*One* man in the line, *six* to bring up the Coca-Cola!" they wisecracked bitterly. They, the combat infantry, bearded, unwashed, worn, more often than not, hungry, looked like a bunch of human wrecks.

* * *

But the fate of his infantry little concerned Patton. When the time came to get up and fight one more, they would—or else. His mind was full of glory and how he would achieve his great aim—to be on the Rhine before the "Field Marshal" or any of his fellow U.S. army commanders for that matter. For he had a low opinion of the whole bunch of them.

Montgomery was "that little fart." Eisenhower was "yellow." Bradley and the First Army Commander Hodges were "nothings." "Even the tent maker admits that Courtney [Hodges] is dumb. He is also very jealous of me."[6] And so the litany of his disrespect and dislike continued. Patton thought every one of his superiors and fellow commanders were trying to stop him conducting the war the way he wanted to do. As he confided to his diary, "I have to battle for every yard. It is not the enemy who is trying to stop me, it is *they*."[7]

Even his corps commanders, loyal as they were to him, did not escape his disdain and contempt. "Middleton and Milliken . . . are too cautious."[8] "General Eddy is very nervous, very much inclined to be grasping and always worrying that some other Corps Commander is getting a better deal than he is."[9] But, as he said of his fourth corps commander, Walker, all of them would "fight anytime, anyplace, with anything that the Army Commander would give him."[10]

Now, convinced that all four of them would obey him on the continuation of his drive into Germany, he put them through a detailed rehearsal of the briefing he had worked out for General Bradley. For now as he stabilized his front on the Kyll, he intended to convince the Army Group Commander that his Third Army should continue fighting.

Bradley arrived, and Patton got down to business at once. "General," he snapped in that squeaky voice of his, "Third Army wants to fight. It can do so victoriously if it is allowed. That's all that is standing in our way, and that's all we're asking. The chance to fight for our country and to lick the goddam Hun whom we've got on the run! I asked the Corps Commanders to come here to outline their situations to you. They will tell you the whole story."[11]

Middleton stepped to the map and delivered the briefing in which Patton had rehearsed him. He was followed by Walker, who explained that he could capture Trier within two days if he were allowed to retain the 10th Armored Division, which had been allotted to him for a brief period out of SHAEF reserve. Bradley listened quietly, face revealing nothing. Then it was his turn. He stated that Eisenhower was under the strictest instructions from Gen. George Marshall in Washington to keep a certain number of divisions, including the 10th Armored, in reserve. Then he detailed the plan that Marshall wanted Eisenhower to carry out.

Patton, who thought "Marshall lacks imagination,"[12] was nevertheless afraid of him. Marshall had made all of them— and Patton knew he could *break* them just as easily. Indeed, after the war it was stated by President Truman that Marshall had threatened to break even Eisenhower himself on account of his affair with Kay Summersby. But now he was too bitter even to be afraid. He rose and said, "That's a fine plan all right, General. It sounds very impressive on paper. But it sure is one hell-of-a-note to have this war run 5,000 miles away from here! We are trying to fight the enemy according to the situation on the ground. Not on a map or by theory. . . . Third Army wants to fight. It wants to get this goddamned war over with. We can take Trier in two days and be in Koblenz in a week. . . . The Hun can't stop us now!"[13]

Bradley made no reply to Patton's impassioned outburst. He knew "Georgie" of old. He needed him, admittedly, but he no longer had much respect for his judgment. Instead he asked Walker a few questions about the situation around Trier. Then he turned slyly to a fuming Patton and said, "George, if you do take Trier you may be sorry. SHAEF may change Army boundaries on you and give that sector to Jakie Devers."[14]

Patton's face flushed even deeper. General Jacob Devers, the Commander of the U.S. Sixth Army Group to the south of Patton, was a West Point classmate, a fellow cavalryman, and the two of them had played polo together in the U.S. team in the late twenties, but there was no love lost between them. Bradley was being deliberately malicious. Patton flared up and declared, "It doesn't matter who gets the goddam place [Trier] just as long as it isn't the Hun! If, after we take it, it's turned over to Jakie then it will give him a strong position for an offensive through the Palatinate*—damn him!"[15]

Bradley laughed, and the two generals got down to some horse-trading, which ended with Bradley agreeing to accept that the 90th Infantry Division be put in the SHAEF reserve. In its place, Patton could retain the 10th Armored for a further forty-eight hours.

Patton had done it again. Now he could attack Trier, the ancient Roman capital of the north, a city "which was old when Rome was young" as its citizens boasted. The "armored reconnaissance" could continue for a further two days. Thanks to his corps commanders who knew there wasn't a chance that Trier could be taken within that time limit, Patton's Third could carry on "sidling, edging, and maneuvering" their way to the Rhine.

The U.S. 10th Armored and its commander, Maj. Gen. W.H. Morris, were not particularly well regarded by Patton. Morris had graduated from West Point in the same year as Patton had, had gone to France briefly in 1918, and had been wounded there as Patton had. But he did not possess the same fire and flare as his illustrious contemporary, and the Army Commander thought he had achieved his limit as a divisional general.

During the previous year's fighting on the Saar, his 10th Division had done well, but not brilliantly. Patton felt that Morris had not led it correctly. Morris, too, was prone to mistakes. Like General Malony, who commanded the 94th Infantry Division, which would fight alongside the 10th, he was currently on Patton's "shit list."

Visiting their corps commander, Walker, shortly after the Bradley decision to allow him to keep the 10th for two more days, Patton learned that Morris had managed to lose the bridging train vitally needed for the operation against Trier. Patton flew into a rage. Glowering at the portly, undersized Corps Commander, he squeaked, "You should have seen it was in place. So should I. We have all three fallen down on the job." A little later Patton snapped, "General Morris will

*That area of S.W. Germany roughly between the Sauer/Saar River and the Rhine.

lead his division across the river in the first boat, or, if necessary, *swim!*''[16]

It was obvious to Walker's staff officers that Patton—
worried by his efforts to capture Trier by Bradley's deadline,
using only two divisions (most of the staff thought that four
were needed), both of which he did not trust—was letting his
nerves run away with him. Trier would have to be captured
soon—or heads would roll.

But while Patton was engaged in his own much more weighty
battle with authority on account of his employment of Morris's 10th Armored, he also found himself fighting a minor
battle—*with a mere sergeant!* But it was one that illustrated
Patton's basic attitude to the common soldier and his autocratic manner.

The sergeant in question was 21-year-old cartoonist Bill
Mauldin, who had come from a kind of background that was
totally foreign to Patton, growing up ''in the rural Southwest,
with coal-oil lamps and wind through the walls, where we
shot our meat and could never pay our bills.''[17]

In 1943 as a sergeant, Mauldin had landed in Sicily under
Patton's command with the 45th Infantry Division. From the
infantry he had graduated to the Army newspaper, *Stars and
Stripes*, where he had created the famous, unforgettable Willie and Joe: two weary, anti-bull, unshaven infantrymen.

During the harsh winter of 1943/44 in southern Italy, where
the terrain and weather were as much an enemy as the
''Teds,''* Mauldin produced a number of biting cartoons that
some of the top brass thought were ''un-American.'' Indeed
the deputy theater commander ordered they should be banned
in his area.

Naturally Patton, whose men were forced to wear neckties
in the battle zone and helmets in the rear areas on the pain
of severe money fines, was an implacable opponent of Mauldin and his two unsoldierly characters, Willie and Joe.

He contacted the military officer in charge of the *Stars and
Stripes* and suggested their youngest cartoonist should either
shave his creations or be dropped from the paper. Colonel
White, the publisher, refused. Patton took up the matter with

---

*GI nickname for the German, taken from the Italian *tedeschi*.

Eisenhower himself. But the Supreme Commander dismissed the matter, and Mauldin continued to draw his Willie and Joe, as unshaven and war-weary as ever.

Now, as Patton prepared for the coming battle for Trier, his chief-of-staff, General Gay, was informed by SHAEF in a telephone call: "Sergeant Bill Mauldin is scheduled to spend thirty days in your theater, so it may not be a bad idea if Mauldin and General Patton got together and had a little chat."[18]

Gay's reply is not recorded, but one can imagine what he thought of the idea.

In due course, Mauldin arrived in the Third Army area, to be stopped by the first military policeman he encountered, who bawled, "Where the hell is yer gawdam helmet?" For in the Third, even cartoonists were supposed to wear helmets.

Mauldin tried to explain that he had just forgotten it, but the MP cut him off harshly. "Don't you gimme none of yer gawdam lip," he snapped. "Dammit—I heard that one before!"[19]

One word led to another. Tempers flared. Mauldin, who admitted himself that he felt "a terrible need to feel respected, upright and important,"[20] finally shouted at the MP. The result was that the MP gave him a ticket and dismissed him.

Now Mauldin went to work with his pencil. He drew a bitter cartoon depicting what the ordinary "dogface" thought of Patton's Third Army. It showed a weary, unshaven GI (minus helmet), staring at a notice that stated, "You are entering the Third Army." Below were listed the fines that a soldier would pay for various infringements, ranging from "No helmet—$25" to "Trousers down—$50" and "Enforced by order of Ol' Blood and Guts." The dogface's comment is: "Radio th' ol' man we'll be late on account of a thousand-mile detour."[21]

Patton's reaction was predictable. He kept his temper, but was icy in his treatment of the young NCO. After Mauldin left, he ordered that a young artist at his own HQ, Tom Hudson, should draw a series of cartoons that would put Mauldin's Willie and Joe in the shade. They would depict his Third Army men as Patton visualized them: virile, masculine—and clean-shaven!

Hudson made a promising start. His cartoons emphasized sex rather than combat. It was something that Patton approved of. After all, he maintained himself that a ''man who won't fuck, won't fight!'' But after Hudson's creations started to show more than a touch of the Mauldin style, Patton ordered him to cease drawing—and that was that . . .

In itself the episode was of little importance. Its significance lies in the fact that it illustrates just how out of tune Patton was of the spirit of the American Army and the country it represented. The American Army could engineer a meeting between a twenty-one-year-old sergeant and one of its top leaders commanding an army a third of a million strong. Very democratic indeed. But Patton was *not* a democrat.

Of course, he knew it was expected of an American general to pay lip service to the concept of democracy. That is why he agreed to meet the lowly sergeant with his antiestablishment ideas. But in his heart, he was against the concept. Patton fought not for American democracy, but for America. ''Politicians,'' he once wrote, ''are the lowest form of life on earth. Liberal democrats are the lowest form of politician!''[22]

If Patton subscribed to any kind of creed, beyond the belief in his own star, it was surely that expressed by the motto of the United States Military Academy: ''Duty, Honor, Country!''

Patton believed in older values that were probably anathema to most of his soldiers, who were concerned basically with *surviving* the coming battle. For him ''the flag is to the patriot what the cross is to the Christian.''[23] For that flag he was prepared to die, if necessary; for he regarded battle in a completely different manner than they did. ''Battle,'' he once told his aide, Colonel Codman, ''is the most magnificent competition in which a human being can indulge. It brings out all that is best; it removes all that is base.''[24] On another occasion, viewing a battlefield littered with German dead, with blackened corpses everywhere, he shouted, ''Just look at that, Codman. Could anything be more magnificent? Compared with war, all other forms of human endeavor shrink to insignificance.''

As Codman recorded it, "Patton's voice shook with emotion," as he cried: "God, how I love it!"[25]

Now, as his men prepared to attack and capture Trier, Patton did not really consider the cost in human lives—the butcher's bill that his young soldiers would have to pay to win the city. With his keen sense of history, Patton knew not only was he going to attack his first great German city, but that it was also a city with a long historical tradition: one that had been taken by his glorious predecessors: Julius Caesar, Gustavus Adolphus of Sweden, Louis 14th, "the Sun King," etc., etc. Hadn't the Great Napoleon himself captured it!

He, who would be dead before this year was out, could state, "You have but one life, live it to the fullest of glory and be willing to pay any price."[26] But were his young soldiers, most of whom had never even heard of Trier up to this February and had not the slightest interest in the city's history and the great military leaders who had conquered it, prepared to pay that price?

Patton neither knew nor cared. As February 1945 started to give way to March, there was only one overriding consideration in his mind: *when will Trier fall?*

Six

Now Trier was six miles away.

The way here had been tough. The 94th Infantry Division's assault crossing of the Saar River had been a total failure. The two battalions selected to carry out the task had been caught in midstream by German artillery. It had been too much for the infantrymen. They had broken, fleeing back to their own shore and leaving a score of boats filled with dead and dying men behind them.

Elements of the 10th Armored Division had tangled with men of the 94th clearing out some woods near the river. A regular firefight developed that ceased only when someone discovered American was fighting American! But by that time the 94th had lost half a company in killed and wounded.

Finally the 94th and the 10th managed to cross the Saar, only to be attacked by elements of the 6th SS Mountain, 2nd Mountain, and 11th Panzer Divisions. These outfits were shadows of their former selves, but the young men of the two mountain divisions were in peak condition and tough, in most cases, and they made the Americans pay heavily for the ground they gained. For a while the 5th Ranger Battalion, fighting with the 94th, was cut off and was asked by the attacking Germans to surrender—this with the war almost ended! They refused. They managed to get a message through to the 94th that they would continue fighting if ammunition and medical supplies were air-dropped to them.

That day the Piper Cubs of the divisional artillery flew fifty-six sorties in face of intense German machine-gun fire to drop supplies to the hard-pressed Rangers cut off by the SS at Serrig. The Rangers held, but the toll was high.

A German mine field was discovered protecting the villages of Pellingen and Ollmuth. It stopped the advance dead. Engineers were rushed up and began to tackle the mines un-

63

der heavy German fire. In the end they managed to clear it. But again the cost was very high. Forty percent of the brave combat engineers were killed and wounded by the enemy artillery fire or the mines. The advance continued, while in Berlin the "Poison Dwarf,"* Minister of Propaganda Dr. Josef Goebbels, boasted, "No foreign invader will ever enter the city [Trier], even if we've got to beat him to death with our fists or strangle him. Trier will remain free!"[1]

The Americans ran into a bunker line. Captain Miles Standish's company of the 94th was ordered into the attack. They encountered a large force of Germans, and bitter hand-to-hand fighting developed. The Germans and Americans fought all night. Finally the men of the 94th broke, and those who were left crawled and straggled back to their own lines. Three days later Captain Standish was found, absolutely alone, half-starved, and in a state of complete shock.

With time running out fast, Patton hounded Morris and Malony all the time, urging them to ever greater efforts, visiting their headquarters repeatedly.

On February 28, with Trier still not captured, Colonel Codman had telephoned General Morris to arrange a meeting between him and his boss, Patton. Just as Patton's car reached the spot where the two generals had agreed to meet, a military policeman directed it to another place. Fortunately so for Patton. Minutes later a heavy salvo of shells fell on the spot. The Germans had been tapping Third Army's phone lines: Thus Patton lost his last opportunity to die in battle.

Now, however, the 10th Armored Division was within striking distance of Trier. The battered ancient city, which had been under American artillery fire from Luxembourg off and on since September 1944, was held by a rabble of *Wehrmacht* second-line troops and two *Volkssturm*** battalions under the command of Colonel Ernst Bachmann.

Unknown to the hapless "fortress commandant," Hitler personally had ordered that "Trier is to be defended as fortress." When his corps commander had received the order from the headquarters of the Seventh German Army, he had

*On account of his vitriolic tongue and small stature.
**The German Home Guard.

snapped bitterly, "I cannot and will not pass on the order. You can't expect me to pass on an order which it is impossible to carry out. But *you* can pass on what I say—you can't defend Trier with six hundred drunken Volkssturm men!"[2]

In essence, Trier was wide open, ready for the taking. But SHAEF and Bradley were breathing down Patton's neck, demanding the return of the 10th Armored to the SHAEF reserve. The forty-eight hours respite that Bradley had given him were up. Patton took a gamble. Trier was, as Colonel Allen expressed it, "the crux of his secret plan to make a breakthrough dash to the Rhine and a sweep of the Palatinate. VIII and XII Corps were poised on the Kyll for the Rhine Drive. All he needed was Trier to set his daring plan in motion."[3] Patton cut all lines to higher authority, save to Bradley.

On the night of February 27, he phoned Bradley and told the latter that he was within sight of Trier and requested permission to just keep going, even though the 10th was supposed to return to the reserve that night. Bradley gave in. He told Patton to keep on going until Eisenhower *personally* ordered the 10th to be withdrawn from the battle. He chuckled and told Patton that he, too, was going to keep away from the phone for the next few hours. Patton had his green light!

On March 1, the 10th Armored, with a regiment of the 94th (376th Infantry) attached, attacked Trier. During the night an armored task force under the command of Lt. Col. Jack Richardson—"a brave son-of-a-bitch," as Patton called him, who was currently under open arrest awaiting a court-martial*—had successfully captured intact a bridge across the Moselle by a bold *coup-de-main*. Now American troops could be easily brought across the river to support the attackers, who were meeting stiff resistance from Bachmann's rabble of *Wehrmacht* units.

In the main, the Germans used mortars and machine guns to hold up the Americans. With Patton breathing fire, the chief-of-staff of the 10th went up to find out what was holding his men up. He was caught in mortar barrage and was wounded in the head. The house-to-house fighting continued.

*Why is not known, but Richardson never was court-martialed. He was killed in action a little later.

But the resistance was weakening rapidly. Both *Volkssturm* battalions, one of them named after the ancient city's most famous monument, the *Porta Nigra*,* started on a massive binge, looting the abandoned wine cellars that were everywhere in the nearly deserted city. Then, as the German Seventh Army was to record angrily, "As soon as the Americans attacked, the *Porta Nigra* ran away for the most part, while the *Volkssturmbattalion* got blind drunk."[4]

Now with contingents from two combat commands of the 10th and the 376th Regiment of the 94th within the city, more and more Germans began to surrender. Task Force Richardson alone took 800, and in the end 3,000 gave in. Bachmann radioed the German Seventh Army, "The remaining garrison in Trier is surrounded. Can't recapture the Romerbrucke** with my present strength. Intend to break out this night as soon as it is dark,"[5] and that was the last that was heard of the hapless *Oberst* Bachmann.

"Nix Trier . . . Trier kaput," was the comment of one weary GI in broken German to the first frightened civilian he discovered among the smoking ruins. He was right. Trier *was* kaput. As one of the first of Patton's staff to enter the city recorded later: "Aside from its strategic value, Trier was a sorry prize. Founded by the Romans and the oldest city in northern Europe, it was a complete ruin from months of air bombing and artillery pounding. The only thing unscarred in the town was the Porta Negra[sic], a huge stone remnant of a wall built by the Romans."[6]

Ruin or not, Patton was overjoyed when he heard the great news that Trier had fallen at last. This was perhaps the greatest day of what remained of his life. He had taken a major German city, his first, tricked the top brass, and showed just what he and his Third Army could do when "they" stopped interfering in his affairs.

More! Now after two months of fighting, which had cost him 42,000 battle and non-battle casualties, the gate to the Moselle, Trier, was open. He could head up the river to where it joined the Rhine at Koblenz and cross. Or he could turn

---

*The Black Gate, built in the second century by the Romans.
**The Roman Bridge captured by Richardson.

southeast, dash behind the West Wall defenses still holding up the U.S. Seventh Army in the Saar, capture the Saar Basin, and then hit the Rhine below Mainz. Either way he could beat "the little fart" Montgomery. For the Britisher was not scheduled to launch his great set-piece crossing of the Rhine for another three weeks yet.

That March 1, 1945, Patton felt he had the world at his feet. He had thumbed his nose at Eisenhower and his gamble with the 10th Armored Division had paid off. Now, as he received an urgent message from SHAEF, urging him to bypass Trier because it would take four divisions to capture it, he radioed back, his triumph all too obvious: "Have taken Trier with two divisions. What do you want me to do? Give it back?"[7]

Now Patton set in motion the start of his drive for the Rhine. He ordered an immediate attack that night on the Kyll River line. Once it had been successfully assaulted in the region of Bitburg by the 5th Infantry Division, the 4th Armored Division, which had made a spectacular advance across Brittany the previous August, would break out of the bridgehead and barrel for the Rhine. It would be followed by a relatively green armored division, the 11th, breaking out of the bridgehead gained for it by the 90th Infantry Division.

That afternoon, in high spirits, he interrupted the daily briefing, which dealt with the confusion presently reigning on the Third Army front, with: "You mean everything is as confused as hell and nobody really is sure where the Germans are? . . . Well, I'll tell you what I'm going to do. I'm going to drive through Trier and see how things are and then go and find out exactly where this damned war is today."[8]

One hundred percent the conqueror, Patton drove through the smoking ruins of the old Roman city, past the *Judengasse*, the medieval ghetto, and the eighteenth-century house where Karl Marx had been born. Next to the *Porta Nigra*, which no less a person than Napoleon had ordered restored when he had captured the city nearly 150 years before, he found XX Corps Commander Walton Walker, short, rugged, and pugnacious, known as "Bulldog." Of all Patton's generals, he would be the only one to attend Patton's funeral, flying over from Texas for the ceremony in Luxembourg at his own expense.

Now "Ol' Blood and Guts" and "Bulldog," immaculate in their "Ike" jackets and custom-tailored cavalry breeches, complete with polished riding boots, set off to find the war.

They found it in the shape of two German artillery units blindly mortaring *each other*. The little convoy stopped, and Patton got out to study the situation. Finally he said to "Hap" Gay, his chief-of-staff, "Hap, in my considered judgment, the thing to do is get the hell out of here, drive home, and have a drink."

Rank hath privileges and triumphant generals fight office-hour wars. On their way back to Luxembourg, however, the little convoy was stopped by a huge column of stalled vehicles and men, a perfect target for any German bomber. The cause of the jam was a great 155mm cannon trapped under a railway bridge. Patton flew into one of his impressive rages. He found the colonel in charge halfway down the column instead of up front where he should have been. "Listen," he exploded, his face red with fury, "you can blow up that goddam gun, you can blow up the goddam bridge, or you can blow out your goddam brains—and I don't care which!"[9]

And with that Patton drove on "back home." It had been a tremendous day. Now he needed a drink to celebrate.

That night Patton did exactly that. As the guns on the Kyll rumbled, and the men of the 5th and 90th divisions prepared for the assault, Patton killed a whole bottle of bourbon together with his nephew Frey Ayer, while smoking expensive cigars, one after another.

As the evening progressed, Patton grew mellow under the influence of the alcohol, telling his nephew, who was with the FBI, that his Third Army men should enjoy everything they captured, including German women. For his part he wanted no women around his HQ. "He was convinced," he told his nephew, "that those with whom he was unpopular at home had been trying and would continue to try in some way to destroy him. He felt that it was possible for someone to use a woman and a slanted press release to blacken his reputation."[10] One wonders what Fred Ayer knew of his cousin Jean Gordon and her presence at his uncle's HQ.

Patton offered his relative some insight into his personal psychology, too. "In any war," he lectured, "a commander, no matter what his rank, has to send to sure death, nearly every day, by his own orders, a certain number of men. Some are his personal friends. All are his personal responsibility. Any man with a heart would like to sit down and bawl, but he can't. So he sticks out his jaw and swaggers and swears."[11]

As the level of the bourbon got lower and lower, Patton launched into his assessment of current American politics. "We've got a President who's a great politician and who pulled things together, when they had to be. But Goddamn it, the man has never read history. He doesn't understand the Russians and he never will. . . . From Genghis Khan to Stalin they haven't changed. They never will and we, we'll never learn, not anyway until it's too damned late. . . . There's another thing people in our government can't understand. They can't even understand the Germans. It is either that or they're too much influenced by the Jews who understandably want revenge. Look at this fool unconditional surrender announcement. If the Hun ever needed anything to put a burr under his saddle, that's it. He'll now fight like the devil because he'll be ordered to do so."[12]

That night Patton let loose all his rancor at the men in Washington: "Politicians are the worst. They'll wear their country's flag in public, but they'll use it to wipe their behinds in the caucus room, if they think it will win them a vote. I know. I wish I could get some of the bastards into the front lines here. It might be even better than making some read history."[13]

But not even Patton's bitter dislike of the politicians back home could spoil this glorious day. "Now there's almost nothing to stop me," he proclaimed. "We have fresh divisions arriving. We've mastered the air. We have . . . the best weapons in the world. We can soon march into Berlin, Vienna, Prague, and Belgrade with people throwing flowers in our path."[14]

Thus Patton philosophized, as a heavy silence fell over the big, sprawling headquarters, broken only by the rumble of the guns on the Kyll, where already his young men were dying once more for final objectives that would never be attained. Their commander's willfully independent strategy would now ensure that the bulk of the U.S. forces would swing southeast into the strategically unimportant Bavaria. There would be no triumphal march into Berlin, Vienna, Prague, and Belgrade for the survivors, with "people throwing flowers in our path." All their youthful effort, their courage, their sacrifice would be in vain. One tyranny would be defeated admittedly, but another would replace it in Central Europe; and the actions and decisions of that gray-haired old man on that March 1 so long ago played as much a role as any in allowing that new tyranny to be set up.

Now it was three in the morning. The bourbon bottle was empty at last. "Uncle George" ground out his last cigar and rose easily to his feet. "And now," he growled, "by God we can go to bed. See you at breakfast."[15]

George S. Patton had enjoyed his last great triumph. Soon his bitter decline would commence.

PART II

☆ ☆ ☆ ☆ ☆

OVER THE RHINE

Seven

Down in a steep gorge of the Kyll River, below the heights that house the American air base at Bitburg, there is an eighteenth-century water mill, a shabby, rambling structure painted white, surrounded by a little straggle of cottages that housed the workers. Its name is the *Mettericher Mühle*.

Even today, forty-odd years or so after the event that made the mill at Metterich famous for a day and put it so briefly on newspaper maps throughout the world, it is a remote place. The stranger coming down that long, steep slope, which was once churned to mud by the wheels and tracks of a thousand vehicles, to the mill at the side of the fast-flowing Kyll is surrounded by excited old peasants, all talking at once, with dogs snapping threateningly at his feet. The men smell of animal manure and despair. The women, as is common in this region, have their necks disfigured by goiter. The dogs are lean and underfed. It is a poor place—and its inhabitants are poor, too.

Yet their memories are good. In the manner of old people, they remember the events of forty-odd years ago better than they do what happened the day before.

The *Amis*, as they call the Americans, had taken up their positions beyond the railway line on the other side of the Kyll, coming down from newly captured Bitburg. For a day or so nothing happened, and then the Americans set up a choking, white smoke screen the length of their stretch of the river. The few German engineers, busy mining the shallows (for here at Metterich was the only ford for many miles), said it meant the *Amis* would attempt a crossing soon, but it wouldn't be here. Only a handful of local people knew that there was a ford here. The *Amis* wouldn't know that!* Then the engi-

*Amazingly enough, in 1985, forty years afterward, local German Army

73

neers vanished, and the peasants were left to their own devices. So with two whole enemy divisions forming up behind the cover of the smoke, they did what they always had done. They baked their heavy, two-pound, dark-crusted "wheels," as they called their loaves.

Before daylight on the morning of March 2, 1945, they came, wading and splashing through the water out of the choking fog: the infantry of the 5th Division. They caught the peasants completely by surprise. To the undersized civilians they were big tall fellows, "as tall as a tree." Hurriedly, the peasants were forced outside and the straggle of houses searched. "The *Amis* didn't do anything to us," old Frau Lichtner, who was young then, remembers. "One of the soldiers saw all the flour inside the mill and said in German, 'You're not starving in Germany are you?' and then they were gone."[1]

But there were more to come. As the infantrymen clambered up the heights to the winding, twisting road beyond and the hamlet of Metterich, the first of the 30-ton Shermans came clattering through the water, riding unscathed over the antitank mines that the engineers had laid. First a handful, then a score, a hundred . . . two hundred . . . two hundred and fifty. While the peasants stood open-mouthed watching the steel monsters churning up the ford and the fields beyond, two whole combat commands of Gen. Hugh Gaffey's 4th Armored Division rolled to the heights and the road network beyond. At last Patton had launched his drive for the Rhine, sending in his favorite armored division, knowing that if any division of the three American armies, the First, Ninth, and Third, could win the race to the great river, it would be his 4th.

Then they were gone and peace and calm returned to the mill. Once more those humble peasants at the *Mettericher Mühle* returned to their former obscurity, a footnote in the history of World War II.

General Gaffey, formerly of Patton's staff and now commanding the 4th, had only one real concern as he commenced his

---

reservists carried out an exercise the length of the Kyll trying to find a ford and were surprised to find it at Metterich. Seemingly the "secret" ford had been lost again.

drive to the Rhine: not the enemy as represented by General von Rothkirch's LIII Corps, but the weather.

It had been raining and sleeting now for days and the poor-quality Eifel mountain roads were in a terrible state. Continued rain would not help his plan to strike boldly for the Rhine along the roads over the mountains.

But Patton brooked no hesitation. His two combat commands, barreling forward over parallel roads, were to head for the river near Andernach, famed locally for its lunatic asylum. Here with any luck, Gaffey might seize a bridge and cross before the Krauts knew what had hit them. He ordered his Combat Command B to roll.

At dawn on March 5, the tankers broke out of the bridgehead. An hour after they had begun to move, Patton telephoned Bradley and told him what he had done. According to Colonel Allen of Patton's staff, "He [Bradley] was a little startled but not wholly surprised,"[2] which he should have been. For he was already in possession of a "Letter of Instruction" from the U.S. chiefs-of-staff detailing SHAEF's plans for the future. In it there was no mention of Trier or the clearing of the Saar-Moselle triangle. The Third Army, it seemed, was running a private war of which Washington knew nothing!

After the initial German opposition was broken, the 4th's drive to the Rhine began to read like a railroad timetable. Eight o'clock the village of Orself, twelve o'clock Steinborn. . . . By the end of the first day the tankers had reached Weidenbach, twelve miles from the Kyll River.

A desperate Gen. Edwin von Rothkirch, knowing now that his flank had been turned, rushed a brigade of Germany's most feared weapon, the "moaning Minnie," six-barreled electric mortars, to Weidenbach. At the same time he ordered the last drops of fuel to be drained from his own headquarter vehicles in order to provide some for a handful of Tiger tanks in his workshops. But neither could stop the advance the next day; and the 4th shot up the great sixty-ton German tanks, individually.

Rothkirch ordered a blocking position set up at Oberstadtfeld so that the survivors of his battered 340th Division could escape through it during the hours of darkness. The local *Volkssturm* was called out to provide "the heroic reargurard" cover. Heinz Hennen, a local farmer, was one of them. When he heard what his collection of "old buffers and green kids" were going to do, he "sprang over a fence and headed for the hills—like most of the rest of them. From the nearest one I could watch the Americans through my spyglass. Tanks rolling ceaselessly eastward. It was impressive—and frightening."[3]

Oberstadtfeld was taken and the 340th abandoned its transport and tried to break through in small groups. Not many of them made it. Prisoners were flooding in on all sides. At the hamlet of Putzborn, the next settlement on the way from Oberstadtfeld to the larger township of Daun, a handful of SS men tried to blow up the bridge, while behind them the locals looted a burning army depot. But their explosives were not strong enough, and as the thunder of the advancing Shermans grew ever closer, they fled Putzborn. The little hamlet below Daun was immediately turned into a POW camp where the first German prisoner to come in was greeted with a glass of whiskey by a grinning 4th man. Later they received kicks.

Peering out of the window of his father's house, six-year-old Fritz Gehendges thought it strange to see "a German soldier trudging through the rain with his hands up—surrendering in his own country."[4]

But everything was strange, wild, and chaotic now. At one point in the advance, there were so many Germans wishing to surrender, clustered around a column from the 37th Tank Battalion, that General von Rothkirch, hurrying to the rear, took them for one of his own formations. He ordered his car stopped and saw to his horror he was trapped.

"Where do you think you're going?" asked 1st Lt. Joe Liese of Company B.

The Corps Commander, in his immaculate, red-tabbed uniform, displayed an un-German sense of humor. With an ironic smile, he replied, "It looks like I'm going to the American rear."[5] And he was right.

Now the prisoners were coming in by the thousands, as the 4th plunged deeper and deeper into the enemy's rear, a thin, blue line on Patton's situation map, getting ever closer to the Rhine. In spite of the fact that the terrible weather made it virtually impossible for air to give its usual support to the ground troops, nothing seemed able to stop the 4th's drive.

Nor was it alone. The 5th Infantry Division was doing its best on the clogged roads to keep up, with its orders being dropped to it by means of liaison planes; the distances were too great for the radio. The green 11th Armored Division was rampaging eastward as well, cleaving through the demoralized enemy at nine to *twenty-two miles* a day, heading for Andernach and Brohl on the Rhine.

The 4th bypassed the ugly *Vulkaneifel** city of Mayen. It was too heavily defended, though its citizens were only too eager to surrender and were threatened with death by the Army for their pains. Kehrig surrendered after a short artillery bombardment: bombardments that Patton had ordered to be fired at every German town that showed the least sign of resistance. "Third Army Memorial Bombardments," he called them cynically, to remind the Krauts by the ruins that resulted that his famous Third had passed this way. (Patton could not have imagined the speed with which the Germans would rebuild; by the end of the decade the ruins had all vanished.)

Now the advance was little more than a road march, urged on by the many thousands of "slave laborers" from every country in Europe who cheered and waved to their liberators. Flying an artillery spotting plane way ahead of the leading tanks, Lieutenant Smith, the pilot, spotted a column of fleeing Germans, obscured from the tankers by the rolling countryside. He signaled the Shermans, "They're only 1,500 yards from you now. . . . Go faster!" The drivers put their foots down.

The distance between the two enemies narrowed rapidly. "Now they're a thousand yards away," Smith radioed from above. Another pause, and then Smith cried excitedly, "They're around the next curve . . . Go and get 'em!"[6]

The Shermans clattered around the bend. There were the totally surprised Germans! Immediately the Shermans' machine guns chattered, sending white tracer racing toward the

*Volcanic Eifel, due to the fact that there are many extinct volcanoes in the area.

enemy. Within minutes it was all over. Those who didn't surrender swiftly enough, didn't survive.

Now it had all become something of a joke, a comic opera war, with—occasionally—a lethal outcome. Minutes after preventing some Americans of the 4th from shooting his cousin (because the latter had harassed them), Herr Nannen was given a Hershey bar by a grateful U.S. sergeant, "Because I'd chanced some German fire from up the road to pull in a dead American," as he recalled many years later. "The irony of it all was that he had been crushed to death in a passage by one of their own tanks."[7]

A few villages further on, German soldiers who had continued to resist the advancing Americans were protected *by their American captors*—from the wrath of the local villagers who were threatening to lynch them.

Now the German commanders were relaying from phone booths and village post offices what orders they still thought it worthwhile to pass on to their scattered forces. Even the Army Commander of the German Seventh Army was on the run with what was left of his staff, dodging the Americans who were everywhere, or so it seemed. Once they were surprised to find themselves in the midst of an American armored column. Hastily they pulled out, hid their vehicles, and spent several hours concealed in a haystack, a handful of frightened middle-aged men who had once commanded the destinies of hundreds of thousands of men.

In the end the American armor had spread havoc through whatever cohesion still remained in the German defenses west of the Rhine and north of the Moselle River, and there before the weary, begrimed tankers lay the silver snake of the Rhine itself. For the loss of twenty-eight men killed, eighty wounded, and two missing, the 4th had taken five thousand prisoners, killed or wounded seven hundred Germans and knocked out thirty to forty tanks and assault guns. As James Wellard, a correspondent attached to the Third Arms HQ gushed: "One night Patton had been fighting in the Siegfried Line; the next he was on the Rhine sixty-five miles to the east. His tanks had just gone. They roared along the mountain roads in one of those terrifying maneuvers when they just disappear over some distant hilltop and are not heard of again for forty-eight hours. They had gone into the mountains and crossed rivers without the benefit of infantry, supply columns, or supporting artillery. Now the head of this armored column was nearly a hundred miles in advance of the main infantry units. It stuck out on a long slender neck. On the maps it looked impossible . . . It was not only possible. It was brilliantly right. . . . The blitz of the 4th Armored Division represented the greatest action in the world.''[8] It was headline news back in the States. ''Patton storms to Rhine,'' ran the banner headlines. ''Takes Thousands in Rout!'' ''Patton Menaces Coblenz, Bonn,'' announced the *Boston Daily Globe* and ran its account above the tall soldiers' tale of Patton having swum the Sauer River, taking it to be a true story. ''Patton Inspired Troops. Icy Swim Under Fire'' were the headlines.[9]

It was all good heady stuff. The publicity back home must have delighted Patton. But the 4th's bold dash for the Rhine must have been soured for him by the fact that his Third was *not* the first to reach the Rhine. The plodding infantryman General Hodges, whom he detested, had beaten him to that great prize. *By three days!*

Not only that. On the very same day that the 4th reached the Rhine, what was the ''most famous bridge in the world'' that March—fell into the hands of Hodges's First Army! At five on the morning of March 7, the first tanks of the 4th reached the Rhine. Ten hours later Hodges's men of the 9th Armored Division were crossing the great river under fire, courtesy the Ludendorff Bridge, and Hitler could lament, ''Two bridgeheads have decided Germany's fate—Normandy and Remagen!''[10]

In the manner that the top brass conducted the war in the spring of 1945, Patton was called up on the phone the following morning by an old friend, Alexander ''Alec'' Patch, the Commander of the U.S. Seventh Army, which was fighting to the south of Patton's Third. ''George,'' he cried, ''I want to congratulate you.''

Patton was puzzled. ''What about, Alec?'' he asked.

''For being the last Army to reach the Rhine,'' Patch answered with a malicious chuckle.

But Patton could give as good as he took. "Thanks, Alec," he replied pleasantly, "And I want to congratulate you, too."

Now it was Patch's turn to be surprised. "For what?" he asked.

Patton snorted with laughter and yelled, "For being the first Army to be kicked off the Rhine!"[11]*

It was recorded that Patch joined in the laughter.

Thus the games generals played that spring, and while they did, the young men with their broken bodies—and often broken minds, too—piled up in the first aid stations, with the same old sentences being used over and over again, "Next man, come in . . . Where ya wounded . . . ? Name . . . rank . . . serial number . . . Take your wound tablets?" And then grisly business would commence, lying on the floor in the straw of a barn stinking of animals, on the table in some kitchen farmhouse, on the shattered altar of a bombed-out church . . . in a muddy hole, with the dead sprawled out in the extravagant poses of those done to death violently.

Medic Atwell, just behind the forward troops in the Eifel that first week of March, saw one such first aid station. "In close now, I saw bloody stumps where feet had been blown off, caved-in ribs, shattered heads, arms and bodies, backs ripped open as if by giant can openers. 'Quick, carry this man out.' Turn, hoist, strap. And another . . . The tough little Chipman from Company C crying and shivering among the walking wounded, saying, 'Atwell, come here. Help me.'

"Why," Atwell asked, "are you wounded?"

But Chipman wasn't wounded. He was one of those broken, not in body, but in mind. He could take no more combat. Atwell pushed him aside; the wounded came first and yet another batch of walking wounded were straggling in, eyes wild with shock and pain, displaying their shattered limbs as if they couldn't believe this was happening to them. "The sense of time disappeared. Turn, hold, strap. Up the stairs with the walking wounded. More salvage to be thrown away in a heap that rapidly grew higher than my head. . . . Back

---

*The Seventh had been forced to withdraw from its Rhine positions in December 1944 in order to take over the Third Army's sector at the time of the Battle of the Bulge. See C. Whiting, *Operation Northwind: The Unknown Battle of the Bulge* for further details.

to the blazing light. More wounded. 'Hey, Doc, when are they gonna look at us? I'm shot up here . . . my knee. . . . Hey, Doc, I'm bleeding here. . . . Hey, this guy has passed out!' ''[12]

Drenched with sweat, fearing he might pass out himself with the horror and exhaustion of it all, Atwell did his best to reassure the new casualties. ''The first they get. . . . As soon as they get rid of these three men on litters,'' he gasped. And as he passed at the double, someone cried plaintively behind him, ''Hey, Doc, wait a second—where can I get a shit?''[13]

In the end the race to the Rhine cost Patton's Third Army (from January 29), 2,706 killed, 16,779 wounded and 1,081 missing, some twenty thousand young men. But it had not succeeded in obtaining a bridge across the great river for its commander. *Yet for three whole days there was one remaining bridge intact in the 4th Armored area!* Due to the fact that the division had been ordered not to go down to the banks of the Rhine itself, in order to avoid casualties, but to keep to the cover of the reverse slopes of the high ground just short of the river, the 4th was unaware that the bridge at Urmitz (between Andernach and Koblenz) still stood. It was only three days after the bridge at Remagen was captured that it was finally blown. It would take General Patton another two weeks before he achieved his aim of crossing the Rhine.

Now that Hodges had beaten him across the Rhine, Patton rationalized to his staff that ''there is no tactical advantage to be gained by crossing the Rhine now. If that bridge had not been captured, an assault of the river probably would have been the best thing we could have done.''[14]

Instead, Patton dreamed up another battle for his Army, again without permission from the chiefs-of-staff. He told his planners, ''Now our most profitable target is the Palatinate. They've got an Army Group down there holding the Siegfried Line against the Seventh Army [in the west] and the Hunsrück Mountains [in the north] against us. G-2 reports they haven't got much on that flank as they are counting on the Hunsrück to hold us off.''[15] Patton flashed a grin at his staff. ''Well we've cracked that kind of terrain before. We did it in the Eifel and we can do it just as fast in the Hunsrück.'' He concluded by stating, "I don't see any reason why we shouldn't turn the German rear in a matter of days . . . and then we can cross [the Rhine] at will. It will be a cinch!"[16] Thus again Patton prepared to commit his army, almost as if it were a personal chattel, with which he could do just as he willed.

Eight

On March 9, Patton, together with Bradley, Hodges, and others of the top brass, were in Liège, Belgium, to receive yet another honor. The French were going to decorate them with the French Legion of Honour, Grand Officer grade, and the Croix de Guerre with Palm—and decorations were always very important for the top brass.

Just as the ceremony was commencing, with its speeches and references to *la gloire* and *patrie* and all the rest of those high-sounding phrases, General Gay back at Patton's HQ in Luxembourg received an excited phone call from General Eddy. He told Patton's chief-of-staff that "the Second Cavalry under [Col.] Charles H. Reed had secured a bridge intact across the Moselle River."[1] What was he to do?

The one-eyed Gay, of whom Patton said, "he's not a world-beater," made a snap decision. He took it upon himself to tell the Corps Commander to exploit the success and establish a firm bridgehead on the other side of the river. Thereupon he called Patton at Liège and suggested he try to obtain Eisenhower's permission to launch his Palatinate campaign at the lunch that followed the investiture.

That morning Patton had already discussed with Bradley the possibility of involving his Third Army in new fighting "so that Montgomery's plan to use most of the divisions on the western front, British and American under his command, for an attack on the Ruhr plains could not come off, and the First and Third Armies be left out on a limb."[2] He liked Gay's new idea. Immediately he had the chance he conferred with Bradley and Eisenhower, explaining the new situation. They both gave permission to exploit the capture of the bridge over the Moselle. Patton was delighted. He called Gay and ordered him to launch the Palatinate Campaign.

The new campaign soon hit problems. On the following

day, while Patton was still in Liège, Eddy called Gay to tell him the bridge had not been captured after all. Gay responded in true Patton fashion. He told Eddy the telephone was out of order and he was unable to hear what the Corps Commander was saying. The Palatinate Campaign was to continue.

Eddy, his blood pressure reaching danger point, persisted. "I'm telling you we haven't got a bridge! It was blown up!" he cried.

Gay said, "You must be mistaken. We've got to have a bridge across the Moselle by tomorrow morning. If you can't do it, they'll reduce me to private in short notice!"[3]

Naturally the bad news could not be kept from Patton when he returned to the headquarters the next day. Just before leaving the conference at Liège he had said to French General A. Juin, who had needled him a little for having allowed Hodges to steal a march on him by capturing a bridge across the Rhine first, "When you get back to Paris, don't fail to read your favorite newspaper. Within a day or two you will see who is stealing a march on whom!"[4] Now he had to make that boast come true. For the bridge between Carden and Treis on the Moselle had really been blown. Just before a unit of the 4th Armored had approached Carden, there had been a fierce argument between the local villagers and a Captain von Hack, who commanded the bridge between the two Moselle villages. "He was a great monster of a man," one of the villagers, Herr Zimmermann, remembered years later, "from Westphalia, well over one meter ninety tall. We told him, 'if you blow up the bridge, we won't be able to get any food supplies through.' It meant nothing to him. He blew it up just as the *Amis* started arriving. Some years afterward when he returned here, we said to him, 'and where were you, friend, when we had to rebuild the bridge you blew up?' To that he had no answer."[5]

But Patton *had* in 1945. He ordered all lines to higher authority cut while Eddy built a bridge across the damned river (in the end he built three). He would kick off the assault across the Moselle with the 5th and 90th Infantry Divisions, sixteen miles south of Koblenz. Once they had established a bridgehead, the 4th Armored would thrust out of the bridgehead. Thereupon, ten miles north and south of that bridgehead, the 87th and 89th Divisions would attack across; while the 10th Armored, 26th Infantry, 80th, and 94th Infantry pushed up from the general direction of Trier. It was a massive force aimed at trapping the German Seventh Army and creating another Falaise Pocket, similar to the one in which the German Army in France had been virtually decimated the previous August.

Only bespectacled General Middleton, Commander of Patton's VIII Corps, was not happy with the plan. It meant that he would be left with only one division (Patton needed his other divisions to strengthen the attack lower down the Moselle). Middleton carefully guarded—as all the generals did—his personal power and prestige, and now he took "a leaf from George's book" and "asked him to let me capture Koblenz with the Eighty-seventh."

Patton laughed at him and said, "Only a fool would attempt such an operation with so few troops."

Middleton pleaded, "Let me try. If I find it too well organized, I can suspend the operation."[6]

Patton gave in, and Middleton started to plan his attack: an assault across the Moselle against a major city, well defended by the dreaded 88mm antiaircraft guns that could be used in a ground role, and held by an unknown number of German troops, with one lone division. It was a tall order.

Outside the little village of Guels, where the assault crossing would take place, the infantry practiced "dummy rowing" in a large boat "anchored" in the middle of a farmer's field. Amused and a little apprehensive, too, Medic Lester Atwell watched as an officer instructed the men, while the top brass looked on. "The lieutenant, sweating and red-faced, had an extremely loud voice, and there was something wild and disheveled about his gestures. 'Now pay attention. This line here, when I give you the signal, you start forward, you understand?' For no reason he began to push at the line, shoving one man one way, pulling another another way.

" 'Look at the crazy bastard,' a C Company man said. 'He's drunk and they're trying to keep him away from the brass.' There was a little convoy about him, consisting of a few lieutenants and staff sergeants. 'Now tonight when you get in these boats, you wanna be absolutely quiet.' The lieu-

tenant, slightly unsteady, raised his elbow and wiped the
sweat from his face. 'D'you get that? Quiet! Your entrenching
tools are gonna be all padded so that they don't make any
noise banging against the boat. We don't want a sound because the Jerries will be waiting for us on the other bank. . . .
Now the idea is to row in time. All right, now begin, One
pull! Two *pull*! No, together.' "[7]

As the awkward infantrymen did their best, turfing up
chunks of grass and dirt in their efforts, making a hopeless
mess of it, Atwell's buddy De Vroom commented, "This is
the most fucked up thing I ever saw!" Atwell, for his part,
told himself miserably, "Jesus, this is gonna be a slaughter."[8]

A dozen miles downstream at Karden, the men of the 5th and
4th Armored Divisions preparing for the crossing were also
finding it not so easy. For over twenty-four hours their engineers had covered the Moselle with a thick, white smoke
screen. But that had not put Captain von Hack off. His artillery shells pounded the village, killing both Americans and
German alike. Nerves and tempers became frayed. The German civilians blamed both their own soldiers and the Americans for their ordeal, as the German guns thundered from
the vineyards at the other side of the river and the shells fell
on their picturesque houses. The Americans took their rage
and nervousness out on the villagers, more than once threatening some of them with a speedy death if they weren't careful.

Even further downstream where the 76th Division, which
was not going to take part in the initial assault, had closed
with the river, the recently "blooded" greenhorns took their
revenge for the slaughter on the Sauer.

In those pretty, medieval Moselle villages, whose names
were known throughout the world on account of the wines
they produced—Wehlen, Ürzig, Bernkastel and the like—they
took over the riverside villas of the prominent wine-growers.
First—naturally—they looted the wine cellars. Young men
who thought that wine could be "slugged" just like the weak
3.5 percent Stateside beer soon became drunk—and aggressive—very aggressive.

Forty years later Herr Hans Ahrends of Ürzig remembers

the young men of the 76th as they "took over my balcony
which overlooked the river. All day long they drank my wine
and fired at anything that moved on the opposite side. Naturally the German soldiers were smart enough not to venture
out by daylight. But the civilians were not so smart. Mostly
the *Amis* were too drunk to hit anything. But once they spotted an old man pulling a handcart. He had wrapped himself
in a bed sheet to show he was harmless. But that didn't stop
them. They shot him and he lay there dead for three days
until he finally disappeared during the night."[9]

Drink also led to the desire for sex. There had already been
unfortunate incidents at Wittlich, the largest German town
captured by the 76th so far. There, houses had been plun-
dered and the wife of a local schoolteacher had been raped
by four soldiers in front of her two children. Later, she had
been placed in a mental home; the shame and shock had been
too much for her.

Now, from the hamlets and villages along the Moselle occupied by the 76th, there came the first reports of rape, attempted rape, and sexual molestations. With the troops strung
out along a wide section of the river, it was difficult for senior
officers to exercise control; and junior officers were sometimes unable to keep their men in check, especially when they
were drinking.

Naturally it wasn't all one-sided. There were plenty of *Veronika Dankeschoens* (Veronica Thankyous) about, easily
available for a can of coffee, cigarettes, and a couple of Hershey bars. Most of these young soldiers had not had any contact with a woman since the States, and they were easily
tempted. But what started as a "business transaction" sometimes turned into a cry of "rape."

And these *Veronika Dankeschoens*, brought up in the easy
sexuality of the war years, their menfolk long away at the
front, sometimes had more to offer the young *Amis* than their
bodies. They often left behind a little "souvenir" of their
easy coupling in a barn, against a door, in the gutter. After
all, their nickname could be shortened to represent the dis-
eases that would soon become epidemic throughout the Allied
armies in Germany—*VD*! . . .

• • •

Bradley gave Patton the green light on March 13. He could start his attack across the Moselle River. He was to attack, with his objective the seizure of the Rhine bank from Koblenz to Mannheim. That night Eddy's XII Corps launched its attack. But he, like Patton's other corps commanders, had received oral instructions from Patton that his objective was different from that ordered by Bradley. He was to head for the Rhine near Oppenheim: an objective that was in the zone allotted to Patch's Seventh Army.

After a two-hour artillery bombardment, the 5th and Walker's 90th divisions stormed across the Moselle. By midmorning both divisions had separate bridgeheads, one mile in depth. Soon they would be ready for the 4th to break out and make its dash for the next river.

Now it was the turn of Middleton's lone division—the 87th. Its commander, Gen. Frank Culin, planned to do the job with two regiments. His 347th Infantry would cross the river before daylight on March 16, five miles upstream from Koblenz. It would be followed by his second regiment, crossing the Moselle opposite Koblenz itself.

Tension mounted as the assault companies began to file down the narrowed, cobbled streets of Guels toward the boats. Once more roll calls were taken in a whisper. Final orders were given in the same tone. Over on the other side of the river the artillery rolled and boomed. Whether it was German or American, no one knew or cared. They were all too preoccupied with their own fates. Here and there the night sky flickered a fitful, ugly pink.

Behind the infantry the medics buckled on full field packs and slung their medical bags. "Well I guess this is it," they whispered. "So long guys," Atwell noted. "Some began to shake hands, but others were ashamed to follow suit."

"Les," Ted De Vroom whispered to Atwell, "pray for us. Take care of my binoculars . . . We'll be seeing you."

"Good luck," Atwell, and the other medics who were going over in the next wave, called softly, and then they were gone and there was nothing left but to wait and worry."[10]

Eisenhower paid a surprise visit to Patton's HQ on that March 16. It was his first visit to the HQ since the previous fall and now he was sporting his fifth star and was in obvious high spirits. After promising Patton he would send him another armored division, he explained his reason for coming. "I want your help to get some favorable press stories about our tanks," he told Patton.

"I received a cable from General Marshall on the matter the other day. It seems that some of our men have returned home and are saying that German tanks are better than ours, that they outshoot us. Also, somebody got up in Congress and said the Germans have better equipment and winter clothing than we have . . . that seventy-five percent of our stuff is inferior to theirs. General Marshall is worried about adverse public reaction to all this criticism, and we'd like to get your help on the matter."[11]

Both generals knew the criticism was true. German weapons and equipment *were* superior to that produced in the U.S.A., and they had known it since 1943. Back in 1944 in Italy, a *New York Times* correspondent had tried to expose the scandal of just how inferior the Sherman's armor and gun were to those of the German Tiger and Panther. Instead of action being taken, correspondent C. L. Sulzberger was banned from the theater by General Devers.

All along the line, German equipment was better. They had better tanks; better guns, especially their feared, all-purpose 88mm; better mortars, in particular, their multiple, mobile six-barreled one; better antitank weapons. The American-built bazooka, for example, had so little punch that American infantrymen were trained to use captured German *panzerfaust* launchers or their older "stove pipes," as the German soldiers nicknamed the rocket launcher, which could punch through thick armored plate at a considerable distance. For most of the 1944/45 campaign in Europe, Eisenhower's soldiers had to fight the Germans with weapons that were decidedly inferior to theirs. Indeed, Eisenhower himself had cabled the War Department just after the invasion to complain about the inferior guns and armor of the U.S. forces.

Patton, who knew well just how deficient American weapons were, readily complied. He told Eisenhower, "I'll be glad to cooperate, General. I'll do the best I can for you and General Marshall."

"I hope you will, George," Eisenhower said. "Give your PRO statements [to pass onto trusted war correspondents] on how good our tanks are. . . . I am anxious to get some good stories. General Marshall needs help on this matter and we want to do all we can for him."[12]

The incident in itself is of no importance. But it was typical of the way the top brass was running the war in Europe in early 1945. It was their personal publicity and public opinion that counted most; not the conduct of the war and the safety of the men's lives entrusted to them.

Patton, normally so hot-tempered and so opinionated, tamely acquiesced, though he knew that for every German tank knocked out, his men usually lost three of their Shermans; and that a regular "Tiger phobia" existed among his infantry. At the very mention of the word "Tiger," his riflemen were inclined to get out of their foxholes and run! Again, however, public opinion back home counted more than the lives of his young men.*

Just before he left, Eisenhower referred to the attack on Koblenz by the 87th. "George," he quipped, "be sure to take a shot for me at that big iron statue of some Kaiser the Germans have at the bend of the Rhine at Koblenz. That hunk of metal would look a lot better at the bottom of the river than stuck up in the air. It would do their culture a lot more good that way."

"Be delighted, General," Patton promised dutifully. "We'll take care of that little matter for you without delay. It will be a pleasure."[13]

A hundred miles away, up where that equestrian statue of Kaiser Wilhelm I towered above Koblenz's *Deutsches Eck*, "the German Corner," where the Moselle, Lahn, and Rhine rivers join, Patton's young infantrymen of the 87th were fighting for their lives.

---

*Third Army finally received a few M-26 tanks, capable of tackling the Tigers and Panthers, in the very last weeks of the war, when it was already too late.

Nine

☆

Amazingly enough the 347th Infantry Regiment of General Culin's 87th Division crossed the Moselle without a shot being fired at it! The utter ease of the crossing surprised Culin, even though he knew from Intelligence just how thinly spread the German defenses were.

As dawn broke, the two assault battalions advanced toward the nearest village with the countryside strangely empty of the enemy. Then a single shot, and the riflemen knew they had a fight on their hands. The 347th had now bumped into elements of one of Germany's remaining elite formations— the 6th SS Mountain Division. The 6th SS had spent most of its war fighting in the remote tundra of Finland and northern Russia, where they had helped the Finns to successfully resist the might of the Red Army for years. When, however, tiny Finland succumbed to the Russians in September 1944 and sued for peace, the 6th fled the country, making a tortuous journey from the frozen north to Alsace, where in January they first went into action against the Americans. There they had participated in the surprise attack on the American Seventh Army, code-named Operation Northwind,* and had achieved considerable success before being withdrawn.

Although they had suffered grievous losses in Alsace during the month-long fighting there, they had again dealt the Americans some hard blows in the fighting around Trier. There they had counterattacked more than once, helping to surround the 5th Ranger Battalion and wiping out one whole company of the 94th Infantry Division.

Now they fought back stubbornly although they were hopelessly outnumbered (true to the tradition of the SS, whose

*See C. Whiting, *Operation Northwind: The Unknown Battle of the Bulge* for further details.

wounded in Russia had shot themselves rather than surrender to the hated Red Army), making the men of the 87th pay for every yard of ground they captured. But not only the Americans paid. German civilians on the American side of the Moselle did too.

Many years later, the local teacher at the village school of Guels remembered how, "The SS started shelling the village from the school building at Moselweiss on the other side. Our people panicked and ran for the cover of a tunnel at the other end of the village. A shell landed right in their midst. Two women were killed outright by their own people and a little boy had both legs severed. Much later the *Amis* brought the first SS prisoners back to Guels. The local people mobbed around them, crying they had shot fellow countrymen and threatening to lynch them. The *Amis* had to protect the SS with their weapons; otherwise the locals would have surely strung them up there and then!"[1]

Order and control were beginning to break down in the Koblenz area. There was worse to come.

Patton was jubilant that day as the 4th Armored broke loose and Walker's 80th and 94th Infantry Divisions began to move into the Hunsrück Mountains to clear the way for the armor of the 4th, 10th, and newly attached 12th Armored Divisions. What if the SS were holding him up in Koblenz and were actually *counterattacking* in Hunsrück. Patton knew that the German Seventh Army was virtually shattered. Ultra had already told him that.

He was right too. Gen. Hans-Gustav Felber, its commander, was on the run, controlling what was left of his shattered units from a *post office* at Bad Kreuznach, waiting for permission to withdraw over the Rhine. What little information he could obtain was telephoned to him by a female "spy": prewar champion lady rider Irmgard von Opel. The little town in which she lived had already been taken by the *Amis* but they had not thought of checking the telephone system. Bravely she observed and reported the number and types of American tanks rolling by her window and, as Felber's chief-of-staff, Freiherr Gero von Gersdorff, recorded after the war "she wasn't the only one."[2]

Indeed Patton was so sure that the war was about over that

on that day he sent a special letter to General Marshall in Washington. It read: "I should like to be considered for any type of combat command, from a division up, against the Japanese. . . . I am sure that my method of fighting would be successful. I am also of such age that this is my last war, and I would therefore like to see it through to the end."[3]

Seemingly the old warrior, now nearing sixty years of age, could not get enough of war. But Fate had other things in mind for George S. Patton.

Now the heart was going out of the Germans. Resistance, save at Koblenz, was crumbling rapidly. In a letter to his wife that March, Lt. Bennett Fisher of the 4th Armored, wrote, "No German village is complete without a full set of white flags, although they are usually impromptu affairs such as tablecloths, napkins, shirts, and grandpa's long winter underpants. If there are some German soldiers to contest our entrance, the reception is a little different at first although later it amounts to the same thing, except that the white flags fly—*from the rubble*! Personally, I don't have a great deal of stomach for this town fighting business, even if they are Kraut towns because it means that there are plenty of non-soldiers involved, but what is necessary is necessary, I suppose."[4] Now town after town began to fall to the victorious Third Army. Some were obscure ones in the poverty-stricken Hunsrück, where in the eighteenth century the peasants had fled the hunger to start a new life in America, including a local blacksmith named "Eisenhauer." Others had names that had graced school history books for centuries and were known to generations of American high school kids: Worms, where Luther had defied the Pope; Mainz, where Gutenberg had printed the first Bible; Ludwigshafen, which had seen the start of a chemical dye industry that had led to the pioneering medical discoveries of Koch, Ehrlich, and the like . . .

In Koblenz, the fight still continued. Middleton's men had faced deadly fire from the ring of 88mm cannon around the city being used in the ground role. The 1,800 strong *Kampfgruppe Koblenz* put up a stout defense as they were pressed back into the ruined city. Heavy fog descended upon the river area during the second night of the battle, and 1,700 men of the German LXXXIX Corps escaped across the Moselle. But the *Kampfgruppe Koblenz* continued their dogged resistance, with their backs now against the river in a city that had now been transformed into a miniature Stalingrad.

Now Middleton, reduced to commanding a single division, was running out of patience. He still had four battalions of artillery under his command. So he ordered the defenders to be informed by means of loudspeakers that if they did not surrender he would rain five thousand shells down upon the city.

The answer was silence. Middleton didn't hesitate. Within the hour, the massed fire of the four artillery battalions descended upon the dying city. One shell struck the base of the equestrian statue of Kaiser Wilhelm and the great bronze and stone figure slipped to the ground. Patton had kept his promise to Eisenhower, at least.

The bombardment had its effect. A group of municipal officials braved the battle to make their way through the grotesque, smoking ruins of the prosperous city they had once administered, to the *Westbunker*. There they convinced the commandant that he should surrender his area of the city. The harassed, worn-out major agreed. So it was that the port manager, a Herr Gerhard Lanters, and another official named Schmitz, who maintained he could speak English, ventured out into no-man's-land to meet the advancing *Amis*.

By this time the GIs battling desperately in the ruins were very trigger-happy, indeed. But fortunately for the two portly, middle-aged Germans, the officer commanding the leading infantry company had his men well under control. He ordered his men to hold their fire. Thus it was that that part of Koblenz finally surrendered and a gleeful General Middleton could inform Patton that, "General, in addition to my other duties, I am now Mayor of Koblenz."[5]

He wasn't! It would take another two days of fighting before Middleton could really justify that claim. Indeed, in that third terrible week of March 1945, no one was really in control in Koblenz.

"The windows of all the houses were shuttered tight," Lester Atwell recalled. "A few dead Germans and American soldiers lay in the streets; jeeps raced by; artillery barrages screamed in, bringing down houses in a thunder of rubble;

fighting continued from street to street. But there was, over-all, the chaotic air of a drunken end-of-the-world carnival. Infantrymen who had been down in the cellars ran crookedly past, firing everywhere, and shrill, overexcited young Ger-man girls, impatient of rape, ran after them through barrages, ducking into almost flat doorways as tiles fell from the roofs in crashing showers.''[6]

Later Atwell found himself in the middle of a crazy, drunken scene, a confused mess of inebriated German and American soldiers, with two of the latter, Jimmy McDonough and ''Horse-Face'' Fogarty, trying drunkenly to loot a living room. ''They had learned to say, *'Achtung, Macht Schnell. Kommen Sie hier!'* and that they repeated to each other over and over. While Fogarty had his back turned, rifling through the ornaments in a corner whatnot, Jimmy McDonough, with mock German gruffness, said just behind him, *'Achtung. Macht schnell!'*

'' 'Hey cut it out, you make me nervous,' Fogarty said, but a moment or two passed and the harsh German voice resumed. 'Cut it *out*, I said,' Fogarty repeated. 'What the hell's the matter with you anyway. Always fucking around!'

''Then he felt something poke him in the back, and when he turned he saw that Jimmy McDonough was at the far side of the room, speechless and shivering, his hands trembling over his head.''[7]

Four armed German soldiers stood there! But they had only come in to surrender, and while one of the medics made love to a German woman on the litter, the Germans and Ameri-cans got drunk, staggering off to the bathroom only to bump ''into German soldiers who had been holding wassail on the second floor and had come downstairs on the same mission, 'Scuse me. Beg your pardon. Wanna get through here,' one American found himself saying to an equally drunken Ger-man in a polite Alphonse-and-Gaston routine.''

That ''chaotic air of a drunken end-of-the-world carnival'' reigned throughout the Palatinate as Patton's tanks neared the Rhine. Everywhere slave laborers and displaced persons from a dozen different European countries looted the farms and depots of their former masters, taking their revenge for the sufferings they had endured during the long years of captivity.

Medieval villages burned by the score, for at the least sign
of resistance, Patton's artillery descended upon them and they
became instant "Third Army memorials." Stragglers from
the beaten German Seventh Army, in their shabby, ankle-
length gray coats and battered, greasy ski caps, tried to slip
through the American lines to escape across the Rhine; or
simply gave in. By their scores, their hundreds, and in the
end, by their thousands. And in their cellars, the cowed civilians, many of them now drunk for days on end, played that
sad little tune of spring 1945 on their phonographs over and
over again in a kind of desperate wishful thinking that the
terror and horror of it all might soon have an end:

> Es geht alles voruber
> Es geht alles vorbei
> Nach jedem Dezember,
> Gibt's wieder ein Mai.*

On March 20, a desperate General Felber received permission from Field Marshal Albert Kesselring to withdraw
what was left of his shattered Seventh Army across the Rhine.
Soon "Smiling Albert," as Kesselring was known to his
troops on account of his fixed smile, would relieve Felber,
but for the time being he needed the unfortunate Felber to
keep some sort of control on his demoralized command. Desperately, as Felber made his plans, Kesselring threw in his
last air reserve—over three hundred fighter-bombers, including the new jet-propelled Messerschmitt 262. They were intended to hold up the columns of the 4th, 10th, 11th, and 12th
Armored Divisions racing across the Palatinate.

The mobile antiaircraft units attached to these columns had
a field day. They boasted they shot down more than twenty-
five German fighter-bombers in one day alone. And the excited gunners could well have been right. Now the *Luftwaffe*
was using pilots with less than twelve hours actual flying
time. The "old hares," as the veterans in the *Luftwaffe* were
called, had vanished into the greedy maws of the God of War
long ago.

---

*"Everything passes, everything goes by. After every December, there
is always a May."

Patton brooked no delay, in spite of the massive air attack on his flying columns and the tiredness of the tankers who had been fighting and rolling now for nearly two months. Time was running out—*fast*. On March 23 "the Field Marshal" was scheduled to launch his great set-piece attack across the Rhine; and the Rhine had become important again to Patton. Hodges had beaten him across it already. He was determined Montgomery wouldn't do the same. As the date of the crossing up north came ever closer, he urged his Third Army on to ever greater efforts, "peeping" here, there, and everywhere, chewing out corps commanders if they were too slow, sacking generals, including the commanding general of the 11th Armored Division if they were not aggressive enough.

Once he discovered that replacement tanks were not reaching his fighting division quickly enough. Swiftly he made his own personal survey and found the huge tank transporters laid up in villages, woods, and other places and concluded that the drivers were "whooping it up with the local damery." In fact they were being mostly stopped by the lack of bridges, which the Germans had destroyed in their headlong retreat. Such considerations didn't worry Patton. He ordered every sergeant commanding one of those tank transporters to be "busted to buck private." Fair and unfair, it worked. His rampaging armored divisions received their Shermans on time.

On March 21, General Felber's front fell apart completely. As Lieutenant Max Gissen of the 26th Infantry Division recorded: "What had been a stubborn retreat began a real rout. The Air Force had a field day, the infantry no longer walked, but mounted everything on wheels and pushed on as much as 25 miles a day, leaving behind pockets of Germans to be mopped up or taken prisoner without resistance. Some of course fought on and raised the devil with the few rear-echelon troops. But after the Bulge and before that the dreary, muddy, inch-by-inch crawl through Lorraine, the few days before we reached the Rhine seemed a lark."[8]

But it was not that funny for the fleeing Germans. Following up in the wake of his armor near the small German town of Frankenstein, Patton and his aide, Codman, came across the carnage left when the armor had bumped into a German supply column. "It was all there," Codman wrote after the war, "but no longer on the road. Cannoned, machine-gunned or simply pushed over the edge, hundreds of splintered vehicles, dead horses and Germans literally filled the deep gully below. For a time we viewed it in silence."[9]

Finally Patton broke the heavy, brooding silence of that place of death. In an awed voice, he said, "That is the greatest scene of carnage I have ever witnessed . . . Let's go home."[10]

And then there it was at last—*the Rhine!*

On the night of March 21/22, patrols of General Patton's Third Army were probing the whole length of the Rhine River from Mainz to Worms, cutting into the sector originally allotted to General Patch's Seventh Army. Not that such considerations worried Patton any more than the fact that there were still thousands of armed German soldiers at large in the Palatinate. For him the campaign was over. His gaze was now firmly fixed on the Frankfurt-Kassel "corridor," which would take him into central Germany. But first he had to cross the Rhine, *with or without permission!*

"We've got to get a bridgehead at once!" he told his staff excitedly. "The enemy is in chaos on our front. But if we delay 72 hours, he will reorganize and we'll have to fight to push him out of our way. We must not give him that chance, regardless of what political machinations are going on up above. . . . We destroyed two armies in one week with a handful of losses to ourselves and I don't propose to give the bastards the chance to reorganize."[11]

Flashing a smile at his admiring staff he added, "We're going to make a crossing at once. I don't care how or where we get the necessary equipment, but it must be got. Steal it, beg it or make it. But I want it and it had better be there where we need it, when we need it." He pointed his big cigar at them like an offensive weapon. "We're going to cross the Rhine and we're going to do it before I'm a day older."[12]

Ten

For once Patton had both Bradley's—and Hodges's—support for the unauthorized plan to cross the Rhine immediately. While Patton's staff worked feverishly on the plan, Bradley and Hodges arrived at Patton's HQ to discuss what could be done. It was the First Army commander's first visit there, and Colonel Allen could not refrain from making a comparison between the two army commanders. Patton was "a towering statue of gleaming magnificence. Twelve stars on his short collar and shoulders. His tailor-made, form-fitting battle jacket surmounted by glistening brass buttons and high-polished, leather waist belt with a large, embossed brass buckle. Below the waist, skin-tight, whipcord riding breeches and two-buckled cavalry riding boots that came up to his calves, leaving the rest of his lower legs uncovered. The unique combination was his own original conception."[1]

It must have been, for General Hodges was clad in regulation uniform. He wore a "neat, issue battle jacket and combat shoes. No brass buttons or any other shiny ornaments. . . . The only marked difference was the poor fit of his trousers in the rear, the seat hanging down like a sack."[2]

But for once Patton was friendly to the poor "sad sack" of a plodding infantryman. Why not? After all, Hodges had come to support him. Both Bradley and Hodges were concerned about the situation up north where Montgomery was still assembling his great force to cross the Rhine. They were afraid that he would wheedle Eisenhower, "the best general the British have," as Patton had once sneered, into taking more divisions from the Twelfth Army Group to reinforce him. That would mean that both Hodges and Patton would lose men. Again the generals were playing games, more concerned about their personal prestige than the conduct of the war.

Patton reassured them immediately. "That's simple," he said. "I'll cross down here and once the divisions are committed, they can't take them." Bradley nodded his agreement and said slowly, "Ike has to make the main effort in the north. That's the decision and he has no choice in the matter. We may not like it, but that's what will have to be done. But we've got to act quickly to avoid losing some more divisions to Montgomery." Bradley then considered who should make the first attack: Hodges's First Army out of its bridgehead on the eastern bank of the Rhine or Patton at Oppenheim.

In essence, he already knew who should jump off first, but for a little while he attempted to save Hodges's face by appearing to discuss the matter seriously. In the end he said, "I'm afraid that if Courtney [Hodges] jumps off first, he will run into the full weight of the Germans. If you [Patton] cross first, that will tend to pull some of them down to your area and split them up. How do you feel about that, Courtney?"

"I would like to jump off several days after George," Hodges replied dutifully.

"My thought is," Bradley said to him, "that you will come down toward Limburg [twenty-five miles east of Koblenz] and by that time George can prove whether he can go on to Kassel."

"Oh, I don't have to prove that," Patton said with a big smile. "We'll just go ahead and do it. There'll be nothing to it."

"All right," Bradley concluded, "then we'll leave it that way. You will cross first, and Courtney will then break out and contact you at Limburg. Seventh Army will come up from the north and then we can go up and help . . ."[3]

Bradley didn't end his sentence. Instead he grinned and left his final thought unspoken. But the other two generals knew what he meant. The "Field Marshal" was still sitting on his "butt" up north. If their plans worked out well, they could turn north too, if they wished to go and help him. Thus was grand strategy decided in the final weeks of World War II in Europe.

• • •

If Patton was supremely confident that he "could take the Rhine on the run," his men—from corps commander to humble private—were not so sanguine. Eddy, whose corps had been selected for the assault crossing, protested to Patton, "I'm not ready yet."

Patton overruled his objectives. He knew that Eddy was always unready. What he didn't know was that Eddy was hanging onto his job desperately, concealing his ill-health, afraid that Patton would send him home if he knew just how sick he was. Soon, however, he would no longer be able to conceal it. A heart attack would send him back to the States on a stretcher.

"What are you waiting for?" Patton growled. "We can take the river on the run."[4]

Eddy passed the buck to the General "Red" Irwin, commander of the 5th Infantry Division, which had made nearly a score of river crossings under fire since the breakout from the Normandy beaches. He didn't like the task either. But having served under Patton since the early days in North Africa, he knew better than to protest. Patton had a nasty habit of sacking divisional commanders who didn't see eye-to-eye with him. Hastily he began to gather the equipment he would need for the crossing.

The men weren't overjoyed at the prospect either. In Sergeant Giles's combat engineer battalion, "Everybody is talking about what it's going to be like to cross the Rhine. That's where we're headed. 'Rough,' they say, 'plenty rough.' They'll make it hot for us on the Rhine. It's their last stand.

"Black Mac started singing 'One More River to Cross' but didn't get beyond the first line when someone threw a shoe at him.

"Somebody said, 'How big is the damned thing?'

" 'I dunno. Big as the Mississippi, I guess.'

" 'Oh my God!'

"Somebody else said, 'I sure wish it *would* be the last one we have to do.'

"Somebody else, 'It'll be the last one for some of us.'

" 'Shuddup! *You wanta jinx us?* ' "[5]

Lieutenant Max Gissen of the 26th Infantry Division was apprehensive, too. "Some, like myself, knowing that Rhine was a holy word to most Germans and especially to the wretched little house painter, expected a terrific battle and even a crossing under intense fire. It seems, from my subsequent reading that Allied intelligence was aware that the area was lightly defended, but to those of us who were in ignorance of what the Germans had there, it was a certainty that all hell would break loose once we started across. There was no 'jostling in the line' to be first into the attack.

"There were commanders who couldn't wait to be committed and our own first Colonel was one. But the men and junior officers? Nonsense. Everyone was exhausted by the time we reached the Rhine. We had suffered heavy casualties in the preceding week and nothing would have pleased us better than a longish leave (say about a year) in Paris or Biarritz or even what was left of St. Lô Of course there was great excitement when we saw the Rhine. Even the deepest dyed half-wit in the outfit knew that we'd be crossing and in addition to the natural apprehension there was a sense of history in the situation that no one tried to laugh off. But forget all that about being wild for the chance to have the first go."[6]

The moon shone far too brightly as the GIs of the 11th Infantry's 3rd Battalion crept down to the Rhine at Nierstein, just above Oppenheim. The soldiers were tense and nervous. All hell could break loose at any moment. But there was no going back now. Softly the orders were whispered from man to man, and they began to climb gingerly into the boats which would take them across. They were half an hour behind schedule. Not that that mattered to them. For all they cared they could have been half a century behind time. For these men of Company K, commanded by Lt. Irven Jacobs, were going to be the first of the 300,000-strong Third Army to assault Germany's last great natural barrier. Now they were moving, a company of scared infantrymen sailing out into the bright, silver snake of the Rhine. All was silent on the far bank. What were they up to? Were the Krauts just waiting for them to come within range before they opened fire? The suspense was terrific. The Company K men pressed their heads down even lower.

Midstream. Still nothing. Not one sign of protest—even of life—came from the far shore. It was too good to be true. Surely the slaughter *must* start soon! They gripped their weapons tighter in hands that were wet with sweat. Some of them began to breathe faster as if they were taking part in some great race. Then the boat carrying Lieutenant Jacobs and ten more men grated against the rocks on the far side to come to a sudden halt. Hastily the eleven of them climbed up the muddy bank, bodies tensed for the first frightening burst of machine-gun fire.

But none came. Moments later, the rest of Company K were across. Seven surprised Germans promptly surrendered and obligingly paddled themselves back to the other side and the waiting POW cage.

A few hundred yards away Companies A and B of the 1st Battalion crossing at Oppenheim were less fortunate. They were caught in midstream by a terrific burst of machine-gun fire. More followed, the white tracer zipping lethally low across the surface of the water. There was nothing for it but to go forward. This they did, paddling furiously right into the deadly maelstrom. Surprisingly enough most of them made it, but there was a fierce little skirmish on the other side before the German defenders finally gave in.

By midnight the whole of the 11th Infantry Regiment of the 5th Division was across at a cost of twenty casualties. Now as the night hours raced by speedily and the Germans awoke—slowly—to the new threat, a second regiment of the 5th was thrown across.

German artillery started to shell the crossing sites. A U.S. battalion command post was hit at Oppenheim, and an ammunition truck was set on fire. Still Irwin persisted, readying another regiment of his 5th for crossing and one attached from the 90th Division.

At dawn German jets came howling in, streaking across the ugly white sky at a tremendous rate, with the antiaircraft guns peppering the air around them with shells so that they seemed to be sailing through a black lace curtain.

Waiting to cross that day with his men of the 4th Armored, which would pass through the 5th once the bridgehead had been secured, Lt. Bennett Fisher watched as a Piper Cub "attached to our division circled the crossing area constantly acting as a spotter for artillery in the event we got any fire. None ever came . . . The opposition was very scant at the crossing . . . What opposition there was came from old men and young boys who had hand grenades and old rifles and hearts full of hate.''[7]

Once he was sure that the crossing would be a success, Patton no longer hid the fact from the world. Earlier on the morning of March 23, he called Bradley and told the latter, ''Brad, don't tell anyone, but I'm across.''

''Well, I'll be damned. You mean across the Rhine?'' Bradley queried excitedly.

''Sure I am. I sneaked a division over last night. But there are so few Krauts around there they don't know it yet. So don't make any announcement—we'll keep it secret until we see how it goes.''[8] But Patton couldn't wait now. That evening he again telephoned Bradley and yelled, ''Brad, for God's sake, tell the world we're across! We knocked down thirty-three Krauts today when they came after our pontoon bridges. I want the world to know that Third Army made it before Monty starts across.''[9]

But the ''world'' had already been told. At the morning briefing at Bradley's HQ, the Third Army representative had stated, ''Without benefit of aerial bombing, ground smoke, artillery preparation and airborne assistance, the Third Army at 2200 hours, Thursday evening, March 22, crossed the Rhine River.''[10]

The dig was obvious. It was aimed at Montgomery, who crossed with exactly such assistance as detailed above, twenty-three hours later. Maliciously, Patton's representative was turning the knife in the wound.

Shortly afterward, Bradley himself announced that the U.S. Army could cross the Rhine almost at will, almost anywhere, without air bombardment, and sometimes even without artillery. His subsequent criticism revealed his motive: ''Had Monty crashed the river on the run as Patton had done, he might have averted the momentous effort required in that heavily publicized crossing.''[11]

When the future of a whole continent was at stake, it seemed as if the top brass was mainly concerned with the headlines, jealous of those who might take away their personal publicity. Neither did they appear very concerned with the anonymous mass of young men in olive drab who fought—and died—to gain those headlines for them. For even as the banner headlines proclaimed Patton's triumphant crossing of the Rhine back in the States, other of his outfits were assaulting the same river—*unsuccessfully*.

The deaths of these scores of young men, who died for objectives of little military importance, were quietly overlooked in the general back-slapping, congratulatory telegrams, and euphoria. Who remembers today the two assaults made by Patton's 87th Division at Rhens on the night of March 24/25, 1945? There the 87th Infantry Division's assault force was pounded even before it commenced the attack, and it took an hour before the attack companies could be reorganized for the crossing. The battalion concerned lost one-fifth of its strength before it even attacked.

It was no different at St. Goar, where the 89th Division attacked. Here flares and flames from a burning fuel barge set alight by the Germans made the infantry in their boats a perfect target. Many of the assault boats were hit and sank. Others, their occupants wounded and helpless, were carried away by the swift current never to be seen again. That night the assault battalion lost 29 men killed, 102 wounded, and 146 missing—one-third of its strength.

In the end the two divisions made it across, but the cost at this stage of the war was too high. With seven weeks to go before it ended, why sacrifice precious young lives in order to raise the American flag above the Lorelei for the sake of the newsreel cameramen?

Such considerations seemingly did not bother the top brass. All that Corps Commander Middleton, whose divisions made the assault at St. Goar and Rhens, has to say of the attack is that he warned his son, Troy Jr., to get in a ditch. "One of those bullets may have your number on it." To which his son, who was his aide, bravely replied, "None of them has hit me yet."[12] And that after crossing the Rhine himself he came across one of his soldiers who held up a four-foot string of fish and said, "Look what I got, General."[13] No mention at all of the fact that some four hundred of his soldiers had been killed, wounded, or listed missing on that same stretch of river the previous night. The way General Middleton described the assault to his biographer, it had all gone off bloodlessly and according to plan.

• • •

On that same day, the March 24 that the 87th and 89th Divisions attacked, Patton crossed the pontoon bridge built by the 5th Division at Oppenheim. Halfway across he unbuttoned his fly and urinated contemptuously in the Rhine. (He would be followed by a whole procession of generals doing the same. Indeed one of them—Gen. Robert Grow of the 6th Armored Division—proudly had himself *photographed* doing so.) Then, where the bridge met the opposite bank, where it had been churned to mud by the tanks of the 4th Armored, Patton appeared to slip, sinking to one knee, before steadying himself with both hands.

When he rose, his two hands were filled with handfuls of muddy earth, which he allowed to drop slowly to the ground, saying to his surprised staff, "Thus William the Conqueror!"

Historically unversed as most of them were, they did not know the reference was to the legend that maintains that when William commenced his invasion of England at Hastings in 1066, he fell. Realizing that his men in the invasion fleet would regard this as a bad omen, he had quickly seized two handfuls of sand and cried, "See, I have taken England with both hands!"

That afternoon, Patton reported what he had done in a much more down-to-earth manner to his boss, Eisenhower: "Today, I pissed in the Rhine!" he scrawled proudly in his own hand on the daily official report.

It was typical of him. The crude comment emphasized his contempt for the "gentlemen up north," including Eisenhower. It mattered nothing to him that the Red Army was sweeping across Central Europe at a tremendous rate, but not in the broad front manner that Patton and Bradley had now forced on Eisenhower by the crossings at Remagen and Oppenheim. The Russians were making their drives for key political objectives, such as Berlin and the gateway to the Baltic. Such political considerations played no role in Patton's thinking.

Now the final destruction of the German Army was only secondary. The "1,000 Year Reich" was already beaten. Montgomery, as vain, as publicity-conscious, and as jealous as Patton himself, did, however, realize that what mattered now was the attainment of a geographical line that would deny the Russians any further foothold in Western Europe.

And in the end he did just that. His armies, "British and American, just managed to beat the Russians to Lübeck and Wismar on the Baltic and thus prevented the Red Army from taking over the Schleswig-Holstein peninsula and perhaps Denmark and Norway, too. For his part, Patton would now find his Third Army driving through weak resistance for objectives that had little strategic and no political value. The end of his Rhine run would be a compulsory halt just over the Czech border, waiting for the Soviets to take over Central Europe. But such political considerations were foreign to his nature—*then*. The main thing was that he had "pissed in the Rhine" and thumbed his nose at authority yet once again. It would be the last time he would do so.

Eleven

On March 24th, the 4th Armored Division, which had spear-headed Patton's drive across the Rhine, had reached the next river, the Main. Soon the division was scheduled to cross the river at Hanau and Aschaffenburg. But on this fine spring morning, with the sun a full gold in the crisp blue sky, the men of the division rested. Others stripped in the muddy fields and washed themselves as best they could, using their helmets as bowls. Here and there amateur barbers tried their hands, clipping their comrades' hair while their "clients" read old copies of the *Stars and Stripes* and *Yank* magazine.

But there was no rest that spring morning for Corps Commander General Eddy, for he had just received an order from General Patton, which he didn't quite understand and which he *definitely* did not like. As he pondered the order, he felt that old sensation of nausea, which indicated rising blood pressure, and wished to God that *he* didn't have to pass it onto the commander of the 4th Armored. That was William Hoge who had just taken over Patton's favorite division, being promoted to the command after his sensational capture of the bridge at Remagen.

Reluctantly Eddy picked up the telephone and called Hoge. After a few preliminaries, he came to the point. "Bill," he said, "George wants a special expedition sent behind the lines to pick up nine hundred prisoners at Hammelburg."

We do not know Hoge's reaction to that strange order—to penetrate sixty miles behind enemy lines and rescue nine hundred American prisoners at the German POW camp located above Hammelburg; it is not recorded. We *do* know, however, that he had not much time to consider it, for a few hours later no less a person than the Army Commander personally called him on the phone. Again it was Hammelburg. Swiftly Patton related what he expected the 4th to do, ending excitedly with, "This is going to make the MacArthur raid on Cabanatuan look like peanuts, Bill.''*[1]

Outspoken and honest as he was, General Hoge decided it was no use trying to talk Patton out of what he planned. Instead he called Eddy to register his protest against the "raid," as Patton called it.

Eddy listened attentively and then said soothingly, "All right, Bill, I'll take it up with George." And there for the time being the matter rested.

One day later Hoge received a surprising visitor at his head-quarters: a short, stocky major in his late forties with a tough, no-nonsense face. He introduced himself as Maj. Alexander Stiller and said he was General Patton's senior aide. What he didn't tell Hoge was that he had been Patton's senior tank sergeant in World War I and that he had gone to Africa with Patton, still dressed in World War I uniform, complete with flat pancake helmet. Now the ex-Arizona cowboy and former Texas Ranger had been with the "boss" for nearly three years and was devoted to him body and soul.

Hoge looked at the aide, whose pistol bore several notches on the butt, with a certain amount of suspicion and asked what had brought him to the 4th.

Stiller replied he was going to go along on the raid.

"But I thought the idea was shelved," Hoge replied, rising to his feet with surprise.

"No sir," Stiller drawled, no emotion showing on his leathery killer's face, which Patton so envied. "The General wants it to go as planned."

Again a worried Hoge got on the phone to Eddy and again the Corps Commander appeased him with, "Don't worry, I'll handle the matter personally."[2]

Another day passed and now it was Eddy's turn to receive an unexpected visitor, no less a person than Patton himself, accompanied by his other aide, Colonel Codman. They were

---

*A month earlier Gen. Douglas MacArthur, another U.S. general with an eye for publicity, had attracted considerable press attention with his successful raid on two POW camps in the Philippines and the rescue of five thousand POWs.

met by Eddy's chief-of-staff, Gen. Ralph Canine, who was a little embarrassed that his boss wasn't there personally to receive the Army Commander.

"Where's Matty?" Patton demanded, as if in a great hurry, though Canine later began to suspect that Patton, for reasons known to himself, had deliberately picked this moment when Eddy was absent.

"He's not here, Sir," Canine began. "He didn't expect—"

"Pick up the phone," Patton cut him short, "and get Bill Hoge. And tell him to cross the Main River and get over to Hammelburg."

Canine hesitated, feeling himself going red, knowing just how explosive Patton's temper was. Finally he plucked up enough courage to tell Patton what Eddy had told him to say should the Army Commander appear: "General, the last thing Matt told me before he left was that if you came by and told us to issue that order, I was to tell you I wasn't to do it." He paused and waited for the hail of invective to descend upon him.*

None came.

"Get Hoge on the phone," Patton snapped, "and I'll tell him myself."

Reluctantly Canine agreed.

Hoge was made of sterner stuff than Canine. He was surprised, shocked, and not a little angry at what Patton was ordering him to do. He said he had not a single man or vehicle to spare for the "raid" on Hammelburg.

Patton didn't lose his temper as he usually did when he was thwarted. Instead, he wheedled in a tone that distinctly embarrassed Hoge, "Bill, I promise I'll replace every man and every vehicle you lose . . . I *promise!*"[3]

After the line went dead, Hoge, completely bewildered, turned to Stiller, who had listened to the conversation, for enlightenment. What was so damned important about Hammelburg?

For a while Stiller hesitated then he came out with it. *The Old Man wanted the Hammelburg POW camp liberated be-*

---

*One wonders if Eddy, expecting this confrontation, decided it would be safer to be away at the front when Patton appeared.

cause his favorite son-in-law, Col. John Waters, was a prisoner there!

When the scandal of the Hammelburg fiasco finally spread outside the inner circle of the Third Army, Patton would flatly deny to the press, the public, his superiors, even to his own family (in the shape of Colonel Waters when he was finally rescued) that he had ordered the raid to rescue the husband of his beloved daughter "Little B."

He told Bradley that he "did not learn of his son-in-law's incarceration until nine days after the raid."[4] He told the press, showing the correspondents his personal diary for that week, that he had first learned of Waters's presence in the camp after one of the few survivors of the raid reached the lines of General Patch's Seventh Army. The latter had informed him that Waters had been in Hammelburg and had been wounded in the escape attempt. That had been on April 4, 1945. When his father-in-law visited the wounded Waters in the hospital, the latter asked him point-blank, "Did you know I was in Hammelburg?" Patton replied, "No I did not . . . I knew there were Americans POWs in the camp and that's why I went in."[5] To the very end, Patton maintained in his memoirs: "I can say through the campaign in Europe I know of no error I made except that of failing to send a Combat Command to take Hammelburg."[6] There was, of course, not one word of regret for the three-hundred-odd men killed, wounded, or captured during the abortive raid.

Well, was Patton lying?

Until John Toland wrote his account of the raid in his *Last One Hundred Days* in 1965, those who knew the truth kept loyally silent. As late as June 1965, after it had become clear that Patton *had* known his son-in-law was in Hammelburg Camp, the now *General* Waters could write to *Army Magazine* stating that Patton hadn't known. How could he have in the conditions prevailing in a crumbling Germany of March 1945? Huge numbers of people were on the move in both east and west, trying to escape the advancing Russians and Western Allies. These included over a hundred thousand Allied POWs being shuttled back and forth by their German captors to prevent them from falling into Allied hands. Virtually all communication and control had broken down. How could

Allied Intelligence or even the Swiss and Swedish Red Cross, which looked after the welfare of Allied prisoners in German imprisonment, know the whereabouts of one single American prisoner, who had last been in a camp in Poland before the great flight had commenced?

General Sir Kenneth Strong, Eisenhower's chief-of-intelligence, when asked for an opinion,* wrote: "If the transfer [of Waters from Poland] took place when the fighting was on, then I do not think Intelligence would have been able or had the time to follow it."[7]

Toland, however, after questioning the key officers concerned, wrote: "One month before, three U.S. officers who had escaped from Poland to Russia told Major General John Deane, head of the U.S. Military Mission in Moscow, that Waters and other Yanks marched west. Deane wired the information to Eisenhower who passed it on to Patton."[8]

This is confirmed by the entry in the Gay diary for February 9, 1945.[9] It is probable that the escaped U.S. officer who informed Deane of Waters's departure from the Polish POW camp was Lt. Craig Campbell. Campbell, who had been one of Eisenhower's aides, had been captured in North Africa at the same time as Colonel Waters and had been in the same camp with him in Poland. As Captain Butcher, Eisenhower's senior aide, noted in his diary for March 12, 1945: "General Deane, head of the American Military Mission to Moscow, had radioed that among American prisoners of war released by the Russians in their great advance is our friend and my brother aide, Lieutenant Craig Campbell, who had been captured in Tunisia during the battle of the Kasserine."[10]**

But how would Patton know where Waters had gone after he had left Poland? It could not have been too difficult to work his destination out. By March 1945, the territory left to the German authorities in which they could hold prisoners was limited to the areas around Hamburg, Munich, and the Franconian area, which included the long-established officers' POW camp at Hammelburg. In February 1945 the Swiss Red Cross reported that seven large columns of prisoners

---

*By the author.
**See C. Whiting, *Kasserine*. Stein and Day, 1984, for further details.

from Poland, including Waters's group, were passing through the city of Dresden heading for the Franconian area.

General Ernst von Goeckel, Waters's last jailer, certainly thought the raid had been launched specifically to free Waters. He wrote, "I visited several of my new prisoners [the survivors of the abortive raid]. Among them was a major—in civilian life, a farmer in Texas*—who told me he wasn't the leader of the operation, but the liaison officer with the American Third Army. Whether the name Patton was mentioned or not, I can't remember, but we were all convinced at that time that the operation had been conducted solely on Waters's behalf."[11]

General von Goeckel's belief was strengthened further by the fact that some years after the war he was visited by a former major on Patton's staff who told him that the Third Army commander had known that his son-in-law was in the camp when he had ordered the raid.

But perhaps the most convincing evidence of all comes from the man who was going to lead that disastrous raid. In an interview given nearly fifteen years after the event, he stated categorically, "Not till hours later [after the raid had started] did I learn that Patton's son-in-law, captured in Tunisia in 1943, was reported to be a prisoner in Hammelburg."[12]

That man was Capt. Abe Baum, a tall, tough twenty-four-year-old who, as a well-brought-up Jewish boy, had been shocked by Patton's crudities at the beginning of his army career, but who now was as tough and cocky as his commander himself. Already the former pattern cutter in New York's rag district (the army had first assigned him to the engineers because it had thought pattern-cutting had something to do with engineering) had earned himself a batch of medals, including Purple Hearts, during the five campaigns in which he had already fought. Soon he was to gain some more—and it would be painful, very painful, indeed. Now on the afternoon of March 26, he was awakened from an exhausted sleep and told to report to the headquarters of Col. Creighton Abrams's command post.

*This was obviously Major Stiller.

There awaiting him was the future Commander-in-Chief of the U.S. Army in Vietnam, his own battalion commander Col. Harold Cohen, and a tough looking major from the staff, who wore World War I decorations. It was Stiller, of course.

"We have a special mission for you," Abrams snapped. "Orders come directly from General Patton." He paused to let the full import of his words sink in. "Do you know where Hammelburg is?"

"Yessir," Baum answered promptly. The rumors of a top-secret suicidal mission to the place had been kicking around the division for forty-eight hours now; and he had helped Colonel Cohen to do the planning of the proposed raid on the place the day before. "It's about sixty miles from here."

Abrams nodded. "Yes, there's a prisoner-of-war camp at Hammelburg. We want you to take a task force and liberate as many Americans as you can. We think there are about three hundred American officers at the *Oflag*."* Abrams hesitated. "The division is not to follow you—you'll be on your own. We'll give you the best we have available. You're to get back to us whichever way you can. You understand?"

Baum didn't speak.

Abrams looked at him hard. "If anyone can get there, Able,** you will," he said softly.

Baum smiled. "This is no way to get rid of me," he wisecracked. "I'll be back."

Later, as Abe Baum left the command post, an almost embarrassed silence fell over the place, broken only when an angry Abrams snorted, "If this mission is accomplished, that guy"—he frowned hard—"deserves a Congressional Medal of Honor."[13]

The breakthrough commenced precisely at nine o'clock that evening. Startlingly, the preliminary artillery barrage stopped. There was a moment's loud, echoing silence, as the thunder of guns reverberated around the surrounding hills. Next instant the first of Baum's tanks began to crawl toward the first German-held village, Schweinheim.

---

*Officers' POW camp.
**Abe Baum's nickname on account of his ability to carry out every mission.

Suddenly a German armed with a panzerfaust sprang out of the doorway. He aimed and fired in the same movement. The Sherman shuddered to a stop, as if halted by a giant fist. For a moment nothing happened. Then there was a sudden sucking in of air, as if the metal monster had lungs, and the Sherman went up in flames.

The American armored infantrymen ran forward in the lurid light of the burning tank and crouched low, as fire erupted on both sides of the little village street. Angrily the officer in charge of the tank column called the commander of the tank stalled behind the burning one, ''Get that fucking thing out of the way!'' he yelled over the radio.

The sergeant needed no urging. His driver rattled on, while the gunner sprayed the houses to both sides with his turret machine gun. Another crew member dropped off and at the risk of his own life started the stalled tank's engine (its crew had fled). With a creak of protesting metal, the stricken Sherman limped to the side of the road. The way ahead was free once more.

But Baum had a hard battle on his hands. The Germans fought back fanatically. Another tank was hit. Again its crew fled, bullets kicking up sparks at their flying feet. Corporal Smith of Baum's B Company, who was there, recalled afterward, ''The Nazis mounted the crippled tank and began firing its 76mm at us. The building beside us was hit and started to burn. Suddenly the company commander radioed we were to withdraw because the task force had gone through. The burning building threw plenty of light so I put the tank in reverse and backed out the street. It was much safer now, but I was still sweating.''[14]

Finally Baum had broken through, but it had taken him three hours to do so. Now he had to ''make miles'' before the Krauts spotted him. But unfortunately for the Baum task force, the column had already been sighted by no less a person than the chief-of-staff of the German Seventh Army, Major General von Gersdorff.

On the same night that Baum started his breakthrough, the staff of the Seventh, established in their command post at a little inn in the village of Heidenbrucken, had spent several hours in some hard drinking. Their chief, General Felber, had finally been relieved by Marshal Kesselring, being replaced by hard-liner Gen. Hans von Obstfelder, the fifth commander of the Seventh Army within six months!

Suddenly the staff, drinking with their departing chief, became "aware of the rattle of tanks coming closer," as von Gersdorff recorded after the war. "As I knew that in the whole Army area we didn't have a single tank or tracked vehicle, we left the inn carefully and stood outside in the darkness."[15]

Moments later the first tanks appeared and von Gersdorff recognized them for what they were—American Shermans. They moved by, "without seeming to notice us at about twenty metres' distance and disappeared into the night."[16] The energetic, aristocratic chief-of-staff acted immediately. He ordered the staff and General Felber into the nearby woods, though he did forget the new Army Commander, who was sound asleep in a bedroom. Then he reentered the inn and grabbed the phone. "I knew there was a large prisoner-of-war camp for U.S. officers and guessed the Americans would attempt to liberate their prisoners."[17] Why von Gersdorff guessed so accurately has never been explained. Now he called the local town commander at Hammelburg village itself. The latter handed him over to a major, home on leave from the front.

Von Gersdorff made him responsible for the defense of the place, warning him that the American armored column was probably heading for the POW camp and asking what he possessed in the way of troops. The major, who apparently had served a long time on the Russian front, had good news for von Gersdorff. That very afternoon a troop of tank destroyers had been unloaded at Hammelburg Station, complete with crews.

Von Gersdorff was delighted. He knew just how vulnerable the Sherman was; the German tank destroyer armed with a 90mm cannon would soon make short work of it. The unknown American task force was riding straight into a trap.

Twelve

On the morning of Tuesday, March 27, things started to go wrong for the Baum force. That morning Burgomaster Clement of Hammelburg ordered his town crier into the streets to warn the inhabitants to evacuate the place. The *Amis* were coming and there was going to be a battle.

"Chaos reigned in the narrow streets as the crowd of refugees hastened to north and east," an eyewitness remembered long afterward. "Hurrying women, children and old men rushed down the main escape route, their baggage loaded on little handcarts. There were also wagons, pulled by horses and slow plodding oxen. . . . Even the pigs and chickens were loaded and taken away."[1]

Now the town was empty save for a few invalids. An expectant silence fell over the place, broken only by the muted sound of firing to the west.

Up in the camp on the heights beyond, General von Goeckel organized his force for the attack to come. It wasn't much, as he told his second-in-command, Colonel Hoppe, a former NCO who had worked himself up through the ranks. "You with your twenty-man staff and your company of snipers, I with my three-hundred cripples and congenital idiots. And against American tanks at that!"

"What are we going to do, Sir?" a hollow-eyed Hoppe asked.

"What we have always done all our lives, Hoppe," von Goeckel, who had been severely wounded in World War I, snapped, "Obey orders!"[2]

Not far away at the little village of Bonnland, another tough old soldier, named Major Otto Diefenbek, was also readying his small force of combat engineers to meet the coming threat. He had already agreed upon a code word with the local farmers along the route that Baum must take. It was

117

"wasp's nest." Once it was given, he would move into the attack.

But it was the great metal monsters now clanking their way down from Hammelburg Railway Station who were going to be the biggest threat to the approaching *Amis*. They were Captain Fritz Koehl's detachment of Ferdinand tank destroyers. With their great guns they could knock out a Sherman frontally, where its armor was thickest, at eight hundred yards. The Sherman, to have the same effect, would have to approach to within two hundred yards and *place a shell through the Ferdinand's periscope, measuring all of two by eight inches!* It seemed that Baum hadn't a chance.

One of the few civilians to remain behind at Hammelburg spotted the first of Baum's force at about two o'clock that afternoon. "Two hours later," he recalled many years later, "the first enemy tank appeared and began to crawl forward very slowly and cautiously. One by one, six tanks came in sight, followed by armored personnel carriers. There must have been forty vehicles in all."[3]

Just about then Koehl spotted them, too, and cursed because among the enemy Shermans he could see an American tank destroyer armed with a 105mm cannon, which was more powerful than his own 90mms. It was a TD commanded by a Sergeant Graham, who would be one of the few survivors of the raid.

But there was no time to worry about the *Ami* 105. Koehl rapped out his orders, and the tank destroyers strung out along the ridge line prepared to fire. Koehl waited no longer. *"Feuer Frei!"* he cried, and his first gunner fired—*and missed*!

Baum reacted immediately. He called Graham over the radio and yelled, "Get up onto that knoll at two o'clock and engage the enemy!"[4] Graham yelled he would, as the rest of the force scattered, and the leading Sherman engaged the German TDs. But not for long. It was hit almost immediately and started burning furiously. A Sherman was struck and skidded to a stop.

But it wasn't all one-sided. Gunner Reynolds in the leading TD lined up a convoy of trucks speeding away to his front. His first shells exploded harmlessly, and there was a tremendous roar and one of the fleeing German trucks simply disappeared. He had struck very lucky indeed. He had hit a truck carrying ammunition for the Ferdinands.

Now the Americans began to take serious casualties. The steep, winding road leading up to the camp was littered with damaged and destroyed Shermans. And not only tanks. Baum's "soft" vehicles, the ones he needed to evacuate the prisoners, were also taking losses. After the war he recalled, "The Kraut tanks knocked out five of my half-tracks and three peeps—one was the medic peep. One of the half-tracks that was hit was filled with gasoline and the other carried 105mm ammunition."[5] But still the tough New Yorker determined to carry out his mission. Gathering together what was left of his force, he ordered them to make a run for it up the hill where they would be in dead ground under the cover of smoke laid by Sergeant Graham's TD. And he made it. Just as it began to darken he reached the outskirts of the camp, where the Sherman gunners started to pound the stockade— and the quarters of the Serbian officer prisoners—manned by von Goeckel's "cripples and congenital idiots." And there the Baum force remained for three long hours, doing nothing. As General von Goeckel recalled after the war, "It was no advertisement for the U.S. Army. . . . I expected then they would overrun the wire. . . . After all there was nothing to stop them. But to my surprise they did nothing. Instead they remained at 500 to 800 meters distance, firing their cannon from time to time."[6]

Now, Colonel Waters, the man they had come to rescue, felt it was time that he took a part in the action. If this went on, he reasoned, the tankers would only succeed in killing their own men. So, with a Colonel "Pop" Goode, who had been captured fighting with the 29th Division in Normandy and played the bagpipes, and the German liaison officer Captain Fuchs, he decided to go out and surrender the camp to them.

Under an improvised white flag and a large Stars and Stripes banner, the three stepped out into the darkness, braving the shells that were still falling all over the camp. They didn't get far. Suddenly a soldier, dressed in what looked like a camouflage suit, popped up out of a hole. Waters knew

American paratroopers wore camouflaged uniforms; perhaps this was one. Hesitantly he called, "*Amerikanisch?*"

The unknown soldier's reaction was instantaneous. He poked his rifle through the fence and fired. At that range he couldn't miss. Waters was lifted from his feet and flung into a ditch, feeling as if he had been "hit with a baseball bat."

Lying there in the ditch while the soldier threatened Fuchs with his rifle, a half-conscious Waters thought miserably, "Goddamnit, you've ruined my hunting and fishing now!"[7]

After that strange halt in front of the wire, Baum started to move forward again. One of his surviving Shermans hit the wire fence and tried to break through. To no avail, the wire wouldn't give. The tank's motor stalled, and it hung there helplessly like a metallic fly trapped in a metallic spiderweb, while the slugs howled off its sides. But others did break through, and suddenly, crazily happy "kriegies"* were streaming toward their liberators yelling and waving. They were free at last!

But in the midst of the general jubilation, Captain Baum, who had been wounded in the fighting, remained grim and unsmiling. For he was worried. How was he going to get the kriegies home? There were hundreds more of them than he had anticipated and he had lost about half his tracked vehicles already. Looking at their pale faces and skinny bodies, emaciated from a diet of cabbage, rotten potatoes, and what they called "green hornet" soup,**, he couldn't imagine them hiking the sixty miles back to their own lines. And then there was the biggest headache of all—*which was the way back*; for already he knew he was surrounded on two sides by Diefenbek's and Koehl's soldiers, and unknown to him, a third column of enemy infantry was on the way to Hammelburg. He was virtually trapped. But Baum kept his glum thoughts to himself in the middle of all the wild shouting and rejoicing. Instead he ordered a radio message sent back to 4th Armored Division HQ.

*POWs' nickname for themselves from the German *Kriegsgefangene* (prisoner-of-war).
**A soup made of horsemeat and beet tops, always covered with maggots and stained green by the maggots.

It was received there at 0300 hours on the morning of March 28 and read simply: "MISSION ACCOMPLISHED."

It was the last message anyone was to receive from Task Force Baum.

That same day Patton, obviously "greatly agitated," burst into General Middleton's HQ and cried, "Troy, I'm in trouble again. This time I've really done it. I've sent Alex Stiller off to his death. He kept nagging me until I told him to go ahead on a special mission to this prisoner of war camp at Hammelburg with this outfit I was sending."

"Wait a minute, George," Middleton interrupted, for this was the first he had heard of the raid. "Let's have that again."

Patton explained what he had done, making no mention of Waters, but saying that the force had "been badly shot up," lamenting that he "loved that boy [Stiller] like a son. Why did I let him talk me into letting him go along?" No mention at all was made of the other three-hundred-odd American soldiers who had gone with him. Middleton was sympathetic. He asked Patton, "What sort of outfit did you send?"

Patton answered, "Oh, something like a reinforced company."

"A reinforced company," Middleton exclaimed. "You surely have played it!"[8]

Patton certainly had. Now as March '45 gave way to April, the first reports of what had happened to Baum's force came in, and they were alarming. German radio, controlled by the "Poison Dwarf," as Dr. Goebbels was nicknamed on account of his vitriolic tongue and small stature, crowed, "South of Aschaffenburg, the 4th American Armored Division has attacked through Loehr to East Gemuenden. This force is being attacked on all sides. All thirteen enemy tanks in Gemuenden have been destroyed and the town recaptured. . . . The first attack of extreme right wing of the U.S. Third Army has ended in total failure."[9]

Here and there a wild-eyed, tattered survivor was beginning to reach the lines of General Patch's Seventh Army to tell his tragic tale; of how Task Force Baum and the POWs who had gone with them had been trapped on a hill near the

camp and had decimated by heavy fire before being attacked
and overrun. Baum had been killed or wounded, as had been
most of his force and the liberated ex-prisoners. Those who
had attempted to make a run for it through the hills had been
chased by soldiers with bloodhounds.

Angry rumors of what had happened to Baum and their
comrades spread through the 4th Armored and indeed
throughout Eddy's corps HQ, which, try as he might, Eddy
could not prevent "traveling the grapevine to Army Group,"
as Bradley put it later when he explained how he first learned
of the "wild goose chase"—his own description of the Hammelburg raid.

Naturally the war correspondents attached to the Army
Group became interested. Patton and his exploits were always
good for copy. The rumor grew that a son-in-law of the Third
Army Commander was involved. A correspondent discovered
that tough, swaggering, highly conspicuous Maj. Al Stiller
had mysteriously disappeared from the Patton entourage. Malicious speculation began.

Patton decided to act. At the beginning of April he decided
to hold a press conference to explain his position, for as he
confessed to Bradley later, "he [Patton] was worried for fear
that the newsmen might draw their own implications." Bradley who had little need of Patton now, agreed. "Certainly
had George consulted me on the mission, I would have for-
bidden him to have gone ahead with it," he wrote later."[10]
He had washed his hands of the affair. Patton was his own
worst enemy; see how he would get out of this one.

The conference was staged in the best Patton manner. Dis-
daining the use of a press officer, Patton talked to the correspondents personally. Displaying his personal diary to prove
his innocence, he denied he had known his son-in-law had
been in the camp. He had only become aware of that fact on
April 4, when one of the survivors had reported it to General
Patch, who had informed him. The correspondents were convinced. Even the hard-boiled newspapermen couldn't believe
that "ol' Blood and Guts" would run to such an extravagant
folly as risking the lives of three hundred young men to rescue a relative. Thus it was that all that came out of the conference of any importance was a quarter column report in

Time, stating: "Why did Patton order such a desperate un-
dertaking [the Hammelburg raid]? One of the prisoners was
Patton's son-in-law, Lt. Col. J. K. Waters, who was badly
wounded in the fracas. Patton, denying that he ever knew
Waters was there when he launched the operation, displayed
his personal diary to prove it; his motive, he said, was concern for Allied prisoners. Some men (including Hearst correspondent Austin Lake, who was with the Third Army and
told the story last week) wondered if Patton should not have
shown more concern for his own soldiers."[11]

One wonders.

Now Patton set about cleaning up the mess hurriedly. When
thirty-five wounded members of the Baum Task Force were
liberated, together with Colonel Waters, by the 14th Armored
Division, they were speedily forwarded to Camp Lucky Strike
at Cherbourg, France. Here released "kriegies" were shipped
home to the States, and since the Allied armies had begun to
liberate prisoners-of-war in large numbers, there had been a
number of bitter complaints on the slowness of the proce-
dure. Indeed a senatorial investigating committee would soon
visit the repatriation camp to look into the matter. These
thirty-five men of the 4th Armored, however, were shipped
home *immediately*.

Captain Baum, who had been wounded three times, including the inner thigh (he had thought the "Krauts had shot
my nuts off"), was also rescued. But he didn't want to be
repatriated. He wanted to fight on. Promoted to major,
awarded to D.S.C., visited in hospital by no less a person
than Patton himself, he was allowed to return to his old unit
where he was greeted by his C.O., Colonel Cohen, with the
words, "I thought I got rid of you."

But he didn't stay long. After testing his nerve at the front
with a combat outfit, he was ordered by the divisional psy-
chiatrist with the amazing name of Earl Miracle to report to
HQ. Miracle told him to take a rest. Baum refused. Then
Hoge stepped in and said, "I've got news for you. You're on
the way to the Riviera."

When Miracle heard this, he gasped, "Maybe I made a
mistake. *I* should be so sick!"[12] Thus it happened that the

aggressive young soldier was relaxing in the warm sun of the
French coast at the U.S. Army rest center there when World
War II came to an end.

By the end of the first week of April, with five weeks to go
before the end of the war, George S. Patton must have felt
that he had swept the problem of the Hammelburg raid neatly
under the carpet. The wounded survivors had been repatriated. Baum was out of the way. Stiller had been found "with
ten new notches" on the butt of his pistol, as Colonel Codman noted. He was well and happy, though ten pounds
lighter, and could be depended upon to keep his mouth shut.
Just as Eddy, Hoge, and Abrams would. (Even as late as
1973, General Middleton was maintaining to his biographer
that he didn't think Patton had known Waters was in Hammelburg when he launched the great raid. "My opinion then
and now is that the raid was a damn fool stunt attempted with
a pitifully under-strength force."[13])

More importantly the press, which was the main link with
the Great American Public back home, was appeased. The
correspondents had not taken up the story of the Hammelburg
raid; that week there were many more exciting and dramatic
incidents to report than the minor skirmish. What did it matter that there were still some two hundred American soldiers
unaccounted for? (Patton had quickly replaced the two missing companies from the 10th Armored Infantry and 37th Tank
Battalions.) There would be no public scandal such as in Sicily in '43 and Knutsford in '44.

It must have seemed to him that he had even concealed the
incident from the Supreme Commander, for so far there had
been no queries or comments from the "gentlemen up
north." And if Eisenhower didn't know, then the most feared
and influential man in the U.S. Army, General Marshall,
would not learn of the incident.

Thus Patton must have satisfied himself that the unfortunate business at Hammelburg had been dealt with once and
for all. Now he could get on with the business of enjoying
what was left of the war before he ran out of those battles
that he loved so dearly.

But Patton was wrong. The "Hammelburg Incident" was

not going to go away, in spite of the strict censorship that Patton had now ordered clamped down on the story. Soon it would resurface with decisive results for the rest of Patton's remaining career. Now the final break with Eisenhower could commence.

Christmas Eve, 1944, in the Hotel Alfa, Luxembourg City. From left to right: Colonel Koch, Brigadier General Sibert, Brigadier General Moses, Lt. Gen. George S. Patton, Jr., Gen. Omar N. Bradley, Major General Allen, Brigadier General Kibler, Brigadier General Maddox, Colonel Harkins.

Patton and Bradley with officers from their staffs in Luxembourg City.

January 1945: An American soldier works on a frozen .50 caliber machine gun atop a tank of the 6th Armored Division.

American tanks cross the Our River in February 1945 and enter Germany.

The barrage commences on the Our-Sauer river line, as Third Army prepares to fight through the German Eifel Moselle region, prior to making a dash for the Rhine.

Terrified German villagers forced out of their homes by American soldiers on the lookout for snipers.

A portion of Wittlich's main street after the bombardments of March 1945.

Suspected snipers are brought in by men of the 76th Infantry Division in the town of Wittlich.

The key town of Bitburg after its capture. From here, Patton's 4th Armored Division made its celebrated dash to the Rhine.

One reason for continued German resistance is documented in this photo near a town taken back from the Red Army by the Germans in January 1945. The picture shows the bodies of women and girls raped by the Russians.

BRITISH COMBINE PHOTO

While civilians walk about the city of Mainz, GI's stay close to the buildings in the background, ready to take cover from snipers.

Troops, boats, and paddles crowd the street as the men make ready to attempt another crossing of the Rhine.

Some of Patton's infantry make an assault crossing of the Rhine under enemy fire.

"Radio th' ol' man we'll be late on account of a thousand-mile detour."

Sgt. Bill Mauldin's celebrated lampoon of Patton's Third Army after his meeting with Patton, March 1945.

March 1945: A German toddler starts to rebuild.

In shattered postwar Germany, civilians unload supplies from a river barge.

Germans line up to surrender weapons in Patton's kingdom—Bavaria, 1945.

Citizens of Frankfurt-on-Main stand in a line three blocks long waiting for food rations.

IMPERIAL WAR MUSEUM

Patton the victor—and newly appointed governor of Bavaria. He will have plenty of problems to face.

In mid-1945, Patton—still an energetic ladies' man—stands surrounded by female admirers.

Here at the army hospital in Heidelberg, Patton breathed his last in December 1945, one year after his last great triumph in the Battle of the Bulge.

Patton's casket is borne to the grave. On the left is Master Sergeant Meeks, Patton's faithful servant.

General Patton's grave in Hamm/Luxembourg.

PART III

THE END RUN

Thirteen

On the morning of April 6, 1945, two military policemen, Privates First Class Clyde Harmon and Anthony Kline, of the 90th Infantry Division, which had just captured the German town of Merkers, were in their jeep patrolling the area. They were on the lookout for any Germans moving about contrary to the divisional order forbidding civilian movement. Just outside the town they came across two civilian women and stopped to reprimand them. It turned out, however, that the women were French DPs and as one of them was pregnant, the two young soldiers decided to give them a ride in their jeep. At least, that was their story—afterward!

For some reason the women were deposited at a local command post and questioned before being driven back into Merkers by a Private Mootz. On their way they passed one of the entrances to the Kaiseroda salt mine. Here one of the French-women exclaimed, ''That's the mine where the gold bullion is kept.'' Mootz took the women back to the command post and let Intelligence have a go at them. Soon a tremendous story began to emerge. Two months before, flatcars had begun to arrive at Merkers from Berlin—thirteen of them in all—bringing with them one hundred tons of gold, worth a staggering $200 million, plus a thousand million Reichsmarks and four million dollar bills! Seventy-two hours later, for it took that time to unload the huge treasure, this tremendous hoard, which was the dying Reich's total financial reserves, was stored at Room 8 deep in the heart of the Kaiseroda mine.

The story was confirmed swiftly by other displaced persons and sergeants of the British 51st Highland Division, who had been captured in 1940 and had helped to unload the treasure. Patton's Third Army was now in possession of the entire reserves of the Berlin *Reichsbank*!

By noon General Eddy, the Corps Commander, had been informed, and he ordered immediate steps to be taken to seal off the mine's five entrances and guard its thirty miles of galleries. One entrance was placed in the care of the 712th Tank Battalion and the other four were taken over by the men of the 357th Infantry. Now under guard, Army experts began to assess what exactly the treasure was worth. By the end of the first day they had figured out the hoard amounted to $315 million, which made it one of the greatest deposits in the whole world.*

By that evening Patton had heard the news that the gold and monetary reserves of the Third Reich had been captured by his Third Army. We do not know why he did so, but Patton ordered a news blackout. That meant banning correspondents from the area. (Perhaps he feared that a public announcement would alert the Germans to their loss and that they would make some attempt to recover it.)

Almost immediately Patton's ban was broken. A SHAEF censor passed the story of the great discovery and something else—*the story of the abortive Hammelburg raid*! The tragic incident that Patton had thought he had been able to hide could now reach the Great American Public. Patton was furious, and his reaction was typical of him when he was angry. He fired the unfortunate SHAEF censor, although he had no jurisdiction over the officer.

His move was unfortunate; it started a chain reaction. When the war correspondents heard of the sacking and its cause, they thought that Patton was trying to censor news, which, of course, he was. Now several of them took it upon themselves to write bitter articles about the Third Army Commander. Newsworthy though he was, Patton was also a heavy-handed autocrat.

Captain Butcher, Eisenhower's public relations man, became alarmed. As this former vice-president of NBC and very influential officer at Eisenhower's HQ put it later, "Because of Patton's attitude, I knew that three or four correspondents had written bitter articles about him. Unfortunately they appeared as examples of 'Army blundering.' "[1] He reported the matter to Eisenhower. The supreme commander,

*Later, a more "conservative" estimate made it out to be $238,490,000.

always conscious of his public image, which depended on good relations with the press and perhaps thinking of his political future, decided to step in. He would have to talk seriously to the general he called his "problem child."*

On the morning of April 12, Eisenhower and Bradley arrived at Merkers to view the great treasure. Together with Eddy and Patton, the top brass were lowered down the 2,000-foot shaft in a primitive elevator operated by a German. As they descended at an ever-increasing speed down the pitch-black shaft, Patton began counting the stars on his neighbors' shoulders, then looked up at the single cable barely visible against the diminishing patch of sky. "If that clothesline should part," he observed, "promotions in the United States Army would be considerably stimulated." Out of the darkness came Eisenhower's voice, "O.K., George, that's enough! No more cracks until we are above ground again."[2]

At the bottom they fumbled their way through a dimly lit tunnel into a large vault, piled high with gold bars, coins, paintings by the great masters, Titian, Van Dyck, Dürer, and other treasures. When the soldier guarding the treasures was suddenly confronted by all this top brass, he said, "Jez-us Christ!"

Patton was not impressed by the artworks. He threw them a bored glance and recorded in his memoirs that, "The ones I saw were worth, in my opinion, two dollars, fifty, and were the type normally seen in bars in America."[3] So much for Patton's aesthetic sense.

Their guide, a German, pointed then to a dozen bales of notes and said they amounted to three thousand million Reichsmark. "They will be badly needed to meet the Army payroll," he said through an interpreter.

Bradley laughed and said, "I doubt the German Army will be meeting payrolls much longer." Then he turned to Patton. "If these were freebooting days when a soldier kept his loot, you'd be the richest man in the world."[4]

Patton grinned . . .

At lunch at Eddy's HQ, Patton told Eisenhower he was not at all disturbed by the uproar caused by the war correspon-

*In a letter to General Marshall.

dents protesting his sacking of the SHAEF censor for having passed the Merkers and Hammelburg stories. "I knew I was right on that," he announced calmly.

"Well, I'll be damned!" Eisenhower snorted. "Until you said that maybe you were. But if you're that positive, then I'm sure you're wrong."

Patton winked across the table at Bradley. The latter laughed and said, "But why keep it a secret, George? What would you do with all that money?"

Patton smiled and said the Third Army was divided into two schools of thought. Half wanted the gold to be made into medallions. "One for every son of a bitch in Third Army." The rest wanted the loot hidden until Congress cracked down on peacetime military appropriation; then "Third Army could drag out the money and buy new weapons."

Eisenhower shook his head in mock wonder and commented to Bradley, "He's always got an answer."[5]

If the visit to the gold hoard at the bottom of the salt mine had about it a quality of unreality, that afternoon was stark and terrible. For after lunch the top brass flew to XX Corps HQ at Gotha, from whence Corps Commander Walker took them to see the newly overrun German concentration camp at Ohrdruf. Their SS guard spared them nothing—the whipping blocks, the butchers' blocks for the cleaving of jaws and the smashing out of gold teeth, the half-filled still smoking ovens, the huge piles of emaciated cadavers everywhere.

Patton walked off and vomited. Bradley was unable to speak. But Eisenhower stuck it out and felt it his duty to visit every section of the horror camp with its 3,200 corpses. Later, while the glumly silent top brass awaited transportation, a GI accidentally bumped into one of the former guards and laughed almost apologetically.

Eisenhower rounded on him icily, snapping, "Still having trouble hating them?" Then he turned to the others and ordered, "I want every American unit not actually in the front lines to see this place. We are told that the American soldier does not know what he is fighting for. Now, at least, he will know what he is fighting against."[6]

That night Eisenhower stayed at Patton's HQ. After dinner he divulged something he had not told to his other army commanders. He was ordering the Ninth and First Armies to halt, while Patton's Third was to turn to the south. "From a tactical point of view," he told Patton, "it is highly inadvisable for the American Army to take Berlin and I hope political influence won't cause me to take the city. It has no tactical or strategic value and would place upon the American forces the burden of caring for thousands and thousands of Germans, displaced persons and Allied prisoners of war."

Patton was dismayed. "Ike," he said, "I don't see how you figure that out. We had better take Berlin and quick—and on to the Oder."

Eisenhower was adamant.

Later Patton tried again. It could be done in forty-eight hours, he stated. But Eisenhower was not impressed. "Well, who would want it?" he demanded.

Patton, who had done as much as anyone to draw away the men and resources from the north where they would have ensured a quick breakthrough to the most important political objective left, placed both his hands on Eisenhower's shoulders and said solemnly, "I think history will answer that question for you."[7]

A little later, just as he was turning in, Patton "noticed that I had failed to wind up my watch, which was run down, so I turned on the radio to get a time signal. Just as I turned it on, the announcer reported the death of President Roosevelt."[8]

Patton got up again and informed Bradley and Eisenhower immediately of the momentous news. So ended that long, bizarre, unreal, sickening thirteenth of April 1945, marked by the death of the man who had taken America into the war and transformed all those there that night, in the heart of conquered Germany, from obscure colonels on the verge of retirement, into generals with household names, commanding the destinies of millions. But that day also marked the last visit that Eisenhower ever paid to Patton. From now onward he would no longer *visit* his "problem child," he would *summon*!

When Eisenhower returned to his own headquarters, Butcher, thinking that his boss had forgotten the sacking of the SHAEF censor over the Merkers-Hammelburg release, tackled the latter on the subject once more. "I told Ike of the flurry at PRD* among the censors because General Patton had arbitrarily fired one of them for passing stories that we had captured some of the German loot and of an expedition Patton had ordered to liberate some American prisoners."[9]

Eisenhower told him, as Butcher confided to his celebrated diary, that he, Eisenhower, "had this chapter and verse while he was visiting Patton and had made it clear to 'Georgie' that he had no right to relieve a SHAEF censor. . . . *Ike had taken Patton's hide off!*" (my italics)[10]

Butcher concluded his entry by confessing ruefully that nevertheless "I think Patton must have as many hides as a cat has lives, for this is at least the fourth time that General Ike has skinned his champion end runner."[11]

But this time Butcher was wrong in his assessment of his boss's attitude to the Third Army commander. The raid on Hammelburg Camp and the sacking of the SHAEF censor marked the decisive turning point in the Eisenhower-Patton relationship. In fact, Eisenhower, who had protected Patton so often in these last three years, felt that a baffling change had come over Patton in the spring of '45; that he was blind to his various faults and shortcomings. As a result he was beginning to make just too many arrogant blunders.

In his full-scale biography of General Patton, Ladislas Farago states that from this time on: "Eisenhower thought . . . something was driving him [Patton] into callous and arbitrary acts; he was arrogating undue privileges to himself; and he was behaving as if his natural place in history had filled him with reckless arrogance."[12]

Two days after he last visited Patton at his headquarters, Eisenhower wrote to Marshall in Washington, inviting him to visit the Army he had created "while we are still conducting a general offensive." Then he went on to state that he was sure Marshall "would be proud of the Army you have produced," detailing the excellence of the troops. All this was a reflection of the "high average ability in our higher command team." The corps commanders were without exception outstanding. There was *only one* weakness at the highest

*Public Relations Dept.

command level, *only one* army commander he could single out.

That army commander was George S. Patton. He, alone of the four army commanders in Bradley's Army Group, could be faulted on account of his "unpredictability."[13]

The writing was on the wall. Now that victory in Europe was clearly in sight, Patton was no longer needed. His flamboyant style and unpredictability was becoming a liability: a liability that Eisenhower could not afford any more. Patton himself had already realized that Eisenhower had political ambitions after the successful conclusion of the war. Could he, Eisenhower, afford to associate himself too closely with a man, who in the eyes of East Coast liberals and much of the press, was—admittedly—a war-winning general; yet at the same time, an autocrat who disdained the "New Deal" and everything that went with it? Indeed, there were some who maintained that one of the great democracy's leading generals was *not* a democrat himself.

Powerful influences behind the scene in Washington would ensure that in June 1945 (one month before the first atom bomb was exploded at Los Alamos), when General Marshall was firmly convinced that the war in the Pacific would last another year, Patton would not be allotted that new command he desired in that theater. At the time it was thought that General MacArthur was opposed to Patton's transfer to his command; that he could not tolerate yet another flamboyant actor in uniform stealing the limelight from himself. But later MacArthur strongly denied that he had anything to do with the Marshall decision not to transfer Patton east after the end of the war in Europe.

Who or what could have influenced Marshall? It certainly was *not* the dawn of the atomic age or the belief that the defeat of Japan was imminent. In June 1945 the bomb, as we have seen, was not tested; and after Okinawa, which had just taken eighty-two days to capture and had cost the U.S. Army some sixty thousand dead and wounded, it seemed hardly likely that the Japanese would give in easily when the homeland was finally invaded.

There can be only one person behind the Marshall decision— *the Supreme Commander, Eisenhower*! The scandals in which Patton had been involved and Eisenhower's reports on those scandals must have influenced Marshall. Roosevelt had promised Patton that he and his Army would be deployed to the Pacific when victory in Europe was ensured. But now Roosevelt was dead and Marshall was making the decisions. Patton would stay in Europe when the war ended. Unknown to the aging general, his fighting career was about over. When Eisenhower left his headquarters for the last time on April 13, Patton had exactly twenty-four days of combat left and Butcher could write in his diary, "Don't know what will happen to him now. . . . He's always said he wanted to die fighting."[14]

Fourteen

☆

It was a crazy time, a time without precedent. The British called it "swanning"; the Americans called it "the rat race." Both phrases meant the armor had cut loose, had almost a free run, barreling straight down the main roads, leaving the infantry to mop up the islands of resistance, bypassing any town that showed any fight. As a result, there were great tracts of "outlaw country" to the left and right of the main roads, which were still in German hands and where there might be resistance.

The tactic the tankers used was simple, but lethal: Reconnaissance elements linked by radio to the main force creeping down the road, "daring" any enemy concealed to their front to take a potshot at them. Sooner or later the men at point would bump into trouble: a lone 88mm intent on suicide, a bunch of unkempt kids armed with a panzerfaust, a platoon of die-hard SS. Then the men at point would die and the "fun" would commence.

Here and there the Germans still launched counterattacks. North of Weimar, Patton's 76th Division was attacked savagely by over two thousand Germans, with a number of assault guns covering them. The attack was repulsed, but only after the 6th Armored Division had launched a full-scale tank assault. The next day General Frederick Hahn, commander of the German LXXXII Corps, walked into the area of a startled black quartermaster outfit and said they wanted to give up. Never before in the history of the U.S. Army had a full general surrendered to a QM unit. The black soldiers talked about it for the rest of the war!

Not far away at Regensburg, the boot was on the other foot. Captain Charles Long, who had once been a cook and was now a company commander in the all-black 761st Tank Battalion, was captured by the Germans and was told that the

137

sergeant who had been taken with him was going to be shot outside.

But the Germans were bluffing. "Soon a general appeared. He asked me, 'What are you doing in Germany, you rich Americans?' "

Long answered, "Sir, we found you in France!"[1]

The German general slapped his thigh and started laughing. Next morning the Germans abandoned Regensburg, and Long and his sergeant found themselves at liberty again and unharmed. Just another tale of the "big war" to tell their grandchildren and prove they had not been "shit-shoveling in Louisiana."

Sometimes, however, prisoners were not treated so considerately during that crazy April. In the second week of that month, Patton's Army finally cut off what was left of the 6th SS Mountain Division, which had been fighting against the Third since the previous January. In the confused fighting some two thousand SS men started to work their way around the Third's rear in an attempt to escape from the trap.

During the course of a night withdrawal, the SS Captured a rear-line U.S. field hospital, complete with doctors and nurses. The next morning the SS men moved out, taking with them the hospital's trucks, but leaving the patients and medical personnel unharmed.

Unfortunately for them, wild rumors began to spread among the men of the 5th Division about what had happened in the hospital. It was said that the SS had murdered the doctors and raped the nurses. Revenge had to be taken. In his diary Patton noted that five hundred SS prisoners were shot in cold blood before the misunderstanding was cleared up.

There were humorous moments, too, during the "rat race." Although Patton personally believed that as long as one of his soldiers kept his helmet on and elbows off the ground while making love a German *Fraulein*, it was not "fraternization but *fornication!*" he knew just how strict Eisenhower was about the implementation of his nonfraternization ban. Thus it was that when he came across two of his GIs talking to German girls on the autobahn he ordered his driver to stop. In a screech of protesting rubber, his jeep skidded to a halt and Patton barked, "what the so-in-so do you mean by fraternizing with those so-in-so German so-in-sos?" (thus Colonel Codman recorded his boss's outburst).

One of the GIs unwound himself from his German partner and said easily, "Sir, these here are two Russian ladies who have lost their way. We are trying to learn their language, sir, so as to direct them properly."

For a moment even Patton was at a loss for words. Then he shook his head in mock wonder and breathed, "Okay, you win." He turned to his driver and snapped, "Go ahead, Mims."

But once out of earshot, he shook his head again at the audacity of the GI, murmuring, "That really is a new one."[2]

Germany had never seen a time like this since the Thirty Years War back in the Seventeenth Century. Millions of slave workers newly liberated, clogging the roads, waving and singing, drunk and mad with hate of the Germans, looting, plundering, raping.

These freed bondsmen, uprooted from a dozen different European countries, were now taking their revenge on he fat, prosperous German civilians, whose pleasant villages and rich farms had been untouched hitherto by the war. The suffering and humiliation they had endured during the last five terrible years now found expression in their terrorization of the German populace.

And they weren't the only ones. During the "rat race" superior officers virtually lost control of their men in these far-ranging mobile units. Previously the men had mostly lived and fought in an empty, desolate countryside, devoid of civilians, their bed for the night a hole in the ground or at the best a shell-shattered barn. Now they were in villages, towns, large cities, taking what they pleased, doing exactly what they wanted without anyone to stop them. For now the only control was in the hands of NCOs or junior officers who were too inexperienced to exercise it. As U.S. General Franklin Davis, then a major, recalled later: "There were new benefits to being victors. . . . They were conquering enemy territory now instead of liberating the countries of the Allies. They often slept in houses, apartments, taverns, hotels, even sumptuous villas. Once a town fell to them, their billeting parties

had only to select a good spot, tell the German inhabitants
'*Raus*' and they were in.''[3]

For the most part the troops looted and stole eggs. Eggs
became an obsession, more highly prized for a while than
schnapps and wine. Everywhere, chicken coops were ran-
sacked, and if the terrified German peasants had already hidden their eggs before the advancing *Amis*, they were forced
to produce them at the muzzle of an M-1. Happy GIs, the
yolks running down their bearded chins, ate ten or twelve
eggs at a sitting. How delightful those fried eggs, "sunny
side up," tasted after months of canned rations!

Medic Private Atwell, up front with one of Patton's infantry divisions, who had become progressively sickened with
the war and the behavior of many of his fellow Americans,
remembered after the war just what it was like when the company he was attached to took another "higgledy-piggledy village" looking "like a page from Mother Goose." He went
into the kitchen of one of the thatched medieval houses to
take a rest when two infantrymen battered down the door,
which was open as it was.

"Has this place been looted yet?" they cried excitedly.

The old woman who owned the place began to weep, covering her wrinkled face with her apron.

"Hey, get her the hell outa here!" one of the infantrymen
yelled. "What's she bitching about anyway? Go on, ya old
bastard—*get out*." The old woman fled, and Atwell went out
into the yard, hardly noticing the sun streaming down. Suddenly he was overwhelmed with misery. "God," he told
himself, "I'm tired of this, tired of the war, of human beings—of everything!"[4]

But it wasn't just eggs that Patton's men—and the vultures
from COMZ who followed them up—looted. As Colonel Allen of Patton's staff noted, "Valuables and treasures such as
art objects, currency and jewels always were meticulously
reported and turned in by the combat troops. But knickknacks
like Lugers and Rolliflex cameras were 'liberated' for secu-
rity and protective reasons. No use leaving pistols and cameras in the hands of the Krauts. . . . Also there were rear
echelon sharpers, always on the prowl for ill-gotten gains.''[5]

There certainly were and some of them were making a fortune. Although regulations prohibited a soldier from sending home more than his normal pay, unless the excess was certified by his personnel officer, the GI usually excused the transfer of larger amounts of money (gained on the black market or through looting) by saying he had won the sums by gambling. As gambling was legal, there was little Patton could do about such money transfers.

But looting was not the only problem in the Third and other armies now sweeping across Germany. The more serious crimes—desertion, murder, rape, assault with intent to commit rape—sharply increased now. The upswing in rape was particularly marked. In January '45, thirty-two men had been brought to trial (naturally there were many more who were never caught). By March the figure had increased to 128 and by April it had doubled to 259.

Naturally there were not the virtually organized mass rapes indulged in by the Red Army as it swept through Germany's eastern provinces; or the terrifying orgy of arson, pillage, and rape carried out by France's colored colonial soldiers in the Black Forest area. There the holiday resort of Freudenstadt was declared an open city by the French commanders for forty-eight hours, open to rape and looting, before it was finally burned to the ground. Or the village of Rohrbach, for instance, where every female "between 12 and 80 was raped" by "Goums from the Sahara, tall, black, strange people in uniforms like grey dressing gowns,"[6] as Englishwoman Christabel Bielenberg recalled after the war. On the other hand, as Bielenberg's husband maintained later, "the black soldiers of the U.S. Army were tremendously popular with the German people. As a result of being underdogs in America, they were humane and sympathetic towards the defeated, and they were the best behaved soldiers of the Occupation— they were gentle, they smiled, they gave the children sweets."[7]

The "rat race," its triumphs and its excesses, bored Patton. What really did it matter that in one day one single division captured twenty-two towns? What did it matter, too, that his stockades were filling up with military criminals, awaiting trial for a whole range of offenses? Whatever regulations stated to the contrary, he had always maintained that that which his soldiers captured should be retained or enjoyed by them. "A soldier who won't fuck, won't fight," was his motto.

Now, however, he found himself at a loose end with no clear military objective in sight, waiting until his Army was ordered to wheel to the south, as Eisenhower, on the thirteenth, had said it would. Then, presumably, it would attack into the new threat: the "Alpine Redoubt," as the "gentlemen up north" were calling that area of Bavaria, Austria, and Northern Italy where the Nazis were supposed to be preparing to make their last stand.

On one day he flew to Mainz to attend the opening of a railway bridge across the Rhine. It had been built by a West Point classmate, Colonel Hulen, who had built it in nine days, eighteen hours and ten minutes. But Hulen was apologetic because Julius Caesar had bridged the river in twelve hours less time.

Patton couldn't have cared less. In a foul mood he snapped at General Plank who had handed him an outsize pair of scissors to cut the ceremonial ribbon, "What are you taking me for?" A *tailor*! Goddamnit, give me a bayonet!"[8]

With an angry sweep, he sliced through the ribbon and declared the bridge open.

In the end Patton decided he would fly to Paris for twenty-four-hours leave until he received the green light to start what was to become his last battle. Together with Codman he flew to Orly, where a car sent by General Hughes, Patton's old crony, was waiting for them. The Packard took them to the Hotel George V, where Patton looked at his watch and said to Codman, "It is now six o'clock [P.M.]. I am going to visit Johnny Waters* and then dine with General Hughes. We take off at two tomorrow afternoon. Between now and then your time is your own."[9]

Codman saluted and departed, leaving Patton to his own devices, glad to be back in Paris once more and away from a very moody boss. Patton, for his part, duly visited his son-

---

*Waters was receiving further treatment in Paris for his wound before being shipped to the States.

in-law and then went off for dinner and a night of drinking with Hughes.

Patton's mood was still bad as he and Hughes drank "until weesome hours," as Hughes noted in his diary in a rather quaint phrase. Eisenhower's last visit to his headquarters after the inspection of the treasure at Merkers still rankled.

Hughes noted: "Geo sore because Ike had cussed him out for taking a gold mine in Russian territory." That wasn't all. Patton was also "sore at Jean* because she broadcast to U.S. that she is here. Bea heard it before Geo did and wrote him. Hell to pay!"[10]

It was not surprising that Patton's mood was black when "Bea," who was his wife, Beatrice (probably the only human being he feared in this world), was after him. Like Eisenhower who lived in dread of his "Mamie" and her bitter, vindictive letters, Patton hated the communications, filled with accusations and recriminations, he received from his plump, homely wife. Above all he trembled at the thought that she might discover his womanizing.

His mood remained black the next day. Earlier on the eighteenth, Codman had discovered that at last Patton had been promoted to four stars—the last of Eisenhower's army commanders to be granted his final star although he was older and more experienced than the others. Hurriedly Codman, the perfect aide, set off on a tour of the quartermaster office in Paris and finally managed to obtain the "last set of Four-Star collar insignia in the E.T.O."[11]

From there he rushed to Orly Airport where the newly promoted general's plane was being refueled. Swiftly he ordered it readied to receive Patton in appropriate fashion. "Four-Star pennants outside, huge Four-Star flag inside, on a table-shelf by his seat, Four-Star auto plates and a bottle of Four-Star Hennessy." Then as an afterthought, "we formed squads of four and stood at rigid attention"[12] to await the new four-star general.

According to the sycophantic aide, Codman, the general "got quite a laugh" out of the gesture. But Hughes knew differently. He had had a hard job getting Patton to read about

*Jean Gordon, his niece, whom Hughes supposed was Patton's mistress.

the promotion on the front page of that morning's *Stars and Stripes*. "He is sore to be promoted as an afterthought," Hughes confided to his dairy. "I don't blame him."[13]

So Patton returned to command his last battle. He was a four-star general, but time and honors were running out fast.

Fifteen

On the evening of Palm Sunday 1945, the American-appointed German burgomaster of Aachen, Franz Oppenhoff, was accosted at the door of his home by three strange men. They told the startled official they were German airmen who had been shot down near Brussels three days before. Now they were trying to make their way back to their own lines on the other side of the Rhine. "What about getting us passes, *Herr Burgermeister*?" their leader, a man named Klaus Wenzel, asked.

Standing there in the moonlight, Franz Oppenhoff, who had been the mayor since the Americans had occupied Aachen the previous October, shook his head. "I can't do that," he said. "You should report to the Americans and give yourselves up. The war's nearly over anyway. It's only a matter of days."

Abruptly another of the men named Leitgeb snapped "Heil Hitler!" and Oppenhoff noted with a shiver of fear that he had a pistol sticking out of his pocket. Fear overcame him, for he knew he was a marked man, threatened with death because he had "collaborated" with the Americans. But he overcame his fear. Turning to his teenage maid, he said, "Don't be alarmed, Elisabeth. They are German fliers. Make them a couple of sandwiches if you can find something. Just a minute," he added for the benefit of the strangers, "I'll help her."

When he was gone, Leitgeb whispered urgently to Wenzel, "When he comes up again."

Wenzel paled and said hoarsely, "Yes, now." Almost hesitantly he drew the pistol with its long silencer, and his companion noticed in the cold, silver rays of the moon that his hand trembled violently.

Footsteps approached down the corridor once more. It was

the burgomaster returning with the sandwiches. The door was opened. There he was—the traitor they had come so far to execute. But Wenzel did not fire!

"Do it!" Leitgeb hissed fervently.

Wenzel did not seem to hear.

"You cowardly sow!" Leitgeb yelled. He snatched the pistol from the other man's hand and pressed the trigger.

Up in the kitchen the maid heard a sound that she later described as being "like an unoiled door creaking."

Outside, Wenzel whispered urgently, "There's someone coming!" He prepared to run across the field that bordered the lonely house on the outskirts of the ruined city.

Leitgeb grabbed him angrily. "Wait a minute, you pig," he snapped. "We've got to have proof." He bent down to where Oppenhoff now lay on the steps, the bullet hole clearly visible on his temple. Swiftly he tugged the armband the Americans had given the mayor from his sleeve and stuffed it in his pocket. Then he and the rest were running for their lives as the first American patrol started to edge its way cautiously up the road. Operation Carnival was over at last.[*1]

The news that the Allied-appointed burgomaster of an occupied German city had been murdered flashed around the world. *The London Times* reported it. *The New York Times* did, too, headlining the story as "Non-Nazi Mayor of Aachen Killed by 3 German Chutists," and commenting, "The assassins shot the Mayor in gangster fashion and escaped. Hitler often has threatened retaliation against Germans who co-operated."[2]

This first major murder and other reported attempts on the American-appointed mayors of Rheydt, Trier, and Heidelberg were followed by an attempt to take over the city of Lüdenscheid. The city had been captured by the Americans on April 13. Now, loosely guarded, it housed some three thousand wounded German soldiers in the *Baukloh-Lazarett*, some of whom had not yet given up the fight for "Folk, Führer, and Fatherland." Weapons had already been smuggled into the hospital, and those who could listened to a clandestine radio broadcasting German news. The mood was tense.

*See C. Whiting, *Hitler's Werewolves*, Stein and Day, for further details.

One evening, as the hospital chaplain, Ernst Boland recalled long afterward, ''I was sitting drinking a bottle of wine with the interpreter when the door was flung open. A huge American officer stood there. He cried, 'take me to the new nurse!' Together we went into the kitchen where a newly appointed nurse was eating her supper. She went pale and with good reason, too. She had been smuggled into the hospital from German-held Hagen. She had brought orders for a captain, whose left leg had been taken off. He was to start a revolt among the lightly wounded. But not only the wounded were concerned. As heavily armed U.S. soldiers encircled the hospital and took up their positions outside the wards (they even guarded the lavatories), it came out that many of the doctors and orderlies were part of the plot. A little later the main conspirators were driven away in buses and the American commandant of the hospital dug out all his knowledge of German to declare angrily, 'What a shit! We didn't need that!' ''[3]

Neither did Shaef. Just when it appeared that the war in Germany was about won, a new menace seemed to be appearing—the nightmare of a German resistance movement, allied to a last-ditch stand in the Alps. In that first week of April 1945, the Allied press suddenly was filled with tales, true and imagined, that maintained that the Western Allies were going to have to fight a protracted partisan war once the *Wehrmacht* had surrendered.

On April 1, the shock caused by the murder of Oppenhoff was heightened by the first broadcast of a new German radio station, which seemingly had borrowed its name from this new German partisan movement—Radio Werewolf.

Masterminded by the ''Poison Dwarf'' himself, it poured out a stream of vitriolic, last-ditch propaganda, hammering home a twin message: Destroy the enemy or destroy yourself! Civilian or soldier, whether you are still unoccupied or deep behind the enemy lines, *fight on*!''[4]

''There is no end to revolution,'' cried the Radio Werewolf speaker fervently. ''A revolution is only doomed to failure if those who make it cease to be revolutionaries. Together with the monuments of culture there crumble also the last obstacles to the fulfillment of our revolutionary task. Now that everything is in ruins we are forced to rebuild Europe. . . . In trying to destroy Europe's future the enemy has only succeeded in smashing the past; and with that everything old and outworn had gone.''⁵

It was the true nihilistic voice of the National Socialist creed, and although the great mass of the German people were war-weary and wanted nothing more than peace, its appeal was felt by Germany's idealistic youth. Schooled in the self-sacrificing philosophy of the Nazi Hitler Youth Organization since their early years, they prepared to fight on, fired by the spate of new slogans launched by Radio Werewolf: ''Rather dead than Red,'' ''People to Arms,'' ''We will win after all,'' and the most popular one of all—''The stronger the storm, the mightier the resistance.''

Later, German General Siegfried Westphal would dismiss these young boys and girls of the Werewolf as a ''rabble of boy scouts,'' but in April Eisenhower and his Intelligence men were taking them seriously, very seriously indeed. Already, in February, *Collier's* back in the States had details of a gigantic guerrilla warfare program being set up by the Nazis in the Alps near Bad Aussee. In this redoubt the cream of the SS and Hitler Youth were being trained already for postwar partisan operations. After the war had been lost these ''Werewolves'' (the journalists already knew the name) would launch attacks from their remote mountain redoubt on the Allied occupation forces. As press comment in the U.S.A. grew in volume, with such reliable correspondents as Drew Pearson and Victor Schiff maintaining that ''Hitler's henchmen in the east of Switzerland are expected to make a final stand,''⁶ Eisenhower's Chief-of-Intelligence Kenneth Strong and Bradley's Gen. Edwin Sibert had begun to investigate the new threat.

On March 11, the *SHAEF Intelligence Summary* reported the ''main trend of German defense policy does seem directed primarily to the safeguarding of the Alpine Zone. Air cover shows at least twenty sites of recent underground activity . . . where ground sources have reported underground accommodation for stores and personnel. The existence of several reported underground factories has also been confirmed. In addition, several new barracks and hutted camps have been seen on air photographs. . . . It thus appears that ground reports of extensive preparations for the accommodation of the German Maquis-to-be are not unfounded.''

Ten days later Sibert followed up with his *Reorientation of Strategy*, which declared that there would be guerrilla warfare conducted in the Alps under the direction of the Werewolves.

Four days after that, General Patch's Seventh Army Intelligence issued a secret report stating that Himmler had ordered provisions for 100,000 SS men, and that the Alpine fortress was going to be defended by eighty crack units. Trains carrying supplies were pouring into the redoubt. New factories to manufacture planes were also being built. When everything was ready, 200,000 veteran SS troops would be withdrawn into the area. Together with the Werewolves—"who were thoroughly imbued with the Nazi spirit"—they would fight to the last man.

By the end of March the top brass was taking the Werewolf and National Redoubt threat so seriously that Eisenhower's chief-of-staff, Walter Bedell Smith, could declare to Strong that, in his opinion, there is "every reason to believe that the Nazis intend to make their last stand among the crags.'"[7] Bradley now proposed that his army group should split Germany in two by driving through the center. This would "prevent German forces from withdrawing" toward the south and "into the Redoubt." As soon as that had been successfully completed, the Twelfth Army Group would swing south to reduce any remaining resistance in the Alpine Redoubt.

If we are to believe Eisenhower's *Crusade in Europe*, his own account of the campaign, he, too, took the "Werewolf Scare" seriously. In it, he writes: "If the German was permitted to establish the Redoubt he might possibly force us to engage in a long-drawn-out guerrilla type of warfare, or a costly siege. Thus he could keep alive his desperate hope that through disagreement among the Allies, he might yet be able to secure terms more favorable than those of unconditional surrender.

"Another Nazi purpose, somewhat akin to that of establishing a mountain fortress, was the organization of an underground army, to which he gave the significant name of 'Werewolves.' The purpose of the Werewolf organization, which was composed only of loyal followers of Hitler, was murder and terrorism. Boys and girls as well as adults were to be absorbed into the secret organization with the hope of so terrifying the countryside and making so difficult the problems of occupation that the conquering forces would presumably be glad to get out.

"The way to stop this project—and such a development was always a possibility because of the passionate devotion to their Führer of many young Germans—was to overrun the entire national territory before its organization could be effected."[8]

But it can also be assumed, now that he had abandoned the idea of driving to Berlin (as he had told Patton on the thirteenth), it had to justify the decision by giving his armies an objective that seemed more important than the capture of the German capital: the capture of the "National Redoubt," the supposed center of guerrilla warfare. There was more to it as well.

Patton had already predicted in March 1945 that Eisenhower would be President of the United States one day, stating cynically that the only reason he, Eisenhower, had visited his Army that month was because his men represented "a lot of votes." R. Ingersoll, a former newspaperman and confidant of Bradley, also made the same point at that time. "The big parades in New York and Washington [are] much closer than they had been six months before."[9] It seems clear, therefore, that Eisenhower was anxious to put himself in a good light. If later there was any criticism of his decision not to go for Berlin, he could always point out he had relinquished it in favor of a genuine military target—the destruction of Germany's last fighting troops and the civilians who might fight on with them in a Maquis-type of war!

When Patton returned to his headquarters after his twenty-four hours' leave in Paris, he was informed by his Intelligence men that there was a serious threat now posed by these new Werewolves. His G-2 warned him that there might be glider-borne raids on his headquarters aimed at assassinating him, and Codman, his aide, was detailed to keep a close watch over his boss during daylight hours. When Patton left his headquarters he did so accompanied by a heavy armored car. Patton laughed at his staff officers' fears. He took little stock of them, saying "like the cries of the Werewolf." All the same, he kept a loaded carbine underneath his bed now.

On the same day, however, that Patton's Third Army started its last offensive, heading south for the National Redoubt, something happened that, at first, seemed to confirm all the Intelligence men's fears: Patton had his closest call since 1943. On that fine spring afternoon, sunny and cloudless, Patton set off to fly to visit his III Corps headquarters at Reidfeld. He flew in front in one Piper Cub, with Codman flying behind in a second one.

Suddenly it happened. The general's plane was about two miles from Reidfeld Field, preparing to make its approach, when abruptly a fighter plane dived out of the sun.

Codman, in the second plane, started. The fighter was zooming in, its guns chattered, aiming directly at Patton's plane!

"The fighter makes a pass. He misses. Now he has the General's Cub lined. The General is pointing something at him. His pistol? No, his camera. What a man!"[10] Thus Codman gushed after the war. But on that spring afternoon in 1945 it was all very different and exceedingly serious. For the plane attacking the general's was a British-made Spitfire. There could be only one explanation. As they had done before, the enemy Werewolves were using a captured Allied plane, and this time it seemed they were about to assassinate General Patton.

Later Patton admitted to Colonel Allen of his staff that he had been frightened, but "after the first pass, I decided I might as well take some pictures of my impending demise. There wasn't anything I could do, so I thought I might as well use the camera. But after it was all over, I found I had been so nervous I had forgotten to take the cover off the lens and all I got were blanks."[11]

By now both Cubs were very low, skipping over wooden fences, dipping into hollows and skirting tree tops. With a terrific, whining scream, the fighter came roaring in once more, guns chattering. Codman could see the heat haze ripple along the wing and the dark, helmeted outline of the pilot as the Spitfire howled by them at less than fifty yards away. Again the pilot missed. But this time he had come in too low. In his eagerness he had followed the leading Cub down to an altitude from which there was no recovery. At four hundred miles an hour the Spitfire hit the knoll of a hill. Like a flat stone skidding across the surface of a still pond, the doomed "murder plane" careened across a field, churning up a wild wake of mud and stones. Then it slowed round and exploded with a great roar. A gray-white mushroom of smoke shot upward. Next instant the Spitfire disintegrated. A few minutes later the two Cubs landed safely. It was Patton's closest call of the war.

As soon as Codman had checked that Patton was all right, a search party was sent out to look for the wreckage of the plane that had attacked them. It was soon confirmed that the plane was indeed a Spitfire with British markings. The news was flashed to III Corps headquarters and for half-an-hour rumor ran riot. There had been the first Werewolf attempt to murder a senior Allied commander. Was this going to be the Battle of the Bulge all over again when it was thought a killer squad was out to gun down the Supreme Commander and there were German commandos in American uniform loose everywhere behind American lines?

But within the hour, the mystery was all cleared up. It had been merely a tragic accident, a young man throwing away his life purposelessly when the war was about over. The Spitfire had been manned by a Polish volunteer with the RAF who had mistakenly flown out of his own sector. He had taken the two Piper Cubs for German Fiesler Storch spotting planes, which they resembled slightly, and had attacked in the belief he was attacking the enemy.

The initial hysteria caused by the incident confirmed Patton's belief that the Werewolves and their Alpine Redoubt were figments of some nervous staff officer's imagination. General James Van Fleet's III Corps was making swift progress through Bavaria, and its commander was confident that he would be on the Danube within a matter of days. Now the Third Army, with its third of a million soldiers, was taking fewer than a hundred casualties a day as it drove on to the Redoubt, and most of these (in the general's opinion) were caused by his young soldiers driving jeeps as if they were tanks and getting themselves killed in the process. As he noted in his diary: "Considering that at this time the Third Army had fourteen divisions in action and an equivalent number of corp and army troops, one gets an idea of how cheap the fighting was.''[12]

Patton was correct in his assessment of the opposition in his last campaign. The National Redoubt existed only in the minds of the scaremongers and those apologists for the change in Eisenhower's strategy. It was the same with the Werewolves. Soon most of them would go home tamely and resume their normal peacetime existences. ''As if,'' as General Westphal, the last German chief-of-staff in the west would say after his capture in May, ''what the *Wehrmacht* had failed to do could be accomplished by a rabble of Boy Scouts.''[13]

It was a fitting enough epitaph for Hitler's Werewolves.

Sixteen

"What's it going to be Sir?" the emaciated POWs continually asked their harassed Scottish padre, as the speed of the Third Army's advance became known to them through the communiqués. "Which is it going to be first? Is it going to be *Parcels, Patton or Peace*?"[1]

Some of them had been prisoners since Dunkirk, moving from camp to camp all over Central Europe, and had now landed here at the huge, sprawling POW camp at Moosburg after marching for forty-three solid days so that they didn't fall into the hands of the Russians. Others were more recent prisoners, the wounded survivors of the Arnhem Bridge debacle, happy to view what was left of the "invincible German army" moving by the camp. "Old men and boys. Tiger tanks and horse-drawn farm carts, captured jeeps and bicycles, with a motley collection of vehicles of all kinds. One could not help wondering why they went on fighting, for if ever there was now a hopeless cause, it was this. I suppose that like their leader they hoped for some miracle. I felt pity." Thus Col. John Frost, the wounded C.O. of that doomed 2nd Parachute Battalion that had fought until it had been cut to ribbons on that bridge at Arnhem.[2]

But now it was going to be definitely not "peace" or "parcels," but Patton. As Frost wrote afterward, "almost as if by magic, the American spearheads were down below. Highly professional, tanks and half-tracks, always covered by fire, all under control."[3] Braving the fire of the German snipers, Colonel Frost hobbled out to view the American advance. "Knowing that I was safe, I put a bold face on it, but some of the American soldiers were doing the crouchy-wouchy act and taking their time. A sergeant, noting this, gave one of the crouchers a kick in the backside, saying "Stand up! Don't you see that there is a British officer watching?""[4]

Inside the camp, the Scottish padre, Capt. H. Read, had just finished his service for the American POWs and was singing the thanksgiving hymn with them—"The Day of Redemption"—when there came a terrific cry, followed by cheering outside. They went out to find "the camp was seething with a mass of people, cheering, laughing, and up in the middle of the camp came an American jeep and the first free Allied soldier that I'd seen for practically five years."[5]

The day afterward, May 1, 1945, Patton and Codman decided to visit Moosburg Camp where Al Stiller had been liberated—"with about ten Boches to his credit and the loss of an equivalent number of pounds around his waistline."[6]

Patton was given an ovation by the thousands of Allied prisoners the camp contained, as they stood there on their spindly legs, dressed in rags of uniform, cheeks sunken with hunger. But one group of prisoners "with their stained, tattered uniforms and scraggly beards" looking "a motley and dejected crew"[7] made a lasting impression on Patton as they formed up outside the barbed wire.

Suddenly the senior Russian office blew his whistle and barked a sharp command. The ex-POWs clicked to attention and marched forward at "a fast rhythmic clip. Bearing, precision, staying power, discipline," as a fascinated Codman, who himself had been a German POW in the old war, noted. "Somehow the beards were no longer unkempt. They bristled with stored energy and the faded tunics took on the lines of dress uniforms."[8]

Patton was equally fascinated as he watched this "endless column of ex-prisoners now magically reconverted into seasoned troops, veterans of a hundred battles, combat soldiers on their way—HOME!"[9] "That's it," he murmured, almost as if to himself, "Russian infantry. Hard to beat."

His eyes flashed suddenly. "But it *can* be done and that is undoubtedly what we shall have to do."[10]

This first meeting with the Red Army, significantly enough on May Day, seemed to spark off yet another of Patton's hates, and yet another race—the Russians—was added to that long "personal shit list" that already included "kikes," "A-rabs," "Wops," "Frogs," "Limeys," and so forth. Again this new hate was a mixture of passionate, subjective emotionalism and professional detachment.

Before the war he had probably shared his class's dislike of communism and fear of the "red menace." But it was only in December 1943 that he first really encountered hard-line, almost fanatical anti-communism when he met the commander of the Polish II Corps, General Anders in Cairo. Anders, who had been a Russian officer in the Tsarist Army in his youth and then their prisoner in World War II, being released in his underpants and shirt (as his only possessions) in order to form his fellow Polish prisoners into fighting force, hated the Russians with a passion.

He told Patton that thousands of his fellow Polish officers had been murdered by their Russian captors in the woods at Katyn and that, "If I ever marched my corps of two divisions in between the Russians and the Germans, I'd attack in *both* directions!"[11]

Later, President Roosevelt's special envoy to Russia, W. Averell Harriman, warned Patton in 1944 that Stalin was a strong, ruthless revolutionist and therefore a "very potential threat to future world conditions." The envoy described the discipline in the Red Army as "the most rigid and ruthless he had ever seen" and its officer caste as "the new nobility."[12]

The dislike was added to by members of his staff who had experience of Russian rule in the east and his few encounters with visiting Red Army officers and observers. He regarded them, in general, as sullen, suspicious, and crude. As he once commented, "I have never seen in any army at any time, including the German Imperial Army of 1912, as severe discipline as exists in the Russian Army. The officers, with few exceptions, give the appearance of recently civilized Mongolian bandits!"[13]

It didn't take Patton long to conclude that sooner or later he would have to fight against the Russians. "At dinner I stated that in my opinion Germany was so completely blacked out that so far as military resistance was concerned they were not a menace and that what we had to look out for was Russia. This caused a considerable furor."[14]

Now it seemed on this same first of May Patton was going to have the opportunity of meeting the Red Army in force at last, and the result of that meeting was anybody's guess. For

Patton had already declared, "if it should be necessary for us to fight the Russians, the sooner we do it, the better."[15]

Now that Berlin had fallen, Prague was the only Central European capital left of any significance. Bearing in mind Bismarck's dictum that whoever held Prague, held Central Europe, Churchill in London cabled Truman on the last day of April that the liberation of Prague by Patton's Third Army "might make the whole difference to the postwar situation in Czechoslovakia" and would influence the politics of the nearby Balkan countries. He warned the new President that Czechoslovakia might "go the way of Yugoslavia" if the West hung back.[16]

Truman turned to Marshall for enlightenment, who in his turn queried Eisenhower. He replied that the Red Army was in a position to capture Prague before Patton and that "I shall not attempt any move I deem militarily unwise, merely to gain a political prize unless I receive specific orders from the combined chiefs of staff."[17]

But on May 1 Patton unexpectedly rolled across the border where Low Bavaria fringes on the Czech frontier. "Thank God, thank God!" exclaimed Dr. Ernst Benes, head of the Czech government-in-exile, when he received the news in London. "Hanicko . . . Hanicko," he said to his wife in a choked voice. "The Americans have just entered Czechoslovakia! Patton is across the border!"[18]

Benes realized that Stalin intended to turn his country into a Russian satellite, once it had been freed of the German occupiers, and he already knew that the government with which he would return to Prague was dominated by communists. If, however, the Americans beat the Russians to Prague, he reasoned, then things might be different. It was the same reasoning that had made Churchill send his cable to Truman.

But Eisenhower remained obstinate. He would not fight for political objectives. It was almost as if he were proud of the fact, forgetting that, in the end, all wars are fought for political aims.

Thus it was that an impatient Patton champed at the bit, halted by Eisenhower's orders at the Czech frontier, waiting for four long days until finally on May 4, at seven-thirty in the evening, Bradley rang him up at his command post. "Ike has just called," he cried, "you have the green light for Czechoslovakia, George. When can you move?"

"Tomorrow morning!" Patton yelled excitedly.[19]

He had already made sure that his 90th and 5th Infantry Divisions, plus Colonel Reed's 2nd Cavalry Group, had secured the mountain passes into the country, writing "in case we had to attack Prague, we would at least be through the passes before anything hit us."[20] Whether he meant he might be attacked by the Germans or Russians, Patton did not specify. Now he prepared to move forward with the largest army he had ever commanded—over 540,000 men, three times the size of the whole of the prewar U.S. Regular Army!

Still, Bradley was skeptical when Patton informed him he could change overnight from attacking the nonexistent National Redoubt into entering Czechoslovakia. Patton's eagerness at this stage of the war puzzled him, too. "Why does everyone in the Third Army want to liberate the Czechs?" he asked the Third Army Commander.

Patton kept his thoughts about a possible confrontation with the Red Army to himself. He told his intimates, "If we have to fight them, now is the time. From now on, we will get weaker and they will get stronger."[21] Instead he joked, "Oh Brad, can't you see? The Czechs are our *allies* and consequently their women aren't off limits. *On to Czechoslovakia and fraternization!*" he yelled over the phone. "How in hell can you stop an army with a battle cry like that?"[22]

On May 5, 1945, five days after Hitler's death, Patton attacked into Czechoslovakia, with the 90th and 5th Divisions. His V Corps, newly allotted to the Third Army, also joined the attack in the shape of the U.S. Army's premier division "the Big Red One," the 1st Infantry. The "Big Red One" prided itself in having fired the first shots of any American unit in France in World War I and having been the first to do so once more in September 1944 when its artillery loosed off the first shells into the Reich near Aachen. Now, however, there were less than one hundred of the veterans left who had originally gone into action with the division back in November 1942 in North Africa.

Now the division's objective was Karlsbad, while its neighbor, the 97th Infantry Division, drove for Pilsen. Meanwhile

the 90th and 5th divisions were opening up the routes needed
for the debouchment of Patton's armor, in particular, his favorite 4th Armored which was being readied for an attack
toward Prague itself.

Naturally Eisenhower knew nothing of this. He had instructed Bradley to direct Patton to restrict his advance to a
northwest-southwest line running through Pilsen. But Bradley
had also added that Patton "could and should reconnoitre
vigorously as far as Prague."[23] It was the old "rock soup"
method all over again.

Unknown to Patton, who eagerly seized the bit in his teeth,
a handful of Americans were already in the Czech capital.
They were the OSS team commanded by a Capt. Eugene
Fodor, who had once been an artilleryman in the Czech Army
himself. In the famed Wenzel Square in the heart of Prague,
General Frantisek Kratochwhil, commander of the local par-
tisans, formally "surrendered" the capital to the secret service captain. Thereupon Fodor turned about and raced back
to a spot near Pilsen. Here he came across General Clarence
Huebner, commanding V Corps, and told him what had happened. Speedily the news was forwarded up the chain of
command to Patton himself.

He was elated by the news. But Eisenhower had stipulated
he should not advance from Pilsen to Prague. What was he to
do? He had not captured an enemy capital since Sicily back in
1943. The prospect of taking a capital city right at the end of
his fighting career in Europe must have seemed very appeal-
ing to him that May 5. Patton sat and thought.

Meanwhile, Churchill made a direct appeal to Eisenhower
himself. He cabled the Supreme Commander, "I am hoping
that your plan does not inhibit you to advance to Prague if
you have the troops and do not meet the Russians earlier. I
thought you did not mean to tie yourself down if you had the
troops and the country was empty. Don't bother to reply by
wire, but tell me when we next have a talk."[24]

Eisenhower had the troops *and* the country was empty; at
least, it was empty of German fighting troops. Now that the
Russians were on their tail, they were only too eager to throw
away their weapons and surrender to the advancing Americans while there was still time. Even the SS could not reach

the U.S. lines quickly enough. But Eisenhower had no intention of moving a single mile east of Pilsen. As far as he, Marshall, and President Truman were concerned, the fate of Prague was not their business. Leave the capital to the Russians and the Czechs.

Patton, unaware that Eisenhower had made up his mind for good, appealed to Bradley. He asked, "Is this stop line through Pilsen really mandatory? Can't you let me go into Prague? For God's sake, Brad, those patriots in the city need our help! *We have no time to lose!*"[25]

Bradley replied that he would refer the matter to Eisenhower once more. Suddenly Patton had a bright idea. He would "get lost" on the next day, as he had done at the time of the Trier crisis. While he was out of touch, his troops would take Prague. The next time Bradley would hear from him would be from a phone booth on Wenzel Square.

Bradley was amused, but he said he had to check with Eisenhower. It was no use. The Russians had already protested Patton's move into Czechoslovakia. Now the Red Army chief-of-staff maintained that there would be "possible confusion of forces, if any further advance" was made and urged Eisenhower "not to move the Allied forces in Czechoslovakia east of the originally intended line."[26]

As a result Eisenhower was at his firmest. He ordered Bradley to find Patton wherever he was and tell him to stop on the prescribed line. Under no circumstances was he to make an attempt to drive to Prague.

On the morning of the sixth, Bradley called Patton and told him, "The halt line through Pilsen is mandatory for V an XII Corps, George. Moreover you must not—I repeat *not*—reconnoitre to a greater depth than five miles northeast of Pilsen. Ike does not want any international complications at this late date."

"For God's sake, Brad," Patton protested, "it seems to me that a great nation like America should let others worry about complications."[27]

But Bradley was adamant. This time Patton's tried and trusted "rock soup method" would not work. To all intents and purposes, General George S. Patton Junior's shooting war was over.

· · ·

On that same day, the long columns of the veterans 12th SS Division, "Hitler Youth"—which had held up Montgomery so long at Caen—began to trudge toward the lines of Patton's 65th Infantry Division in Austria. The divisional general of the "Hitler Youth," Hugo Kraas, and his American counterpart had come to an agreement. The SS men, nearly 10,000 of them, could cross the Enns River beyond the little Austrian township of Amstetten and surrender to the *Amis*.

About midday, as the chief-of-staff of the "Hitler Youth," Colonel Hubert H. Meyer recalled later,[28] "a small column of American ambulances started to whizz in and out of our groups at high speed heading for Amstetten. Then a little while later they came roaring back, dodging in and out of our columns and tanks. . . . We wondered what in three devils' name was going on."

Only later did the SS colonel discover what had happened. A small reconnaissance detachment of the 65th had crossed the Enns River and reached Amstetten, where they had been wildly greeted by the local Austrians who had now conveniently forgotten that they were German and had supported Austrian-born Hitler to the hilt. Now they greeted the handful of GIs as "liberators."

But not for long. Although there were no German troops whatsoever in Amstetten, suddenly seven Russian dive-bombers dropped out of the afternoon sky, machine guns blazing. GIs and civilians went down on all sides, as the Soviet planes commenced beating up the town in approved fashion, "dealing the Fascist troops there an extremely severe blow," as General Biryukov, Commander of the Russian XX Guards Rifle Corps, wrote later.[29]

Whether it was a genuine mistake or not or whether the Red Army now visualized their erstwhile allies as "fascist troops," no one knew that May. Hurriedly the shootings were hushed up,* but the fact remained that with the Second World War having only hours to run, the Russians had already fired upon and killed American soldiers.

---

*Neither the "after-action" reports of the XX U.S. Corps to which the 65th belonged nor that of the 65th mention the incident. But Biryukov and Meyer do.

Seventeen

Passau was the last German city captured by the Third Army before the war ended. For thirty-six hours, Patton's artillery bombarded the place, turning it into another of those "Third Army memorials," a constant reminder to the sorely tried inhabitants that Patton's men had passed this way. Then, as abruptly as it had started, the firing ceased, leaving behind "a silence," as one citizen recalled, "the like of which you've never heard before. Then they were there—*the Amis!*"[1]

These *Amis* were the men of the 26th Infantry Division, entering the still-smoldering, ruined city cautiously, sticking to the shadows of the walls, fearful that the SS who had defended the place might have left snipers behind. They hadn't, but the trigger-happy infantrymen didn't know that. A teacher at the local grammar school turned out to be the only casualty during the capture of Passau. Being hard of hearing, he didn't respond to the Americans' challenge and was shot on the spot.

But for Frau Emma Bauer "the first American I ever had seen in my whole life was the most beautiful and nicest person in the whole world. This man—this angel—came into our cellar, where we crouched in fear and trembling, and said in German '*Grüss Gott. Ihr seid frei.**' "[2]

But all the men of the 26th Infantry Division, which had had a tough campaign with high losses among the ranks of the riflemen, did not possess such "angelic" qualities. Among the prisoners they took were an SS man who possessed some propaganda caricatures of Churchill and Roosevelt, and a civilian fireman who was mistaken for an SS man on account of his black fireman's uniform. The SS man was forced to eat the caricatures, and then he and the fireman

*A Southern German greeting: "Greet God [literally]. You are free."

were told to make a run for it. Both of them were shot as they did so.

A teacher remembers how first the Americans "broke down our glass door. Then they tore off my shirt and that of my brother-in-law to check if we had the tattoed blood-group marking of the SS under our arms. While doing this our wrist-watches "changed ownership." Finally a lieutenant appeared who shouted, "Line them up—and shoot them!"[3] The terri-fied schoolmaster survived to tell the tale.

Everywhere they began to turf out the owners and inhab-itants of those houses that had survived the bombing and bombardment, forcing them to leave with what they could carry in a matter of hours, even minutes. Anything that sym-bolized the old Nazi regime was thrown into the streets, with soldiers taking pot shots at busts of Hitler and wiping their bottoms with Nazi leaflets and thousand-mark notes bearing the Nazi insignia.

Naturally they were after the local women even before the city had been really cleared of the last remaining German soldiers. Apprentice baker Jacob Kurz, who shortly before had fought the Americans in the ranks of the *Volkssturm* as a sixteen-year-old Hitler Youth, now decided it was up to him to save "Germany's honor" as everywhere the local girls chased after the conquerors, impatient to be raped. He col-lected his catapult and went into the nearby wood, where he came across a girl copulating with a GI. "She was on top—you could see her naked bottom. I took out my catapult, loaded it with six lead pellets and aimed. . . . At a distance of twenty meters, I just couldn't miss!"[4]

The first military governor arrived, together with his blond interpreter "Miss Amanda," who "aped her superior, shout-ing and raging just like a sergeant major. With her feet on the table, she lashed out with order after order, speaking in perfect Hamburg German,"[5] frightening the life out of these newly conquered Germans. On May 8, however, her boss, the first of many military governors, a Major Brewster, de-cided it was time to inform the locals that a new age had dawned.

Brewster had the local bigwigs collected together and brought to the Passau District Court, which had not been damaged, one of the few official buildings which hadn't.

Brewster, who had been a college teacher in civilian life, told the locals Germany had been the cause of two world wars. "Don't think," he lectured them, "that the peoples which were overrun by the German war machine will quickly forget. After the First World War, a republic was formed which reintroduced Prussian militarism. You've got to understand that this time nothing like that will happen. Let us work together in order to serve our people and not to prepare for another war. Think about it a little . . . please."[6]

Indeed, on that day when the war ended, a new age had started for the people of Passau and all the rest of the inhabitants of Bavaria. In his modest little speech to the local worthies, that obscure first U.S. military governor of Passau had expressed what would be the style of Bavaria's future—if the Americans had their way. No new German militarism and the two nations—conquered and conqueror—working together for the common good.

For now it was over at last. There would be no more moving up into the line, the guns rumbling uneasily in the distance, the sky ahead a sinister, flickering pink, the soldiers laden with their gear—rifles, grenades, extra ammo, blankets, packs—like pack animals, each man wrapped up in a cocoon of his own brooding apprehension. And all awaiting that first high-pitched hysterical burr of the Spandaus, which signaled that the killing had commenced again. Some indulged in private rituals when they heard the news that May 8. A private of Patton's 76th Division told his buddy to stay in the foxhole they were sharing. "I have some unfinished business to attend to," he said and moved off into some bushes. There, as his buddy reported later, "he raised his MI and fired it into the air, shooting off a whole clip at nothing, at nothing at all."[7]

Others felt a sensation of elation and—at the same time—letdown. Sergeant Giles, serving under Patton in Austria, wrote to his wife: "The war is over! All we can think about is thank God, thank God . . . I'm sure everybody thought exactly what I did. I made it, I made it all the way! Nobody is going to shoot at me any more. I can't be killed. *I have made it!* Yet there is a queer kind of letdown. We have waited for this day so long. We don't yet believe it. My reaction has been a feeling of terrible weariness and then weakness and sleepiness. But I *am* happy! So *damned* happy! It's over!''[8]

Future military historian Capt. Charles MacDonald, serving with Patton's 2nd Infantry Division in Czechoslovakia, felt all these things—and sadness, too. He watched his men's reactions as they marched through a Czech town to the cheers of the locals. ''Brilliant smiles wreathed their faces and they waved cheerfully at the shouting crowds, as if they had just won an election campaign and this was a personal triumph. Hardened, stubble-faced veterans had unashamed tears in their eyes. The unleashed joy of these oppressed people knew no bounds and it was too much for them. ''Suddenly I began to realize what no one thus far had been able to put into words— what we were fighting for. And I found a lump in my throat which I could not swallow.''[9]

And some were simply numb, overwhelmed by a sense of loss. Medic Atwell was munching a sandwich when he heard the news from a comrade. Thereupon the two of them lapsed into silence. ''I searched for some feeling, waited for it to develop. There was hardly any sensation at all. A moment later I was aware of an inward caving in, followed by a sore-throat feeling when I thought of all those who had been forced to give up their lives for this moment.''[10]

Their boss, Patton, was similarly affected by the abrupt ending to World War II.

On that same morning that Major Brewster announced to the local worthies at Passau that a new age had arrived in Bavaria, indeed in conquered Germany as a whole, not far away at a battered *Wehrmacht* barracks at Regensburg, Patton's morning briefing commenced in the ''War Room.'' It was a far cry from Third Army's magnificent headquarters in Luxembourg. The rain-soaked, cracked ceiling sagged in places, and the bullet-scarred and shell-pocked walls looked as if they had caught the symptoms of some loathsome skin disease.

But the briefing didn't get very far. Just as one-eyed General Gay was about to rise to make the morning announcements, Patton restrained him by placing a hand on the chief-of-staff's knee and rose to his feet himself. As trim and as immaculate as ever, he stood there for several minutes wordlessly, simply staring at his staff. Suddenly he broke the heavy silence. "This," he announced in his squeaky voice, "will be our last operational briefing in Europe. I hope and pray that it will be our privilege to resume these briefings in another Theater that still is unfinished business in this war. I know you are as eager to go there as I am. But you know the situation. However, one thing I can promise you. If *I* go, *you* will go!"[11]

He went on to praise his staff in the same way that they had always praised him over the last year, laying it on very thickly indeed, telling them they had an "unsurpassed record" and had done "a magnificent and historic job from start to finish."[12]

He ended the emotional speech with "Well, as the Church says, 'Here endeth the Second Lesson.' "[13]

With that he stood silent for a few minutes before snapping his fingers at his ugly black-and-white pooch, Willie. Obediently the dog, which had once belonged to a dead RAF fighter pilot, trotted behind him toward the door, as Gay announced that from the morrow the Third Army would discard its steel helmets and would wear only the lighter fiber liner.

Patton heard the remark and in typical Patton fashion snapped, "And make damn sure those liners are painted and smart-looking. I don't want any sloppy headgear around here!"[14]

His staff grinned. It was the sort of thing they expected from "Georgie," even on an historic occasion such as this.

But Patton was in no mood for smiling. As he passed through the door of the War Room, whose function had abruptly ceased to matter, he turned to Codman and said miserably, "the best end for an old campaigner is a bullet at the last minute of the last battle."[15] But that wish was not to be granted to George S. Patton. His fighting days were over at last.

Perhaps the war stopped too abruptly for Patton. Suddenly he found himself with time on his hands, with his staff quite capable of running the day-to-day affairs of the Third Army and the local civilian populace—enormous as the problems of the latter were. So the junketing commenced. He went to Luxembourg, Paris, London. There, as he told his crony

General Hughes, he had succeeded "four times in three days."[16]

One evening he invited eight people to dine with him at the Ritz. One of his guests was Jean Gordon, who left in tears, with Hughes taking her home to his apartment to "have a good cry." Hughes knew why. Patton was leaving the next day for his triumphant return to the United States after an absence of nearly three years, though as the conquering hero confessed to Hughes—he was scared stiff of doing so.

His motorcade to Boston was a triumph, with the civilians lining the streets from the military airport to Bedford to cheer him. The *Boston Daily Record* for June 8 headlined his return with "FRENZIED HUB HAILS PATTON." Patton even dared to halt a whole parade in front of his wife, Bea, when he spotted a pretty girl and, raising his hand to halt the brass, said out loud, "God damn, I always did have a quick eye to recognize a pretty girl!"[17]

But inevitably there were some voices raised in disapproval. After addressing a mixed crowd at his boyhood home at Los Angeles, Dwight MacDonald wrote of his speech, "These utterances of Patton are atrocities of the mind; atrocious in being communicated not to a psychoanalyst but to a great number of soldiers, civilians and school children; and atrocious as reflections of what war-making has done to the personality of Patton himself."[18]

At the Church of Our Saviour in San Gabriel, California, which his grandfather had founded, he led the Sunday school in the singing of hymns, then treated the children to one of his more rousing bloodthirsty speeches. Again he was criticized. As he was later by clergymen, middle-class liberals, and even by the *Stars and Stripes*. Patton, it seemed, had lost touch with the reality of the home front. His clash with Bill Mauldin was revived in the papers, and his apparent addiction to war was aired in the media. Patton's image as the conquering hero started to slip a little in an America that desired nothing more than a speedy end to the war with Japan and a return to peacetime normalcy: that comfortable, cozy existence that was anathema to the Commander of the Third Army.

Even his kind of tough humor was not appreciated by the civilians, whom he detested. Speaking to a civilian audience at San Marino, California, he was handed a huge bouquet of flowers by a tiny Cub Scout. For a while he handled the embarrassment to his masculine image like a time bomb, shifting it from one hand to the other. Finally he couldn't stand the flowers any longer. He interrupted his remarks to blurt out, "I know I've made a lot of widows during my life, but this is the first time I've had to stand around looking like a damned bride!"[19] It was recorded that no one laughed. The reference to his "widow-making" hurt.

However, just before he left for Europe once more, he did give some thought to the question of what might happen if—unexpectedly—he made his own wife, Bea, a widow. He told his son, George, and his daughters, Beatrice and Ruth Ellen, "I am soon going back to Germany, to the peaceful occupation, but I'm saying my final goodbye. Because I'll never see you again."

As daughter Ruth Ellen described it, "We were all in the living room of my house on Garfield Street in Washington, Bea and George and myself. Mother was upstairs packing his things. It was the night before Daddy was to go back to Germany. His exact words were: 'I am never going to see you again. I know this. I am going to be buried in foreign soil.' They protested and one said, 'Daddy, don't be silly. The war's all over now.' "

Patton answered, "Yes, I know. But my luck has all run out now. The gold Allenby used to talk about is gone. I've spent it all. I have not been a good enough man in my life to be killed by a bullet like General Bee at Manassas. I don't know how it is going to happen, but I'm going to die over there."

Silence fell over the hot room at this bald declaration, until Patton broke it with, "Promise me one thing, let me be buried over there. In God's name don't bring my body home."[20] Solemnly his children promised, knowing that their father subscribed to Napoleon's dictum that the "boundaries of a nation's empire are marked by the graves of her soldiers."[21] Hadn't he often barked, "Why goddamnit, to bury a soldier anywhere else is simply to cater to a bunch of sniveling sob sisters retained by those carrion-eating ghouls, the coffin makers and undertakers."[22]

His children knew their father was fond of self-dramatization, saying things simply to shock his listeners. They knew, too, that he seemed to have the gift of second sight, seeing things that other people couldn't—a gift that gave Ruth Ellen "the shivers." Now on his last night in the United States, which he had served for over forty years, his daughter felt that his prophesy was one of these occasions. Her father really did believe he was returning to Germany to die there.

Back in Paris, after having failed to gain a command in the Pacific, he reported to his friend Hughes in a more prosaic fashion. Over sandwiches and Scotch in the latter's room, he complained, "Beatrice gave me hell. . . . I'm glad to be in Europe." And just before they parted at Orly, he snorted in his usual style, "Stick around. Maybe you and I will run this theater."[23]

It was a vain hope.

Eighteen

On that May 8, 1945, when it all ended, Patton's Third Army had fought for 281 days and had liberated or captured 81,823 square miles of territory. During this time it had maintained an enormous front, generally 75 to 100 miles wide, but at its longest, in the third week of April 1945, it was 200 miles wide.

At the time the war ended, the numbers of the Third had risen from a strength of 92,187 men to 437,860. It had suffered *battle* casualties of 160,682 men, of which 27,104 had been killed in action. And in its turn the Third had caused an estimated 1,444,388 casualties among the enemy, of whom 47,500 had been killed and 1,280,688 taken prisoner.

Naturally, both sides "cooked the books" and statistical analysis is not the best way to present military history. Those cold statistics reveal nothing of the misery and suffering of those young men who paid the "butcher's bill" so long ago. Yet in Patton's case, the numbers are worthy of consideration for two reasons. They show that Patton's Third caused about ten casualties for every one it suffered. They also show that for most of his campaign in 1944, his losses were remarkably light (half the number suffered by Hodges's First Army, for example, during the same period). Patton's losses only started to rise dramatically during the Battle of the Bulge when his Third lost 27,000 men, over a quarter of the total casualties for the whole battle.

Once over the Our-Sauer line, Patton's losses started to fall sharply, and by the time he had reached the Rhine he was losing, on average, a hundred to two hundred men a day. He commented to his nephew Fred Ayer at the time that "the two most deadly weapons in the German arsenal are our own armored half-track and jeep: the half-track because the boys riding one go all heroic since they think they are in a tank: and the jeep because we have so many god-awful drivers.''[1]

Some analysts surveying these statistics and comparing them with the losses suffered by other Allied armies fighting further north (for instance, the British Army's breakthrough at the Siegfried Line cost it 16,000 dead alone and twice that number wounded), might conclude that for most of his final campaign Patton faced only light opposition; and that the really hard fighting was done by the British, Canadian, and the First and Ninth U.S. Armies further north.

Whatever the truth of the matter may be, Patton was completely satisfied with his conduct of the operations during that final campaign. He wrote: ''I can say throughout the campaign in Europe I know of no error that I made except that of failing to send a Combat Command to take Hammelburg. Otherwise my operations were to me strictly satisfactory. In every case practically throughout the campaign I was under wraps from the Higher Command. This may have been a good thing, as perhaps I am too impetuous. However, I don't believe I was and feel that had I been permitted to go all out, the war would have ended sooner and more lives would have been saved.''[2]

On that typically immodest note Patton said his final words on a campaign in which he played an important role—though not as important as some of his admirers thought—and which will always bring to mind his name and achievements when the Second World War is discussed.

But perhaps at this juncture it is fitting to ask just how good a general George S. Patton was. Eisenhower, who had known him since they had been young officers together, said of him, ''For certain types of action [he] was the most outstanding soldier our country produced.''[3]

Chester Wilmot, the Australian correspondent who went right through the campaign in Northwest Europe and produced perhaps the best overall account of the 1944–1945 battle for Europe, albeit marred by his partisan attitude to Montgomery, called Patton ''a master of exploitation.''[4] These two evaluations point to the area in which Patton did contribute to the campaign.

Naturally, he was no strategist. The ''big picture'' eluded him totally. He simply *would* not and *could* not realize that war is a continuation of politics. The political consequences of any action he took never entered his head. His famed "rock soup" method and those "armored reconnaissance" missions and their consequent impact on the overall political strategy of the war meant nothing to Patton. The fact that he constantly unbalanced Eisenhower's plans from January right to the end of March 1945 did not concern him, and in spite of his almost pathological dislike of the Russians and their political motives, he, indirectly, contributed more than any other American general to their successes in Central Europe in the spring of 1945. It is a weighty accusation to be made, but it *must* be made.

If any one person swayed Eisenhower in his decision not to drive to Berlin, it was Patton, through his willing pawn: Bradley. That "glittering prize" of Berlin, as Eisenhower once called it, was lost to the Western Allies because the general who would have taken it (with the support of at least two American armies) would have been the hated "little fart"—Field Marshal Montgomery; and that was something that Patton—and Bradley, too, naturally—could never have tolerated.

His opponents saw Patton as possessing, primarily, a talent for bold cavalry-type operations. After the war, Gen. Siegfried Westphal, Field Marshal Gerd von Rundstedt's chief-of-staff, wrote: "Above all else, Patton was remarkable for his determined and bold actions. This was quite in contrast to Field Marshal Montgomery who was known to me from North Africa. Montgomery was always extremely cautious, unwilling to take any risks."[5]

Ex-German Army Commander General Guenther Blumentritt regarded Patton in the same manner. "We regarded General Patton extremely highly as the most aggressive panzer general of the Allies, a man of incredible initiative and lightning-like action."[6] Field Marshal von Rundstedt, that wizened, ancient, cognac-drinking genius of the German Army, thought, too, that Patton and Montgomery were "the two best I met, though Montgomery was very systematic."[7]

Indeed of the other American army commanders, Bradley, Devers, Patch, Simpson and Hodges, Patton is the only one to be mentioned *by name* in the postwar accounts and memoirs of the leading German generals. This, I feel, is a sure sign that Patton was highly regarded by his erstwhile opponents, who saw in the American an exponent of the *blitzkrieg* tactics that they had developed themselves.

As a tactician, Patton undoubtedly had a genius for high-speed, mobile warfare, which could not be matched in the Allied command by any other general, American, British, Canadian, or French. He was one of the few Allied generals capable of handling large numbers of tanks, rapidly and effectively, a talent admired by the German commanders.

Yet after having said that, how would Patton have fared as an army group commander, a role that might well have been his, if he had not involved himself in the face-slapping scandal in Sicily in 1943? It is a question that one might well legitimately ask in view of the comparison that is often made between Montgomery and Patton. Indeed, Patton always thought he could have done a better job as army group commander than his onetime subordinate Bradley.

But could he have taken over Montgomery's job or Bradley's, controlling the destinies of not one army but several, managing a million or more men strung out over several varying fronts? I think not. His role was that of a subordinate. As he once told Eisenhower when they were young officers together, "Ike, you will be the Lee of the next war and I will be your Jackson."[8] In spite of his constant complaints about Montgomery and what he regarded as the 'Field Marshal's' instrument—SHAEF—Patton would probably never have felt himself happy at any other level than that of the commander of an army in the field. Up in the rarified atmosphere of SHAEF, the soldiering would have been too impersonal for him, the fronts too broad and far flung, burdened by too much politics. Patton had to be close always to the sound and the fury, the smell of gunpowder.

Patton was excellent in high-speed, mobile warfare. So long as he could keep his enemy off balance and moving, he seldom made a mistake. Too, he was quick to spot a weakness on the part of the enemy and exploit it, for instance, the dash of the 4th Armored through the Eifel to the Rhine, or 5th Infantry's crossing of the great river at Oppenheim.

Fortunately for Patton, during his last campaign he did not experience the kind of opposition he had faced in the previous

year on the Saar and at Metz, where his army became bogged
down for virtually three months. For he had no talent for the
set-piece battle, where the enemy is firmly entrenched and
knows from which direction the attack is coming. Then the
only surprise that can be achieved is of time and the scale of
the attack. To achieve these, careful and extensive preparations must be made. This set-piece type battle was the sort
of thing Montgomery had to fight on the Rhine and of which
Patton was so scathingly contemptuous.

What is it then that made Patton the most memorable of
the American generals fighting in Europe in World War II?
Why is it that Patton has attracted more biographers than all
his fellow U.S. commanders put together, has been the subject of at least two novels, several documentaries, and two full-
scale movies? Why is it that Patton is still well-remembered,
virtually a household name, when Bradley, Simpson, Hodges,
Devers, and Patch have been forgotten, remembered only by
students of World War II?

I think it was Patton's dramatic, imperious personality,
coupled with a strong streak of histrionics. He had a great
deal of the actor in his makeup. The pistols, the elegant uniforms, the delight in pomp and circumstance—all point to his
love of the theatrical gesture. He was indeed a star performer
who hated to be upstaged. His friends were men who couldn't
do this, generals like Hughes or Patch. His enemies were
generals like Montgomery, who had a keen eye for publicity
themselves. Montgomery's eccentric dress—the beret with its
twin badges, the baggy corduroy trousers, the green
"gamp"—made him good copy for the correspondents and a
natural target of Patton's jealousy.

Patton is well remembered by the men of his Third Army,
too. The relationship was not that of a mutual admiration
society. "Our blood and his guts," they grumbled about the
nickname bestowed on their commander by the press. Patton
could drive his men into battle with the unnecessary vulgarity
of his language and later inspect their dead bodies on the
battlefield with apparently no remorse. As we have seen he
showed no concern for the fate of the men he had sent on
the abortive Hammelburg raid, nor did the losses he incurred
on the other less-publicized crossings of the Rhine bother him.

He might weep unashamedly at the sight of his wounded

soldiers in some front-line hospital, but his fighting men knew, as did his staff, that Patton was *performing* for their benefit; it was not a display of genuine emotion. Codman recalled him visiting some wounded in a hospital, handing out the Purple Hearts to the men until they came to the last man who was "unconscious, oxygen mask, probably won't live. The boss pulled one of those quick switches of his—took off his helmet, knelt down, pinned the medal on the pillow, whispered in the guy's ear—stood up at attention. Elementary if you like, but I swear there wasn't a dry eye in the house."[9]

Patton's dogfaces saw through him. As Bradley recorded, "Canny a showman though George was, he failed to grasp the psychology of the combat soldier. . . . He traveled in an entourage of command cars, followed by a string of nattily uniformed staff officers. His own vehicle was gaily decked with oversized stars and the insignia of his command. These exhibitions did not awe the troops as Patton perhaps believed. Instead they offended them as they trudged through the clouds of dust in the wake of the procession."[10]

The present writer can testify to the troops' dislike of such things. Once he saw Field Marshal Montgomery's car, followed by other command cars, crawl slowly by a line of dusty, exhausted infantrymen, while the Great Man, a nonsmoker himself, tossed out packets of cigarettes to the soldiers. One landed at the feet of a red-faced corporal, who instead of picking it up gratefully, as the Great Man obviously expected he would, ground it to shreds savagely with his heavy boot.

What Patton did for his men of the Third Army was to put them on the map. Their commander was such good copy, even for the worldly-wise, cynical war correspondents such as Irishman Cornelius Ryan of the *Daily Telegraph** who was with him to the end, that the Third could always expect to get a write-up in the papers back home. Whereas Hodges's First and Simpson's Ninth were *mentioned* in the media in the States, Patton's Third always grabbed the banner headlines. It meant little back home to say that "I fought with the U.S. Seventh Army." But if the returning hero could boast, "I fought with Patton," he really was somebody. As Patton

---

*Later the author of such bestsellers as *A Bridge Too Far*.

himself put it very succinctly. "When your grandchildren ask you what you did in the war, you can tell them '*I fought with Patton!*' You won't have to shift them to the other knee and say, '*I shoveled shit in Louisiana!*'"

What then is one to make of Patton as a commander:

Perhaps it would be easiest to characterize him as a nineteenth-century man, a Napoleonic-type of general, who lived according to the tenets of a romantic and individualistic code of conduct. Wasn't his own favorite motto based on Napoleon's basic tenet *"activite, vitesse—vitesse"*? This became for Patton: *"L'audace, l'audace, toujours l'audace!"* He might well have been a second Murat or Ney, one of those dashing marshals of Napoleon's—bold, daring, unconventional, foul-mouthed—"follow me, men, the captain's got a hole in his ass!"—and inveterate skirt-chasers. As German General Westphal once put it: "His operations impressed us enormously probably because he came closest to our concept of the classical military commander. He even improved on Napoleon's key motto—*activite, vitesse, vitesse.*"[11]

But already by the mid-forties, Patton was almost an anachronism. Since the 1914–1918 war, war had undergone its industrial revolution. The battlefield had become too large for the lone military genius, hand thrust in jacket à la Grant and standing on a hilltop, as if in some nineteenth-century romantic painting waiting for an opportunity to launch the decisive cavalry charge that would turn the enemy's flank.

By 1944–45 the lone figure had been replaced by a consortium: the team of military experts that were present at Eisenhower's and Bradley's headquarters. Decisions were corporate ones. Army command had almost become what it is today, "trade union operatives," as someone has said, "led by management consultants."[12] Decisions were already having to be made, not solely on the basis of military considerations, but on those of economics, politics, even public relations.

By 1945 Patton was already out-of-date. But Eisenhower still needed him because as Marshall said, "Patton is the man with the drive and imagination to do the dangerous things fast."[13] Yet Eisenhower was forced to keep this "anachronism" under control in case he did anything rash as he had done in Sicily and thereafter. As General Raphael Semmes, one of Patton's most cautious biographers has noted: "It is generally believed that the high command while believing in Patton's great tactical ability, genuinely feared his 'rashness.' "[14] From this statement another biographer, Ladislas Farago, draws the conclusion that "one of Bradley's prime missions was to keep a restraining hand on him [Patton] sometimes by order and sometimes by the diversions of supplies or troops to other armies."[15]

For a time that last spring of World War II there was a limited need for Patton, the anachronism. There was still room for a commander who could impress his flamboyant personality on his troops. It was still a campaign in which the dashing, thrusting commander could go up front and see for himself what was going on; could "chew out" a local commander, put "piss and vinegar" into the troops. Think of Patton telling General Malony he might become a "battle casualty" himself if he didn't get his 94th Division organized or threatening General Morris of the 10th Armored that he'd "goddam swim the river" (the Moselle) if he didn't find his lost bridging equipment!

But now the war was over . . .

Nineteen

Back in the spring of 1943, George Allen, an American who was a highly successful specialist in cultivating the rich and powerful, somehow managed to work his way across the Atlantic. He arrived there shortly before General Eisenhower became the new Supreme Commander. The middle-aged American falsely made it known to everyone that he was a personal friend of this relatively unknown American general. Then when Eisenhower arrived, he confessed his plight to the general and somehow smooth-talked Eisenhower into backing his story up by having lunch together in one of the most conspicuous spots in London—Claridge's.

It was typical of Allen's type of ingratiation (meanwhile, back in the States, Mrs. Allen was becoming a firm friend of Mamie Eisenhower—they were both living in Washington's Wardman Park Hotel*). It would have had no significance, for Eisenhower was to become used to having "visiting firemen" from the States descending upon him, save for one thing: For the very first time, Allen brought up the question of Eisenhower going into politics after the war.

In a letter to Eisenhower dated October 6, 1943, Allen enclosed a clipping from the *Washington Post*. It reported on "Tanks Corps Post No. 715" of the American Legion in New York, which had adopted a resolution boosting Eisenhower for President on account of his "leadership qualities."

Eisenhower's reaction was explosive. "Baloney!" he scribbled in his reply. "Why can't a simple soldier be left alone to carry out his orders. And I furiously object to the word 'candidate'—I ain't and won't!"[1]

But the "Eisenhower-for-President" talk began to swell in volume as 1943 gave way to 1944 and the Invasion of Europe

*Today the Sheraton Park.

178

started to loom larger on the horizon. After D-Day, his headquarters were swamped with hundreds of letters from people back in the States stating that having led "American boys" in war, it was his duty now to lead the country back into peace.

Publicly he brushed aside the campaign as nonsense; he was just a soldier. But those closest to him felt that after the Normandy landings he succumbed to the presidential virus and never recovered from it. Patton certainly thought that Eisenhower was intent on running for the office of President after the war. As early as 1943, he thought that "Ike is bitten by the Presidential Bug" and added bitterly "and he is yellow."[2] On another occasion, when angered by Eisenhower's conduct of operations, he snorted, "How can anyone expect any backbone in a man who is already running for President?"[3]

After Eisenhower left Patton's HQ on his last-but-one visit to Patton on March 16, 1945, the Third Army staff ruminated about the Supreme Commander. Patton said, "I think Ike had a good time. They ought to let him out more often."

"What I can't get over," General Gay said, "was his statement to the effect that Third Army isn't cocky enough. How do you explain it?"

"That's easy," Patton answered, stirring his soup. "Before long Ike will be running for President. Third Army represents a lot of votes." Sensing the half-incredulous smiles, Patton looked up sharply. "You think I'm joking? I'm not. Just wait and see."[4]

Although Patton would not live to see it happen, he was, of course, right. In 1952 Eisenhower would run for—and become—President of the United States. For the man who had been an obscure light colonel in 1941 had now become four years later a kind of twentieth-century Ulysses S. Grant. But a Grant whose power had been increased a thousand times, magnified to world dimensions by virtue of America's new place as the world's greatest nation in 1945. In four short years, Eisenhower had made the transition from being an unknown, middle-aged soldier, contemplating a carpet-slippered retirement, to that of a commander who exercised an authority on a scale granted to only very few mortals. It was heady stuff, calculated to overwhelm most men. While it was obvious that for Patton, at sixty, his career was virtually over, a whole new future, unconnected with the military, was opening itself up for fifty-five-year-old Dwight D. Eisenhower.

Once Patton had moaned, "I wish to God that Ike was more of a soldier and less of a politician."[5] Now as the war came to an end, Eisenhower found himself forced to become even more of a politician. Not only did he have the problem of ruling the newly conquered Germans in the American Zone of Occupation, he was also faced with the problem of the Russians, who were now living cheek by jowl with the Americans all along the zonal frontier stretching through Austria, Czechoslovakia, and into Germany itself.

If that were not enough, he had problems with Gen. Charles de Gaulle about the role France would play in the Occupation; with the British on Anglo-American relations in connection with a joint policy for the Germans; and with the "folks back home," working through the media, who wanted their menfolk returned for separation from the service as quickly as possible, regardless of the effect it would have on the U.S. Army of Occupation. By May 1945 it can be safely said that Eisenhower's role in Germany was no longer *military* but virtually exclusively *political*.

But could a harassed Eisenhower afford to support an unpredictable Patton, now that he no longer needed him as a fighting commander? Patton had just blotted his copybook once more during his visit to the States. His off-the-cuff remarks had generally received a bad press. What was he going to do with a man like Patton, who never seemed able to hold his tongue. Wasn't Patton (as he had told him often enough in the past) his "own worst enemy?"

For his part, Patton harbored no illusions about the kind of person his former friend Eisenhower had become over these last few momentous years. "I feel that as an American it will ill become me to discredit Ike—*yet*," he wrote. "That is until I shall prove even more conclusively that he lacks moral fortitude. This lack has been evident to me since the first landing in Africa, but now that he has been bitten by the Presidential Bee, it is becoming even more pronounced."[6] A little after that, Patton wrote, "Ike made the sensational statement that while hostilities were in progress, the one important thing was order and discipline, but now that hostilities are over the important thing was to stay in with 'world opinion.' "[7] Apparently whether it was right or wrong.

And Patton definitely thought that "world opinion" was wrong, especially on two counts: its attitude to the recently defeated Germans; and its concern not to offend America's erstwhile ally—Soviet Russia.

As we have seen, his critical, pugnacious stance versus the Russians had already begun to harden, fueled by the more right wing of his cronies. Visiting Berlin that summer he was invited to have a drink by one of the Russian welcoming committee. He told his interpreter to "tell that Russian son-ovabitch that from the way they're acting here, I regard them as enemies and I'd rather cut my throat than have a drink with one of my enemies!"

The interpreter paled. "I'm sorry, sir," he stammered. "But I cannot tell the General *that*!"

Patton *ordered* him to translate his words exactly, whereupon the Russian smiled and spoke rapidly to the interpreter. The latter said, "The General says that he feels exactly like that about you, sir. So why, he asks, couldn't you have a drink after all?"[8]

Patton smiled and took the proferred drink, but later he wrote to his wife, "Berlin gave me the blues. We have destroyed what could have been a good race and we [are] about to replace them with Mongolian savages."[9] Later he would note in his diary about the Russians: "I have no particular desire to understand them except to ascertain how much lead or iron it takes to kill them."[10]

Some time afterward, when he met the Victor of Berlin, Marshal G. Zhukov, he wrote to his wife that, "He was in full-dress uniform much like comic opera and covered with medals. He is short, rather fat, and has a prehensile chin like an ape but good blue eyes."[11] Of Marshal Tolbukhin who invested him with the Order of Kutuzoff, he wrote, "He was a very inferior man and sweated profusely at all times."[12] Patton's dislike of "Soviet Man" was not intellectual. It is to be doubted that he knew much about communism. His dislike was based strictly on military considerations. For he believed that sooner or later the United States would have to fight the Red Army and, in his opinion, the sooner the better.

Allied to this intense dislike of the Russians was his growing admiration for the Germans. Everything he saw of the
Russians, Poles, Jews, and sundry Eastern European displaced persons aroused a feeling of loathing in him. Until the
war ended he managed to conceal his feelings. Now he began
to display his feelings in his opposition to the policy of non-
fraternization with the Germans, which Eisenhower wanted
strictly observed, and the denazification of Germany, the approved policy ordered by Washington.

That summer he wrote to his wife, "The stuff in the papers
about fraternization is all wet. . . . All that sort of writing is
done by Jews to get revenge. Actually the Germans are the
only decent people left in Europe. It's a choice between them
and the Russians. I prefer the Germans. So do our cousins
[the British]."[13]

In vain did Eisenhower send his political adviser Robert
Murphy to see Patton. As the veteran diplomat recorded it:
"In two separate talks which we had together, Patton asked
whether I thought he had fought his last battle. He inquired,
with a gleam in his eye, whether there was any chance of
going on to Moscow, which he said he could reach in thirty
days, instead of waiting for the Russians to attack the United
States when we were weak and reduced to two divisions."[14]

Patton expressed this opinion privately to Murphy, but
Murphy knew and so informed Eisenhower that "throughout
his career, this brilliant commander could not desist from
also making controversial remarks publicly."[15]

Murphy spoke with authority for, two and a half years
before, he had experienced Patton as military governor of the
recently occupied state of Morocco. There he had committed
one gaffe after another, associating on extremely friendly
terms with the pro-Axis French commander, General
A. Noguès.

Noguès was a fascist who had introduced the Nazi racial
laws into Morocco and still continued to implement them
against the Jews *after* the American seizure of the country,
with Patton's connivance. (Noguès had told Patton that if the
restrictions on the 200,000 Moroccan Jews were lifted, the
predominantly Arab population of the country might well revolt—and Patton had believed him.) Not only that, Moroccan
radio was still in the hands of pro-Axis operators who were

still broadcasting propaganda on the Nazis' behalf. Intercepts revealed that Noguès himself was in touch with the pro-German Vichy regime in France, discussing with Hitler's henchmen in that country anti-Allied measures, even the possibility of kicking the Americans out of Morocco by force!

Murphy at that time had despaired. As he wrote later, "Milton Eisenhower [Eisenhower's brother] was right in protesting the authority being flaunted by Noguès, but he was mistaken if he thought that I, or even General Eisenhower himself, could take drastic action in Morocco immediately. The expeditionary forces in that area, almost exclusively American, were under the command of Major General George S. Patton, Jr., and relations between that flamboyant warrior and Noguès had become embarrassingly cordial."[16]

In the end Churchill, angered by what was going on in Morocco, wrote directly to President Roosevelt about the situation there. "I have been disturbed by reports received during the last few days from North Africa about conditions in French Morocco and Algeria," he wrote. "These reports show that the SOL* and kindred fascist organizations continue their activities and victimize our former French sympathizers, some of whom have not yet been released from prison. The first reaction of these organizations to the Allied landing was, rightly, one of fear. But it seems that they have now taken courage to regroup themselves and continue their activities. Well-known German sympathizers who have been ousted have been reinstated. Not only have our enemies been thus encouraged but our friends have been correspondingly confused and cast down. There have been cases of French soldiers being punished for desertion because they tried to support the Allied forces during the landing."[17]

Eventually the matter was sorted out and Noguès thrown out of office. Why, however, Patton chose to support a regime that was reactionary, anti-Allied, and had helped to kill one thousand British and American soldiers during the initial landings in North Africa** is not clear. Perhaps Patton just

---

*A pro-Axis group of ex-servicemen.
**Ironically though, the first American soldiers to be killed in the West in WWII were those killed by the very people they had come to "liberate"—the French!

got on better with soldiers like Noguès. Perhaps he was simply politically naive. But as Murphy wrote of the matter: "This was the first time, but by no means the last, when Patton created a problem in public relations for General Eisenhower."[18]

Just what kind of a "problem in public relations" Patton was going to create for Eisenhower no one could have guessed back in 1942. But now, even as Murphy lectured Patton on his mistaken attitude to the Russians and the Germans, the latter was already becoming involved in the first of the scandals that would eventually lead to his disgrace and dismissal.

On a routine visit to a lunatic asylum in Kaufbeuren, which lay in the Third Army area, on July 2, 1945, the American inspectors discovered to their horror that the place was nothing less than a mini-extermination center, where throughout the war the Nazi policy of euthanasia—the killing by injection of mentally retarded adults and children—had been carried out. Worse, two months *after* the Third Army had captured the little Bavarian town, *the place was still operating*!

A matter of hours before the Americans had arrived, German adults and children were still being murdered by injection or slow starvation. In the mortuary the American inspectors found bodies of men and women, none weighing more than seventy-five pounds, who had died within the last few hours.

Later it was impossible to discover how many people, all Germans, had been murdered by their own people in the lunatic asylum. The records had been destroyed. But among the survivors was a ten-year-old German boy weighing exactly twenty-two pounds. The chief nurse, who admitted to having murdered "about two hundred and ten children over the past two years," asked when she was arrested by MPs of the Third Army, "will anything happen to me?" She seemed very surprised when they assured her that something very definitely would.[19]

If Patton ever learned of the shocking incident that had taken place in the area under his command, he makes no mention of it in his diary. He continued his trips around Bavaria, as its newly created Military Governor, occupying himself "with de-Nazification . . . and the recruiting of industries of the German people so that they can be more self-supporting,"[20] greeted, according to General Semmes, "with cheers" and Bavarians "throwing flowers from the windows, shouting, 'He is our saviour. He has saved us from the Russian mob!' "[21]

"Now," Patton wrote in his diary that first summer of the new peace, "all that is left to do is to sit around and await the arrival of the undertaker and posthumous immortality."[22]

But before that event finally took place, Patton would undergo one last venture into the headlines of the world press. They would be his last. Thereafter he would vanish into an embittered obscurity released only by death. Immortality would have to wait.

PART IV

☆ ☆ ☆ ☆ ☆

OCCUPATION

Twenty

They called it *die Stunde Null.**

It was a time without precedent. A chaos without parallel. One of the world's most civilized, most industrialized countries had broken down completely. There was no gas, no electricity, precious little running water. There was no public transport and no mail. The telephones didn't work and only a handful of Allied controlled newspapers, limited mostly to one sheet, appeared. Whole cities had been wiped off the map.

American journalist William Shirer, revisiting Nuremberg after the fighting, recorded in his diary the shock of what he saw: "It is gone! The lovely medieval town behind the moat is utterly destroyed. It is a vast heap of rubble, beyond description, and beyond hope of re-building."[1] Frankfurt, Eisenhower's new headquarters, was so badly destroyed that the Army had to issue street maps so that the troops could find their way through the sea of ruins. In Kassel, where hundreds of dead still lay below the ruins, some streets were labeled "Gruesome" and the citizens talked in whispers when they went down them.

Over three and a half million Germans had been killed fighting with the *Wehrmacht*. Half a million had been killed in the air raids. There were two million cripples, and there were currently one and a half million Germans fleeing eastward from the Russians, Poles, and Czechs. There were ten million displaced persons, former prisoners-of-war, people released from the concentration camps, wandering about the country, some trying to reach the countries of their origin, others simply living by their wits, looting, stealing, raping, trying to make up their minds what to do next.

*Literally "the hour zero."

189

For the great majority of the Germans who had survived the war, especially those who lived in the bomb-shattered cities, life was a matter of squalor and hunger. Some had fashioned themselves caves in the ruins, where they eked out a miserable existence as if they were back in the Stone Age. Others lived high in bombed-out apartment houses, reaching their quarters by rope ladders or planks balanced precariously from one wrecked floor to another. In Germany, now, ten people lived where six had lived before.

Naturally the black market thrived. On the whole the Germans had had a good war, as far as food had been concerned. There had been no "one egg, per week, *perhaps*" for them, as there had been for the British. No stringent food rationing, where even the fish-and-chip shops, which had brought the British poor through the Depression, had been without fish. Now, however, in this summer of defeat the Germans really began to know what hunger really was. Their fat ration was two ounces, meat three and a half, fish was limited to three ounces. Bread, the great staple for the Germans, was cut to two pounds per person, per week. Cabbage was plentiful, though, and it seemed to anyone who was in Germany at that time that the whole place stank of boiled *Weisskohl*.*

To supplement this miserable diet, the Germans turned to the black market for extra food—and the black market was mainly the Allied soldier, with his plentiful supply of Compo ration and K and C ration cans. Family heirlooms went, as did family honor too. For if a hungry woman had nothing else to offer, she gave her body for a can of hash or of corned beef. "Fratting," as it was called in defiance of Eisenhower's non-fraternization edict, was the rage.

"Don't get chummy with Jerry," the *Stars and Stripes* exhorted its readers. "In heart, body, and spirit every German is Hitler," the troops were warned. The warnings had no effect. Nor did the $75 fine that the GI had to pay if he were caught with a German "frowlein." With a pack of Lucky Strikes going for $10 and a Hershey bar for $5 on the black market, the average GI could easily pay any fine leveled.

Not all these Germans *"schatzies"* had sex with soldiers

*White cabbage.

solely for the goods they could earn by spreading their legs. Many of these girls and women sought desperately for some human warmth, the intimate contact that would make them forget the misery and deprivation of their current existence, where most German men were either dead, crippled, missing, or prisoner-of-war. They flung themselves into the arms of these young, healthy, happy men with a kind of joyful despair. If many of the German men remaining were servile lickspittles, bowing and scraping to their conquerors for a pathetic cigarette butt, often thrown away contemptuously and deliberately into the gutter, their womenfolk were bold and fought back.

James McGovern, who was serving then in U.S. Intelligence, vividly portrays the German woman at that time in his novel *Fraulein*:

> There, lying on a slab of concrete six feet square, once part of the facade of a beauty salon, lay the constabulary private and his Frowline half hidden behind a pile of ruins. The young American was naked except for his combat boots and the bright yellow scarf round his neck. The Frowline, whose chubby, cheese-white body and short, powerful piston-legs completely enveloped him, was completely naked. A pitiless moon had suddenly emerged from behind black clouds to light up their bodies like a police spotlight.
>
> They lay coupling, groaning, moaning on a concrete slab in bright moonlight in the dead center of Berlin at the dead center of a dead Germany . . . until the air was split by the Frowline's sudden wail of pleasure and pain. The grunts and the moans stopped. The Frowline rose from the concrete altar of German-American relations. She stood like an avenging Valkyrie, an indestructible Earth-Mother, rising out of the Prussian soil, the bright moonlight shining on the red nipples of her sagging breasts, standing triumphantly over the jagged ruins, living proof that Germany, in whatever form, and by whatever terrible means, was going to survive."[2]

"Fratting" had its consequences of course. Within a year, twenty to thirty thousand illegitimate children would be born in the American Zone of Occupation alone, and in Germany as a whole, the number of illegitimate births rose by ten percent. Today there are thousands of middle-aged Germans whose fathers were American, British, Canadian, French, Russian.

But that was not the only consequence. Venereal disease spread like some medieval plague. Whole divisions of fighting troops were struck down by the several types of the disease. In my own infantry division, a twenty-four-hour leave was promised if a *single* day went by without one case of VD being reported within the division. Over a twelve-month period from June 1945 to the following June, we never got that day off!

The outbreak started in the big cities such as Berlin, Hamburg, and Frankfurt. Here, in the city that housed Eisenhower's headquarters, the syphilis rate increased by a whopping 200 percent on the 1939 figures. From here it spread to the more rural areas, with soldiers taking it to the remotest village.

Desperately, the authorities organized surprise street raids, pulling in any woman between the ages of sixteen and sixty—prostitutes, grandmas, housewives, virgins, schoolgirls—for a medical examination at the nearest hospital. But even if a woman was found to have the disease, there was little that the harassed German doctors could do. The Allies refused to supply them with penicillin to cure the VD, and their own supply of drugs was limited. In the end they had to resort to the kind of treatment that was current before Paul Ehrlich discovered his ''magic bullet'' against syphilis—steam baths, painful scrapings, anti-malaria cures, and the like.

''We cannot expect the GI to behave differently,'' observed one American officer who urged the abandonment of the unworkable ''no-fraternization'' policy. ''After all he is human. He wants companionship—he's lonely and the Germans are past masters at getting around men who feel that way.''[3]

''In this economic set-up, sex relations, which function like any other commodity, assumes a very low value'' explained one U.S. survey. ''Because of this situation, plus the fact that every American soldier is a relative millionaire by virtue of his access to PX rations, the average young man in the occupation army is afforded an unparalleled opportunity for sexual exposure."[4]

As the cynical GIs quipped, *"A can of corned beef means true love."*

Now it became the task of a small group of civilians in uniform and the military to attempt to bring some kind of order and reason to this crazy, corrupt, cynical society that existed in the shattered ruins of Hitler's vaunted "One Thousand Year Reich."

But in many cases these new rulers of a conquered Germany were as crazy, corrupt, and as cynical as the people they were supposed to govern. There was the English homosexual poet Wynstan Auden, for example, masquerading as an American officer, driving about Bavaria in a jeep in a helmet liner and *carpet slippers*, presumably looking for the same kind of *Strichenjungen** he had frequented together with Christopher Isherwood before Hitler had come into power. Or the former member of Roosevelt's White House staff who arrived in Germany to "reeducate" the "natives" in the ways of democracy, armed with fifty cases of cigarettes for the black market!

Or twenty-two-year-old Staff Sergeant Henry Kissinger lording it over the township of Bensheim in Hesse. Here he entertained an old friend who noted in his diary, "What a set-up! Like a castle. Had dinner with him. What an intelligent girl friend."[5] The girl friend was German. So were the cook, the maid, the housekeeper and the secretary. They all went together with the confiscated white Mercedes—*and all for $10 a month!*

Allied with cynicism, corruption, and general craziness were just plain downright stupidity and lack of knowledge of Germany, her people and her history. As one cynical former member of the "Big Red One," now working in Intelligence snorted, "We never occupied a country before. What the hell did we know about occupying Germany? We made so many mistakes. We sent colonels in who needed another year for retirement, we made them military governors of Bavaria. They'd never been in Europe. We taught 'em for a couple of

*Boy prostitutes.

weeks in South Carolina what kind of trees grow in Bavaria!''[6]

The colonel who Patton appointed to run Bavaria for him certainly wasn't old and ready for retirement. Colonel Charles Keegan of the Third Army was very much in the mold of his master—energetic, dynamic, and foul-mouthed. *"Rights!"* he once bawled at a group of Germans who had brought up the topic. "You got no rights. You're conquered, ye'hear. You started the war and you lost. You got no rights. Tell that thick-headed Kraut that there'll be no charges and that I will throw that damned bum into the can if he yells again. Tell that lousy monster I'll put him on ice. . . . I'll throw you all in the can, too, if you don't translate the exact words I said and in the same tone.''[7]

Colonel Keegan's forceful style seemed to set the tone for many other of Patton's appointees. Major Everett S. Cofran, the military governor of Augsburg, for instance, began his short reign by hanging a sign behind his desk that read "I hate all Germans!"

When he was asked why he had put up the sign, he replied bitterly, "Were it not for them I would be America's most famous architect." Apparently before the war he had designed the Bermuda Yacht Club and was now earning two percent of his prewar salary.

He also put up a large card with the total number of Americans killed in the campaign in Europe on it, explaining to the German mayor of Augsburg, "If ever I weaken in the fight against National Socialism, a look at the number of the dead always gives me new strength.''[8]

Cofran made no distinction between Nazis and Germans; they were all the same to him. He treated them all dictatorially, even the mayor, who was supposedly untainted by the National Socialist creed. On one single day, for example, he attempted to fire forty-three of the forty-eight doctors at the city hospital, fifty-eight of the sixty local firemen, the whole of the state forestry staff, and nearly all the policemen on the grounds that they were Nazis, which they probably were!

Like most of Patton's governors, he was a high-liver. He demanded fresh flowers every day in his office, tried to bill Augsburg for five hundred bottles of wine, and demanded two cameras from the harassed mayor as a personal gift. In the end, Cofran's excesses were too much even for Keegan, and he was transferred to Passau, where he was murdered in his sleep six months later by a fellow military government officer who had mistakenly slaughtered two other officers with an axe before he finally found Cofran.

During Cofran's reign over Augsburg, the Americans also began to employ the German later to become known as the "Butcher of Lyons," Klaus Barbie, the notorious SD* officer currently awaiting trial in France for his crimes committed there in World War II. Intelligence officer Erhard Dabringhaus was told by his boss to use Barbie as an informant. Dabringhaus, who already knew something of Barbie's record, exclaimed, "I hope you know what the hell you guys are doing. Okay, if he's the guy I'll work with him. Normally, I would arrest this guy."[9] Later Dabringhaus was astonished to discover that Barbie was being paid "seventeen hundred good green American dollars" for his services, although his boss knew that Barbie was a war criminal who was reported to have killed four thousand Frenchmen during the Occupation. "Yes, we know all about it," his boss told Dabringhaus. "But he's still valuable. In due time, we'll turn him over to the French."[10] But, of course, Barbie was never turned over to the French and was to remain at liberty in South America for nearly forty years.

   The situation was little different at Garmisch, the famous ski resort, where not only did the black market flourish, but also the first great narcotics rings of postwar Europe, covering Germany, Italy, France, and several Eastern European countries. Here, for example, Captain Haig, a Swiss-born U.S. Army Intelligence officer, lived with one of Goebbels's former mistresses—a Czech movie star—while his friend had as his mistress the former girl friend of Gestapo chief Ernst Kaltenbrunner. If that was not bad enough, it was revealed at Haig's court-martial that his pal's mistress was a communist agent who had been pumping Haig for secrets to pass on to the East!

   Indeed these first American rulers appointed by Patton to govern Bavaria were no advertisement for the U.S. Army or

---

Sicherheitsdienst, the secret police of the SS.

the United States itself. There was, for example, the young, rich, and perverted Third Army captain delegated to rule over the sleepy little Bavarian town of Eichstätt. He lives in the folk memory of the place's strictly Catholic citizens as *"Hauptmann Toll"* (literally "Captain Crazy").

"Captain Crazy" ruled Eichstätt like a feudal baron. He walked the town carrying a whip, yelling at the frightened citizens to get out of his way. When a woman made derogatory remarks about the *Amis*, he ordered her stripped naked and frog-marched to the town hall. He declared war on the local Nazis, flinging them into the town's jail, where they were beaten up and robbed. But his chief of police, his superintendent of schools, and his right-hand man, who procured boys for him from the ranks of the Hitler Youth, were all ex-Nazis.

"Captain Crazy" lived in some style, dining off damask tablecloths and using silver tableware. Devout Catholic that he was, when he went to the church—in riding boots and spurs—he sat in solitary splendor at the front of the cathedral in a roped-off area.

He also encouraged local industry—for his own benefit! He had the renowned wood carvers of the area fake copies of antique furniture, which he shipped off to the States to be sold as the genuine article. Yes, "Captain Crazy" lived well, treating life in Eichstätt as a fabulous and profitable adventure before he, too, disappeared, like all the governors did in the end, to return to a dull and prosaic States, where their recent lives in Occupied Germany must have seemed to them like some crazy impossible dream.

As George Kennan of the State Department summed up his impressions of the U.S. Zone of Occupation in his memoirs: "Each time I had come away with a sense of sheer horror at the spectacle of this horde of my compatriots and their dependents camping in luxury amid the ruins of a shattered national community, ignorant of the past, oblivious to the abundant evidences of present tragedy all around them, inhabiting the same sequestered villas that the Gestapo and SS had just abandoned, and enjoying the same privileges, flaunting their silly supermarket luxuries in the face of a veritable ocean of deprivation, hunger and wretchedness, setting an example of empty materialism and cultural poverty before a people desperately in need of spiritual and intellectual guidance, taking for granted—as though it was their natural due—a disparity of privilege and comfort between themselves and their German neighbors no smaller than those that had once divided lord and peasant in that feudal Germany which it had once been our declared purpose in two world wars to destroy.''[11]

These then were the men—the good, the bad, the indifferent—with whom General Patton was going to govern Catholic Bavaria.

Twenty-one

Patton had set up his headquarters in Bad Tölz, an alpine resort in Upper Bavaria. Here the Third Army HQ was housed in the former cadet training school of the *Waffen SS*, many of whose graduates had been quickly seen off by Patton's men in the last eleven months.* For himself he chose the villa once owned by Max Amann, Hitler's former publisher and a first sergeant in World War I. Amann had dreamed up the title of *Mein Kampf* for the book the Führer had written during his imprisonment in Landsberg and had become the head of the publishing firm (by 1940, the biggest in Europe) that continued to churn it out by the hundreds of thousands, year in and year out. By 1942 his wealth was assessed at four million marks and he had used some of that money to have a villa built, which Patton thought was one of the best he had seen. It had, among other things, a boat house, complete with two boats, a swimming pool, and a bowling alley. It suited the general's taste exactly.

Here Patton set about ruling Bavaria, though his major concern was not the Germans under his rule, but his rapidly diminishing Third Army that was being so swiftly run down. More and more units were being broken up and the men were returning to the States for separation from the service. In their place he was receiving green, untrained eighteen-year-olds, who thought they were coming to Occupied Germany for a good time, which indeed they were.

All of them had heard the wild tales of the good times to be had in the American Zone of Occupation, with its thriving black market and more than willing "frowlines." As a con-

---

*Some of Patton's original furniture, including his desk, is still preserved in what has now become the U.S. Seventh Army's NCO Training Academy.

sequence, many of them took badly to the kind of discipline Patton had been able to enforce in his wartime Third Army. Soon discipline would become so bad that four thousand GIs would mob central Frankfurt, catcalling and brawling, shouting up at Eisenhower's HQ in the IG Farben Building, *"We wanna go home!"*

German civilians were beaten up by drunken Third Army GIs. Pedestrians apparently were willfully run down by GI truck drivers. Armed robbery, looting, and theft were rife. Even women attached to the Allied forces were not safe from molestation by these marauding young soldiers unless they carried a little flag on their blouses showing their nationality. Congress was told that violent behavior by American troops was so widespread that their conduct fell far behind that of the German occupiers of conquered Europe. "The German troops occupying France had a better record in their personal contact with the population than the American troops occupying Germany."[1]

Hand in hand with his concern about the conduct of his men and rapid running-down of American forces in Europe, Patton was seized with an almost pathological hatred of the Russians. He felt that Eisenhower in Frankfurt was leaning over backward in his attempts not to offend the Russians. Time and time again he aired his exasperation to his own staff, and then in July he let his temper run away with him in a telephone conversation with Eisenhower's new deputy, General Joseph McNarney, an old friend.

McNarney began to relay a Soviet complaint to Patton about the latter's slowness in disbanding several German units in Bavaria when Patton burst out with, "Hell, why do you care what those Goddamn Russians think? We are going to have to fight them sooner or later, within the next generation. Why not do it now while our Army is intact and the damn Russians can have their hind end kicked back into Russia in three months? We can do it ourselves easily with the help of the German troops we have, if we just arm them and take them with us. They hate the bastards!"

McNarney could hardly believe his own ears. Patton was publicly stating the impossible: that America should re-arm its recent bitter enemies and march with them to fight against their erstwhile ally! He was deeply shocked. "Shut up, George, you fool," he cried over the phone. "This line may be tapped and you will be starting a war with those Russians with your talking!"

But an enraged Patton refused to shut up. "I would like to get it started some way," he exclaimed excitedly. "That is the best thing we can do now. *You* don't have to get mixed up in it at all if you are so damn soft about it and scared of your rank—just let *me* handle it down here. In ten days I can have enough incidents happen to have us at war with those sons of bitches and make it look like their fault. So much so that we will be completely justified in attacking them and running them out!"

Mortified, McNarney hung up. He couldn't believe that a supposedly intelligent man could even *think* that way. Without any recourse to political direction from Washington, Patton seriously thought he could involve the United States in another war. It was incredible.

Patton turned to one of his staff, Colonel Harkins, who happened to be in his office during the heated telephone conversation, and said with a smug smile, "I really believe that we are going to fight them, and if this country does not do it now, it will be taking them on years later when the Russians are ready for it and we will have an awful time whipping them. We will need these Germans," he concluded on a theme that was getting the upper hand with him, dominating his whole thinking, "and I don't think we ought to mistreat people whom we will need so badly."[2] Unknown to Patton, "the little fart" Montgomery still had not demobilized over a *million* Germans in the British Zone of Occupation. Nor did he know that both he and the recently dismissed British premier Churchill were urging that stocks of German weapons, planes, and other matériel should be kept intact just in case there was a need to re-arm German troops in order that they could fight at the side of British soldiers against the Russians. In other words, Patton was not alone in the Allied camp in his fear and distrust of the Soviets.

But Patton had totally misjudged the mood at Eisenhower's Headquarters. Eisenhower believed that, in contrast to the British and the French, the Russians were very much like Americans in being untainted by any kind of colonialism. (Presumably he knew nothing of nineteenth-century Russia, which had been expanding at the expense of its neighbors for over fifty years.) He believed the friendship of his opposite number, Marshal Zhukov, in the Russian Zone of Occupation was genuine and that the Red Army really did want to work together with the Americans. In his memoirs, he wrote that Zhukov and his staff demonstrated only "an intense desire to be friendly and cooperative." Indeed, Eisenhower continued to correspond with the burly, cleft-chinned Russian marshal until April 1946 when the latter fell from grace and was quietly removed from the scene by "Old Leather Face," as he called the Russian dictator Stalin behind his back.

Now McNarney, who was very loyal to his boss and the agreed policy vis-à-vis the Russians, judged that Patton could no longer be allowed to keep his command. With Bavaria bordering on Czechoslovakia, which was now under Russian domination, and the Soviet Zone of Germany, Patton *was* in a position to do something foolish very easily—and start a third world war. Patton, in McNarney's opinion, was simply too politically naive and impetuous. As far as McNarney was concerned, Patton was not fit to govern the Germans or to command what was left of a fighting army.

Unaware of the feelings of the top brass, Patton continued to let his fears of the possible Soviet menace obsess him. Indeed at times, he seemed as paranoic about the Russians as did James Forrestal, the Secretary of the Navy, who committed suicide in 1949 on account of his fears for the future safety of the U.S.A.

In the first week of September 1945, Patton went to Berlin to be present at the great military review that the four occupying powers were putting on to celebrate the successful ending of the war with Japan. Patton made his appearance, resplendent with twenty stars and his ivory-handled pistols, and took his place with the rest of the brass on the reviewing stand. But the parade started with some confusion. As General James "Slim Jim" Gavin of the 82nd Airborne Division wrote later: "A few days earlier, the Russians announced that in the forthcoming victory parade either they or the Americans would lead the parade—no one else! I took exception, pointing out that the British had fought as long as anyone. . . . I therefore suggested that we draw lots, or even that we go in alphabetical order, using the French language as is sometimes diplomatic practice, to establish precedence.''[3]

But the Russians wouldn't have it. So the matter went to Marshal Zhukov himself. However, he started giving Gavin orders. Gavin refused to accept them. Zhukov then told Gavin he would take the matter up with Eisenhower, to which the American airborne commander replied that ''it was fine with me, but I saw no reason to change my position.''[4] And there apparently the storm in a tea cup had ended.

Now, however, as Patton and the rest of the Allied generals waited for the great parade to start, Marshal Zhukov, with medals covering his burly body right down to his ample waist, suddenly jumped into his huge Zis limousine. Unknown to the Westerners, it was the Russian custom for the officer receiving the review to ride around and inspect the troops before the parade itself started. For the Russians this is what they meant by ''leading'' the parade, and Zhukov was determined that the conquerors of Berlin, namely the Red Army, would lead.

Patton, the born showman himself, somehow guessed that the marshal, whom he considered looked ''like an ape,'' was trying to steal a march on the Western Allies. Springing into his own car, followed by a surprised Gavin, he took up the chase. He ordered his driver to put his foot down. The NCO obeyed instantly, and soon they had caught up with Zhukov.

Thus it was that the Red Army marshal rode around proudly, with Patton's car riding exactly parallel with his big Zis. George S. Patton was not going to let any one upstage him—*no sir*!

A little while later, as the armored might of the erstwhile Allies started to rumble by the reviewing stand, Marshal Zhukov proudly pointed to some of the Red Army's most modern tanks, the huge, glistening successor to the famed T-34. ''My dear General Patton,'' he rumbled, talking through his interpreter, ''you see that tank. It carries a cannon which can throw a shell seven miles.''

Patton affected to be unimpressed. ''Indeed,'' he answered icily. ''Well, my dear Marshal Zhukov, let me tell you this. If any of my gunners started firing at your people before they had closed to less than seven hundred yards, I'd have them court-martialed—for cowardice!''[5]

Patton's aide, Major Pat Merle-Smith, who overheard the remark, recorded later: ''It was the first time I saw a Russian commander stunned into silence.''[6]

Naturally, the story of how Patton had upstaged the Russians and had actually mentioned the possibility that Americans might have cause to fire at Russians did the rounds. Patton's cronies and staff obviously thought it was all a good joke, typical of the ''old man.''

Eisenhower when he heard the tale was, like Queen Victoria, definitely ''not amused.'' Already he had cautioned Patton on August 27 at a special conference called to discuss the control of Germany because he, Patton, was being too lenient on the Germans. Not only that, he was now angering the Russians, something that displeased Eisenhower a great deal.

But there was worse to come. Almost as soon as he had been appointed, Colonel Keegan had approached Cardinal Faulhaber, the head of the Catholic Church in Bavaria, for help in finding trustworthy Germans to administer the area. Naively, Keegan had thought that a senior member of the Church and a Bavarian to boot would be untainted by Nazism. According to an Army paper of the time, the Bavarians ''were traditionally against Prussia'' and ''had not been really infected by the Nazi virus.'' (Somehow the Army researchers had overlooked the fact that the Nazi party had been founded in Faulhaber's hometown of Munich!)

With Faulhaber's assistance, Keegan had established a German administration, headed by fifty-seven-year-old Dr. Fritz Schaeffer, who had been briefly arrested the year before after the July attempt on Hitler's life. What Faulhaber had concealed from Keegan, however, was that the Bavarian politician had a long right-wing, anti-democratic history behind him. In 1919 he had joined the Bavarian *Freikorps*, which had revolted against the socialist government in Berlin and had bloodily suppressed the socialist revolt in Bavaria. Two years later, as a minister, he had refused to outlaw the Nazi Party's newly formed paramilitary units, the Storm Troops. In 1932 he had told the then German President Field Marshal von Hindenburg that he and his party ''were not, in principle, opposed to Hitler becoming Chancellor.'' He then told Franz von Papen, the prime minister, that he was ''absolutely available to become a member of any future Hitler government.'' Thereafter, although his own party was banned with all other parties by the Nazis, he supported Hitler almost to the end.

It was not surprising that Dr. Schaeffer filled his administration with men of similar conservative, right-wing views. There was Karl Fischer, for example, the head of the Interior Ministry. He had been a former Nazi official in Czechoslovakia and came under the Allied ''automatic arrest'' category. Or Otto Hipp, the minister of education, who refused to de-Nazify his schools and in whose universities some professors were still teaching the same racist creed that they had in Hitler's time. Or Karl Lange, a businessman, who had made enormous profits during the war thanks to his close contacts with the Nazis.

Later, after the Patton scandal caused their dismissal, Schaeffer would be branded ''a Nazi sympathizer and collaborator'' and his team would be depicted ''as nothing better than a clerical, military clique, filled with senile, obstinate reactionaries.''[7] But that was to be later, when it was too late.

But in September of 1945, Keegan, who was trained for war, not to mastermind a political revolution, concerned himself with getting rid of the outward trappings of National Socialism—the hated swastikas, graven into the walls of swimming pools, barracks, and the like; the removal of street names such as *Adolf Hitler Platz* and *Hermann Goering Strasse*; and the suppression of any kind of Party uniform. He was quite happy to let these competent Bavarians under Schaeffer get on with the mundane business of seeing that there was gas and electricity and that the trains and trams started to run once more.

But Keegan had not reckoned with the flood of reporters and correspondents who had now come to Germany looking for a ''story.'' Many of them were German-speaking, which most of Keegan's American staff weren't; and they started to poke their noses into all sorts of dark and malodorous corners. Their reports began to come to Eisenhower's attention. Sensitive as he always was to press coverage of his affairs and public opinion ''back home,'' he wrote Patton a strong letter on September 12. In it he warned the Third Army Commander he must stop mollycoddling the Nazis in his area and rigorously implement the de-Nazification program that called for the removal of all Nazis from public office.

But Patton refused to listen. Blinded by his own glory and faith in his own assured place in history, he simply could not keep his mouth shut. Throughout the last campaign in Europe, Bradley had warned him several times, "Damnit, George, you're going to get yourself in a terrible doghouse if you don't keep your mouth shut!" Now there was no Bradley to warn and protect him. George S. Patton was going to commit his final blunder.

Twenty-two

It started on Friday, September 21, 1945, when Eisenhower decreed that the ban prohibiting the press directly quoting general officers was now lifted. Patton took the opportunity of calling a press conference for the next day. He had a lot to get off his chest.

The following afternoon Patton and his chief-of-staff, General Gay, faced the press in his walled and turreted headquarters at Bad Tölz. Among the handful of correspondents present were Carl McArdle of the *Philadelphia Bulletin* and Raymond Daniell of *The New York Times*. They waited eagerly for a resplendent Patton to give them the signal to start.

Patton had had a hard day. He and his aide, Merle-Smith, had been to visit a DP camp in which a hunger strike and rioting were going on. As Merle-Smith recalled later, "The refugees had made such an incredible pigsty of the place that the General had to stop the car on the way home and vomit."[1] As a result he was not too happy with his first question. It was if he knew what the *Fragebogen* was?

Now the *Fragebogen* was a questionnaire that every adult German had to fill out and that inquired about his past history, jobs, political affiliation, and so forth. It was essential for obtaining a job under the occupying powers and for obtaining a clean bill of health in the denazification program. In other words, it was the basis of Eisenhower's whole plan to rid German public life of former Nazis. Amazingly enough, therefore, Patton did not know what the form was, and he was fool enough to snort in his usual exasperated manner, "Well, just what in hell is a *Fragebogen*?"

That started it. Now the reporters began to question Patton about his treatment of Nazis in Bavaria and about the new Bavarian premier, Dr. Schaeffer, whom some of them seemed to regard as a Nazi Party member himself. As if hell-bent on self-destruction, Patton defended his policies in Occupied Bavaria, maintaining that if there were free election there he could undoubtedly be "President of Bavaria." The talk became more heated, and Patton grew more outspoken. His aide, Merle-Smith, felt that certain of the correspondents "seemed bound and determined to distort what [Patton] had to say, trap him into an unguarded statement and somehow blacken him."[2]

Raymond Daniell, *The New York Times*'s journalist, who was soon to file the story on Patton that caused the sensation, denies this. He wrote later: "If there was, in fact, any movement in certain quarters to 'get' General Patton, I certainly was not aware of it, although, as I have said earlier, there was widespread talk, both among correspondents and officers, as well as among civilian representatives of various branches of the U.S. Government, of laxity in the enforcement of denazification throughout Bavaria. Whether the talk was set in motion originally by anyone with an ulterior purpose I have no possible way of telling. . . . By the time I decided to look into conditions in Bavaria, whatever pebble had been thrown in the pond had created a ripple of very great dimensions."[3]

Now Patton had on a full head of steam, so much so that he failed to see the trap he was walking straight into when one of the correspondents asked, "Isn't this Nazi thing really just like a Republican-Democratic election fight? The 'outs' calling the 'ins' Nazis?"

Patton never even hesitated. "Yes," he answered promptly, "that's about it. . . . It's just as if the Democrats in power at home threw out every Republican who held any kind of civic job or vice versa," he added, trying to explain his position on denazification and getting ever deeper into the mess he was making for himself. "Nothing would run."[4]

We do not know General Gay's reaction as Patton uttered those fatal words, but we do know that afterward he was supposed to have groaned that Patton had just "given them your head on a platter."[5]

Naturally the journalist—or some of them at least—had a field day. Raymond Daniell filed the scoop immediately with *The New York Times*, and it was taken up by many more Stateside papers roughly under the same provocative headline: "AMERICAN GENERAL SAYS NAZIS ARE JUST LIKE REPUBLICANS AND DEMOCRATS!"

Later Daniell regretted that he had filed the story. In a letter to Fred Ayer, Patton's nephew, he wrote: "While the story I wrote was fully justified, I would feel happier today about the whole incident if I had made a report to General [Walter Bedell] Smith on my observations in Bavaria instead of writing the story for my newspaper. In justification, however, I would say that my mission there was to report the facts as I saw them and not to serve as an unofficial detective for General Eisenhower's Headquarters."[6]

But that was later. Now the fat was in the fire. Patton had just insulted a holy institution—the American two-party system. This time nothing could save him. The storm was about to break over him.

Diplomat Robert Murphy was there when that fateful call came. He had just eaten with Patton, and now the two of them sat smoking while a Polish artist painted the general's portrait. Although Patton knew that a storm was raging in the States over his statement and that this time he would not escape so lightly as he had done before, he remained unbowed, defiant, even truculent, as if he were challenging Eisenhower to do anything to him. Murphy, who was playing this game with his cards held tightly to his chest, made no mention of the fact that Eisenhower had virtually made up his mind what to do with Patton.

Suddenly the group was interrupted by Patton's WAC secretary. It was Bedell Smith calling from Frankfurt. There was no love lost between Eisenhower's chief-of-staff and Patton. Patton thought Smith a coward and the latter thought Patton hotheaded. Now Patton indicated the extension telephone and whispered, "Listen to what the lying SOB will say!"

The "lying SOB" had very little to say, save that Patton was to fly to Frankfurt immediately to meet Eisenhower. If Patton knew why he had been summoned to Eisenhower's headquarters so surprisingly, he did not show it, but kept up his contemptuous attitude toward Bedell Smith, who he once called an "SOB of the first type, selfish, dishonest, and very swell-headed," declaring that "I could not eat at the same table with General Bedell Smith!"[7]

Due to bad weather, Patton could not fly to Frankfurt after all. Instead he drove the three hundred-odd miles in six hours, arriving at the IG Farben Building late in the afternoon. It was clear, in spite of his attitude to Smith on the phone, that he was well aware that this was one of the most solemn and important meetings of his military career. For instead of his usual resplendent custom-made uniform, he wore a plain "Ike jacket," GI trousers instead of the off-white cavalry breeches, and his pistols were conspicuously absent.

For two long hours Eisenhower and Patton were closeted together in the former's office. What went on in there is not known in its totality. One eyewitness states that at one stage, Eisenhower shouted at Patton in exasperation, "What in the devil is the American Army doing in Germany, if not to denazify the German government and administration? The Russians killed their Nazis; the Americans put them in office!"[8]

Patton emerged from Eisenhower's office pale and shaken, his face set and bitter. After all he had done for Eisenhower in the campaign, the Supreme Commander had now taken his beloved Third Army from him. Forthwith he was to hand over to Gen. Lucian Truscott, who had been a mere divisional commander back in 1942 when he, Patton, had been commanding an army. Then he was to take over something named grandly the Fifteenth Army, which, in essence, was a "paper army," concerned with demobilizing German POWs and writing up the history of the recent campaign. After a quarter of a century, Eisenhower, whom he had "gotten out of the hole" after the debacle at the Kasserine Pass* and in the Bulge, had dropped him. He was finished.

On the long journey back to Bad Tölz, Merle-Smith thought his boss was "very calm and very humble," but "I am sure that he was very sad and felt that his lifelong career was over." Afterward, Patton and his aide had dinner together, when suddenly he turned to the younger officer and blurted out, "And now what is there left for me to do? I've obeyed orders and done my best. And now there's nothing left. I think that I'd like to resign from the Army so that I could go home and say what I have to say."[9]

Merle-Smith thought it was typical of Patton that he would

*See C. Whiting. *Kasserine*, Stein and Day, for further details.

ask a much junior officer for his reaction. But he advocated that Patton should stay in the Army. "To resign would be an admission of error."[10]

Patton agreed—for a while . . .

Naturally, in America, where there has always been a great belief in the "conspiracy," in some quarters it was believed that Patton had been trapped at that fatal press interview into saying what he did say; that it was a left-wing plot to oust Patton on account of his anti-Russian views. Right-wing journalist George E. Sokolsky wrote in an editorial in a Cincinnati paper, for example, that "I have been making inquiries, and the story I get is that some newspapermen and left-wing government agents have been laying for George Patton because they do not like him. These left-wingers know that the general has a strong temper, which the Germans found troublesome on the field of battle, and therefore they needled him into outbursts of wrath at them, which, when generalized and repeated out of context, got him into trouble. . . . A tricky reporter can, like a shyster lawyer, cross up an amateur whose business is not asking or answering question. . . . Now, according to the account which was given to me, a number of persons were present at this interview [that of September 22] and some of them discussed Patton before and after it and much of the conversation is recorded in a form which makes ugly reading."[11] Sokolsky concluded with a demand that "I should like to see the heads of the three American news agencies, the Associated Press, the International News Service, and the United Press, investigate this situation thoroughly and make a public report concerning it."[12]

Another journalist, John O'Donnell of the *New York Daily News*, also took up Patton's cause, but he was the kind of ally that the dismissed general could have well done without. "Behind the successful drive to disgrade and remove General George S. Patton," he wrote, "is the secret and astoundingly effective might of this republic's foreign born political leaders—such as Justice of the Supreme Court Felix Frankfurter, of Vienna, White House administrative assistant Dave ("Devious Dave") Niles, alias Neyhus, and the Latvian ex-rabbinical student now known as Sidney Hillman."[13]

According to O'Donnell, Patton had been dismissed at the

urging of Henry Morgenthau, Jr., the Secretary of the Trea-
sury, because he had "used the word 'Jew' in reprimanding
the reluctant warrior" during the 1943 slapping incident in
Sicily. The New York journalist rehashed the whole story,
implying that one of the soldiers slapped was Jewish and
claiming that "the racial issue in the story [had been] suppressed."[14]

It is clear from Patton's private conversations that by 1945
he was sickened by the behavior of the Jews he had met in
the refugee camps; nor was he greatly pleased by the large
number of German Jews who returned to the country of their
birth in the guise of U.S. officers attached to the military
government. By the time September arrived, he was describ-
ing the Jews as "lower than animals."[15]

But he certainly did not subscribe to the kind of racist
nonsense spun by people like O'Donnell that his dismissal
was the result of a "Jewish plot" against him. Hastily he
denied that he had "ever made any statement contrary to the
Jewish or any other faith," emphasizing that he had "never
interferred with or even examined into the religious or racial
antecedents of the men he had the honor to command."[16]

It was statement that one can accept as true. Whatever he
thought about blacks, he was the only senior commander to
ask for them to serve under him at the front—this at a time
when Eisenhower was still calling his colored servants "darkies." Nor did his anti-Semitism in any way stop the promotion of commanders of Jewish faith such as Gen. Maurice
Rose of the 3rd Armored Division, the son of a rabbi, or Col.
Creighton Abrams of the 4th Armored Division, who went
on later to become a four-star general in Vietnam. Indeed
two of Patton's greatest apologists and biographers were both
Jewish.

But on the whole the tone of the American press was set
by the editorial in *The New York Times* entitled "Patton, the
Soldier," which stated, "Perhaps he [Patton] himself will
share the sense of relief his countrymen feel at so safe and
quiet a transfer. He was obviously in a part which he was
unfitted by temperament, training and experience to fill. It
was a mistake to suppose a free-swinging fighter could acquire overnight the capacities of a wise administrator. His
removal by General Eisenhower was an acknowledgment of

that mistake. . . . For all his showmanship he was a scientific soldier, a thorough military student. . . . He reaped no laurels from the peace, but those he won in war will remain green for a long time."[17]

For his part, Patton kept silent as the time came for him to hand over his Third Army to Lucian Truscott. He had to; Eisenhower had specifically ordered him to keep his mouth shut, unless he, Eisenhower, gave him permission to speak publicly to the press, or anyone else for that matter.

To his wife he wrote: "All that I regret is that I have again worried you. I have been helping Lucian to get the hang on the show and he feels rather depressed. I don't blame him."[18] However, old warrior to the bitter end, he maintained that "My head is bloody, but unbowed!"[19]

But a little later his true bitterness at what had been done to him came through. In one of his darker moments, he wrote in his diary "The more I see of people the more I regret that I survived the war."[20]

Twenty-three

Sunday, October 7, 1945, dawned wet and overcast. Soon, it was forecast, there would be further heavy rain in the Bad Tölz area. Hastily the officers responsible for the handing-over ceremony decided to transfer the location from the parade ground to the big gym of the SS, where once those half-naked blond giants had carried out their exercises.

As was his custom on Sundays, General Patton attended a religious service that morning in the onion-roofed church. Whenever it had been possible throughout the campaign in France, Germany, Belgium, and finally Czechoslovakia the general had worshiped formally on Sunday, even at the height of the Battle of the Bulge. A year ago this Sunday he had gone to church in the little Lorraine township of Etain, with the guns thundering in the distance and his troops bogged down before Metz twenty miles away, unable to crack the stubborn defenders, some of them commanded by those same young SS officers who had once learned their handiwork here at Bad Tölz. Now they were dead on the field of battle and he was alive, just hanging on until he died of old age—*in bed*!

Now Patton entered the gym to say his last farewell to that Third Army that he led to victory, "or rather," as he put it himself, "that group of soldiers, mostly recruits, who re-joiced in that historic name."[1] Ever since his dismissal, those who knew him well had expected histrionics or some outburst of rage against a system that had treated him so shabbily. There was none. As Col. George Fisher, who was there, remembers, "Nothing in his dress or bearing reflected the torture of his soul as he stepped forward to hand over the symbol of his command."[2]

When Patton spoke, as his aide Merle-Smith observed, "he

was soft-spoken and carried the thing off with great dignity."[3]

"General Truscott," he commenced, "officers and men. All good things must come to an end. The best thing that has ever come to me thus far is the honor and privilege of having commanded the Third Army. The great successes we have achieved together have been due primarily to the fighting heart of America, but without the coordinating and supply activities of the General and Special Staffs, even American valor would have been impotent. You officers and men here represent the fighting, the administrative, and supply elements of this Army. Please accept my heartfelt congratulations on your valor and devotion to duty, and my fervent gratitude for your unwavering loyalty. When I said that all things come to an end, I was referring to myself and not to you because you will find in General Truscott every characteristic which will inspire in you the same loyalty and devotion which you have so generously afforded me. A man of General Truscott's achievements needs no introduction. His deeds speak for themselves. I know that you will not fail him. Goodbye and God bless you!"[4]

Patton broke off and the military then struck up "Auld Lang Syne," while the general stood there, trying to fight back his emotions; for Patton had always been an emotional man, easily given to tears, as well as anger.

Finally that evocative tune ceased and the Color-Bearer marched up carrying the colors of the Third Army, which had first come into existence on November 15, 1918, at Ligny-en-Barrois, France, intended as an army of occupation.* That month, twenty-seven years before, Patton had been in trouble with his superiors too. He had just deserted the hospital where he was recovering from a serious wound in order to get back into action, and his commanding general had not liked his "desertion" from the hospital one bit.

Now, however, Patton took the treasured flag from the bearer and handed it to General Truscott, who had landed under his command in North Africa back in November 1942, saying that he could think of no more worthy recipient. Trus-

---

*The shoulder patch of the Third was a red "O" with a white "A" on a blue background, signifying "Army of Occupation."

cott murmured his thanks and handed the flag back to the bearer. And that was that, save for the formal lunch with speeches.

It wasn't a happy occasion, as Colonel Fisher remembered: "The luncheon that the headquarters mess officer spread out that noon really deserved a better appetite than most of us could muster. All the old corps and division commanders who could be found were there. Their testimonies varied in length but no wise in sincerity. Some thoughts strayed to George Washington and his farewell address at Fraunces Tavern. Chaplain Eugene O'Neill* may have remembered the Last Supper. Along about mid-afternoon, Patton had had enough. He rose, squared his shoulders, and moved resolutely off to his waiting car."[5]

The car took him to the train station where he boarded a train for his new headquarters at Bad Nauheim. Merle-Smith, who was going into "exile" with his boss, recalled afterward that "He was quite grim-faced when we left to board the train and obviously hurt. When we reached our compartment he took the seat by the window and sat smiling and saluting to the crowd on the platform. Finally he turned to me and said, 'Pat, I hope to God this train starts pretty soon, but until it does I'm going to sit smiling out of this window—even if it kills me!' "[6]

Then, with a shudder and a clatter of steel wheels, a hiss of escaping steam, the train finally started. It was over. Patton's career as a fighting soldier was finished at last.

What must he have pondered as the train clattered through the damp, dripping countryside, littered here and there by the rusty red hulks of tanks and abandoned equipment of the recent fighting, each vehicle ringed by a little circle of crosses—the sad reminder of those young lives spent to achieve final victory. Patton had always wanted to die in battle. Now he was condemned to simply grow old.

What thoughts must have flashed through his mind? At this

*This was the celebrated, if harassed, Chaplain O'Neill of the Third Army, who had been awarded the Bronze Star for having created the prayer to God to stop the inclement weather during the critical phase of the Battle of the Bulge.

most bitter moment of his life, did he recall himself as a young man, bringing in the dead Mexicans of Pancho Villa's bodyguard, strapped to the front of his car; he had shot them with his own pistol. Or did his mind's eye see himself as the dashing Major Patton, commanding America's first tank force in action at the village of Chepy in the French Ardennes? Then, all those years after the Armistice when the U.S. Army had been thought of as refuge for fools and work-shys?

Year in, year out, he had plodded through the hundred-and-one picayune, boring tasks that made up the life of a peacetime soldier. He had sweated through morning parades in the harsh sun of Texas; hiked through the blinding, choking dust of Midwest maneuvers; faced the sullen, resentful eyes of two generations of young soldiers whom he had "gigged" for cursing-out a noncom or failing to salute an officer; listened to the same old boring small talk of the officers' club . . .

Did he think of that great day when, at fifty-seven years of age, he had finally received the call to action once more after half a lifetime awaiting it? And then all those glorious, bold campaigns that had followed—Sicily, Brittany, the Bulge, the attack on the Our-Sauer Line, the dash to the Rhine, the surprise crossing at Oppenheim?

We do not know. All we know is that Patton's resentment started to grow as he pondered the "injustice" that he felt had been done to him after all he had done for Eisenhower during the war.

His new command did not place any great burdens upon him—in essence, it consisted of little more than clerks and cooks and historians—so he began to tour, visiting old friends and units, collecting a caseful of medals and honorary citizenships, or as his aide, Merle-Smith, put it "sufficient certificates of honorary citizenship to paper the walls of a room."[7]

In France he became an honorary citizen of Rennes, Avranches, Chartres, and half a dozen other French cities he had liberated. He took an austere and morose lunch with de Gaulle. The dinner the same night with the head of the French Army, General Juin, was dominated by the fears of the two old campaigners that the Russians might soon attack the West.

He visited Sweden where he was received by the king, in shirt-sleeves, who insisted on taking Patton to see his prized roses. Later Patton was reunited with the Swedish Olympic team of 1912 against whom he had competed thirty-three years before. Some time during the well-oiled celebration in an inn outside Stockholm, the old opponents drew their pistols to see just how good their aim was after all those years. According to Merle-Smith, "The General shot a better score than he had posted for record during the games and brought it back to show around just as delighted with himself as a small boy with a silver cup won for bow-and-arrow shooting, at a summer camp. Things like that pleased him a lot, especially under the circumstances that the Swedes at the party had solemnly declared him their blood brother."[8]

But always events cropped up to remind him of his age and downfall and that he was no longer a person of any significance: an old man with white hair commanding a paper army.

On November 1, for example, Patton decided he would visit the enlisted men's club at the ruined city of Mannheim. Together with Merle-Smith, who had now been promoted to lieutenant-colonel, he made his usual loud entry, surrounded by club officials, flustered as always in the presence of a four-star general.

Most of the enlisted men in there drinking canned beer sprang to attention at the sight of Patton, but not all did. One soldier remained seated, his blouse open, beer can in one hand, his feet propped up on another chair.

Patton rounded on him in his celebrated fashion, with some of that old fire that had so often put the fear of God into many a young officer and soldier during the war. "Goddamnit soldier," he barked, "don't you know enough to stand up when your commanding officer comes into the room?"

The young, sloppily dressed soldier remained unmoved. He did not get up from the chair, while the other enlisted men gaped at him in awe. Now the shit was really going to hit the fan! "The joke's on you, General," he said calmly, staring up at a flushed Patton. "I'm not a soldier any more. My discharge papers came through today. . . six hours ago."

Patton frowned and barked, a note of sadness in his voice, "Then, by God, there's no excuse for you at all, since at least you might show some respect for my gray hairs."[9] According to Colonel Merle-Smith, "the ex-soldier of six hours left very quietly."[10]

On November 11, 1945, Patton celebrated his sixtieth birthday. It couldn't have been a happy occasion, just one more reminder that he was old and unwanted, thrown on the military trash heap, waiting to see what Washington wanted to do with him—if anything. Like an actor, he had always been vain and had been frightened of growing old. When crossing the Atlantic for the invasion of North Africa in '42 he had spent much of his time in his cabin, running four hundred steps in place—that at fifty-seven! At fifty-nine he had still kept trim by running along beaches, counting how many times he could chin the bar. Several times he wrote proudly that "I have not lost my girlish figure." Now he was sixty and did not even have Jean Gordon to comfort him. After that last meeting from which she had departed in tears, she had returned to the States. On hearing of Patton's death soon, she would comment, "I think it is better this way for Uncle Georgie. There is no place for him anymore."

There was no place for Jean Gordon either. Two weeks after Patton's death, she would commit suicide in New York.[11]

And his resentment mounted. Now that there was some talk of sending him back to the States to take over the command of an army there, he began to consider resigning. Somewhere at the beginning of December he told General Gay, who had stayed on loyally as his chief-of-staff, though there was as little for him to do as there was for Patton, "I have given this a great deal of thought. I am going to quit outright, not retire. That's the only way I can be free to live my own way of life. That's the only way I can and will live from now on. For the years that are left to me I am determined to be free to live as I want to live and to say what I want to say. This has occupied my mind almost completely the last two months and I am fully convinced that this is the only *honorable* and proper course to take."

Gay was alarmed with Patton's decision. He felt that there was more to it than just resigning. He was going to attempt to make a scandal, airing his views on Eisenhower and his policy, in general, vis-à-vis the Russians and the Germans.

He urged Patton "not to be hasty. Don't do anything you might regret later." He advised Patton to discuss the matter with the people closest to him. "Talk it over with your wife," he said. "You owe that to her. Also with Fred Ayer [his nephew]. . . . There are others you ought to talk this over with. These people are part of your life and you don't want to make a decision as momentous as this and which will affect them as it will you, without discussing it with them."

"I haven't the slightest doubt that Beatrice and Fred will see it just as I do," Patton replied confidently, "and agree fully with my decision."[12]

Now Patton became increasingly tense and nervous. Often he paced his office and took long drives by himself. At dinner he was not his usual talkative self, taking pleasure in being the center of conversation. Oftentimes he would eat his food and retire to his own quarters early. He started to smoke many more of the big cigars he favored, though he had been warned by his doctor against excessive smoking. As one of his staff observed, "It was obvious that he was undergoing deep and gnawing turmoil."[13]

Early that December he told Gay that he was going to spend Christmas with Beatrice at their home at Hamilton near Boston. "Admiral Hewitt has invited me to the U.S. on his flagship the *Augusta*," he said. "I'll fly to London on Monday and join him there. When I get home I am going through with my plan to resign from the Army."[14] So Patton would return for good to the States the way he had gone to war in what now seemed another age; for it was on Admiral H. K. Hewitt's *Augusta* that he had sailed for North Africa in 1942.

"When I get home," Patton continued, "I am going to make a statement that will be remembered a long time. If it doesn't make the headlines, I will be surprised. I am determined to be free to live my own way of life and I'm going to make that *unforgettably* clear!"[15]

Gay guessed what Patton intended. Patton wasn't really a vindictive man, but Gay knew that his boss felt his honor had been sullied. He knew, too, that Patton thought he was going to disappear from the scene a broken, forgotten man, while Eisenhower, who had been the cause of his downfall, was going to be, not only the U.S. Army's Chief-of-Staff but also probably the President of the United States. During the war, Gay knew, Patton had once stated that, "If Ike, etcetera, don't like what I do, they can relieve me. Then I will resign, *not* retire, and I can tell the world a few truths which will be worth saying."[16]

As a retired general, Patton would still be bound by the Army's code of conduct; he would not be able to say what he felt. But if he resigned, completely severing his connections with the U.S. Army, then things would be different. He could tell the press exactly what he knew and felt about Eisenhower; and Patton knew a great deal that could be extremely harmful to Eisenhower's hopes of one day becoming President.

Gay decided to change the subject. Suddenly he said, striving to be nonchalant, "You haven't done any hunting for quite a while. How about going out tomorrow? They tell me the countryside is overrun with pheasants.* With the men away during the war, the birds have become very plentiful. You could stand a little relaxation before you take off for home."

Gay saw the general was becoming interested and continued hastily, "I'll have the car pick us up early in the morning, and I know exactly where to go for some good shooting. It will do us both a lot of good to tramp around outdoors for a couple of hours. And you can try out that new gun you got a while back. You can see whether it's as good as claimed. It certainly is a beauty and seemed to handle well."

Now Patton really perked up. "You've got something there, Hap," he said. "Doing a little bird-shooting would be good. You're right. I haven't been out much of late and before I leave I ought to see how good that gun is and whether my hunting eye is as sharp as it used to be.

"Yes, let's do it. You arrange to have the car and guns on hand early tomorrow and we'll see how many birds we can bag."[17]

---

*One of the minor mysteries surrounding Patton's subsequent accident is the question of the "pheasants." I chanced to work in that part of Germany for two years after the war, and I never saw a single pheasant in the area; nor did I encounter anyone who had.

So the die was cast that December 8, 1945. Patton would never resign ''with a reverberating blast of indignation.''[18] The next time Patton would hit the main headlines of the Stateside press would be when they reported his death—*in bed*!

Twenty-four

☆

The hunting party set off early on the morning of Sunday December 9, driving along the Frankfurt-Speyer Highway. In front was Patton's big black Cadillac 75 Special, driven by twenty-year-old Pfc Horace L. Woodring, who had been with Patton for four months now. Behind, in a jeep, Sgt. Joe Spruce brought Patton's hunting dog.

For the first stretch of their journey, Patton sat next to Woodring, with General Gay in the rear, the two of them chatting through the opened glass panel that separated the driving seat from the other compartment.

It was a cold, frosty day, and here and there the barren fields were patched with snow. There was more snow, too, when they climbed up into the hills to visit a Roman settlement close to a medieval German village. Patton had always been interested in antiquity ever since he had first read Homer as a seven-year-old boy. Indeed, when he had visited Trier on that great day when his Third Army had captured it, he had astonished his staff by quoting from Caesar.

After the visit to the Roman ruins, Patton got in the back of the car with Gay to his left as military protocol requires (the senior officer always sits on the right), and they drove on toward Mannheim. There they were stopped on the outskirts by American MPs for a check. During this time, Patton had the hunting dog brought to him in the Cadillac so that it wouldn't be too cold for the chase, and Sergeant Spruce took up the lead, driving at a careful thirty miles an hour.

In front now, Sergeant Spruce suddenly spotted a big GMC truck coming up on the other side of the road at about fifteen miles an hour, apparently slowing down as it approached a driveway on the left-hand side.

Behind, in the Cadillac, Patton was apparently quite care-free, chatting easily with Gay, gaze flashing back and forth as he surveyed that lunar, war-shattered landscape. Now it was 11:48 A.M. They were driving through a canyon of wrecked vehicles, piled high on both sides of the road. Patton pointed to the right and said suddenly, "How awful war is! Look at all those derelict vehicles, Hap!" Then he turned in the other direction and cried, "And look at that heap of rubbish!"

Automatically, Woodring, the driver, also looked to the right, taking his eyes off the road in front momentarily.

Just then the driver of the oncoming GMC truck, a T/5 Robert Thompson, who was alone in his cab, signaled that he was about to turn left. He steered the big vehicle at a ninety-degree angle across the road, making for the entrance to his Quartermaster Corps outfit.

Woodring swung his gaze to his front once more. Too late! It seemed he was going to smash into the truck. He hit the brakes and swerved in the same instant. Thompson in the truck did the same. Next moment the Cadillac smashed into the truck's gasoline tank and there was a rending of metal and a splintering of glass as the Cadillac's headlights went. But as the drivers shook their heads and presumably sensed that sinking feeling that always comes after an accident, it seemed to them that it had only been a very minor affair. Gay, Woodring, and Thompson were all uninjured, if a little shaken.

It was different with Patton. Riding on the right-hand side of the back seat, he had been thrown forward and in the very next instant had been jerked backward sharply, to fall limply into Gay's arms, with his head hanging to the left.

Now, as Gay recovered, he saw to his horror that the boss was bleeding profusely from cuts on his forehead and scalp, but that he was fully conscious. Indeed Patton was the first to speak after the shock of the impact. "Are you hurt?" he asked his companion.

"Not a bit, Sir," Gay answered. "Are you, General?"

"I think I'm paralyzed," Patton said. "I'm having trouble in breathing. Work my fingers for me, Hap!"

Frantically Gay tried to move them several times until Patton said again, not realizing seemingly what the other general was doing, "Go ahead, Hap, work my fingers."

Gay knew now that which Patton feared was true; he *was*

paralyzed. So he said simply, "I don't think it's advisable to move you, General."[1]

By now a unit of 8081st Military Police Company, under the command of Lt. Peter Babalas, had arrived on the scene. They took charge immediately. Patton was driven at top speed on the fifteen kilometer stretch of *autobahn* that linked Mannheim with Heidelberg.

Heidelberg had remained an open town during the '44/'45 campaign, as the Germans had used it as a hospital town. In a cavalry barracks there they had set up a small auxiliary hospital just before the end of the war, which had been taken over by the Americans after Heidelberg had been captured in April 1945. Now this hospital—the 130th Station Hospital—was to become the most-known military hospital in the world; for it was here that Patton was admitted for emergency treatment.

Its commander, Colonel Ball, and the chief surgeon, Colonel Hill, had already been alerted and were waiting in the entrance when Patton was brought in. To them it was obvious that he was in shock, but his mind was quite clear. "My neck hurts," was all that Patton said as he was rushed off to surgery.

Now, while Patton was being examined, the wheels started to roll. Patton's old friend General Keyes, who now commanded the U.S. Seventh Army to whose area Heidelberg belonged,* informed the Supreme Command in Frankfurt's IG Farben Building. Headquarters immediately dispatched General Kenner, once Patton's chief surgeon, now Theater Surgeon, to Heidelberg to take charge. Meanwhile from London, Brigadier Hugh Cairns, a famed professor of neurosurgery at Oxford, was flown in to make the first diagnosis.

He viewed the first, hurried X-ray pictures gravely and then helped to prepare the first medical bulletin. It was not very cheerful. It read: "Fracture simple, third cervical vertebra, with posterior dislocation of fourth cervical. Complete paralysis below level of third cervical. Condition critical, prognosis guarded."[2]

---

*Patton regarded Keyes highly. Once, as a corps commander in Italy, he was given a leave, but instead of heading home or to the fleshpots, he came to visit Patton at the front. Patton respected that.

In layman's language, the medical terminology meant that Patton had broken his neck. Now he was paralyzed from the neck downward. After surviving a whole range of accidents in this last year of the war—from the air attack by the Polish Spitfire to a near miss when his sedan almost rammed a German ox cart in the last week of April—Patton had finally done it, with disastrous and, possibly, fatal results . . .

Naturally the rumors started almost immediately. Fred Ayer, his nephew, was back in the States preparing for Christmas when he heard the bad news. Herbert Machon, the family chauffeur and general handyman, walked into the camp where the three generations of the Ayer family would celebrate, in his snowshoes. Fred Ayer could "tell from his expression that he brought bad news."

"Mr. Ayer," the handyman said, "the War Department just called your house to say that General Patton has been badly hurt in an automobile accident and that he may not live."

Ayer's reaction was predictable. As so often in America, Fred Ayer's mind flashed to the conspiracy theory. As he wrote himself later, "My immediate reaction, other than grief, was to blurt out: 'Accident hell! It was murder. Those Communist sons of bitches have killed him!'"[3]

"I know there were many others who felt that Patton had been murdered," he wrote further. "There are some who still do. From all I have since learned I am convinced that they are wrong. There was, however, in the timing, if that be a proper word, a cruel irony. The date of the accident was December 9, 1945. All arrangements had already been made for the General to leave for England and thence for the United States for a Christmas leave. The date scheduled for his departure from Germany was—the next day, December 10!"[4]

Indeed that "cruel irony" of Patton's suffering this grave accident just *one* day before he was scheduled to return to the U.S.A., where he might well resign and cause some sort of sensation by a public announcement, fueled the speculation that it had not been an accident, but an attempted assassination. *But by whom?*

There was, for instance, the current investigation in Germany of what appears to have been the greatest robbery in history. Back in June 1945, Patton's Third Army had its next windfall after the discovery of the Merkers mine in the previous April. It was another huge haul from the German *Reichsbank*, totaling one and a half million dollars (today worth over ten million).

Gay reported the find to Patton who said, "Okay Hap, gimme the sta-goddamn-tistics. How much is this hoard worth all told?"

Gay told Patton what he thought.

"Does the press know about this?" Patton asked.

"No, Sir."

"How many people do?" Patton then asked.

"Well, Sir," said Gay, "Major Allgeier is cognizant, of course, as is Lieutenant Murphy and Captain Biederprum* and—"

"Don't ackack," Patton barked. "You esti-goddamn-mate, General Gay! *How many people know about this fuckin' hoard?*"

A harassed Gay answered, "I'd say a hundred, maybe more."

"You mean the entire Third Army!" Patton snorted. "That's about a hundred too many, Hap. Tell Milliken [Divisional Finance Officer] to pack up this fucking find, all of it, and order Peter Conway to send it to Frankfurt right away. I want the padre to go along to pray all the way that it gets there safely, and Colonel Cheever [Divisional Judge Advocate] should also go to see to it that the receipt we get is legal."

As Gay turned to leave, Patton had another thought.

"And hear this, Hap, I want those civilian bastards handed over to the Criminal Investigation Department, and see to it, Hap, that an investigation is started to find out what happened to the rest of this hoard. I don't want anybody ever to say that sonuvabitch Patton had stolen any part of it."

Later Patton grinned and said about the money that it "was Peanuts, Hap. A million bucks won't buy thirty seconds of war on the black market."[5]

But the missing money had not been "peanuts." It was part of a great hoard, worth about $5 billion by today's val-

*The officers who found the hoard.

ues, which disappeared that summer from Bavaria. Patton's order to Gay to have an investigation launched started an inquiry that would last four years. In turn, the American CID, CIC, CCD, FBI, Inspector General's Department, Public Safety Branch, Military Government Special Branch, and the Theater Provost Marshal all made their own investigations. To no avail. The hoard was never found and forty-odd years later it is listed in the *Guinness Book of World Records* thus: "The greatest robbery on record was that of the German national gold reserves in Bavaria by a combine of U.S. Military Personnel and German civilians in June 1945."[6]

Had these unknown American officers, who knew just how relentless Patton could be when he was angered, anything to do with the accident? There were some at the time who thought so. But, of course, the connection between Patton's threat to spill the beans (and of course he knew a lot) when he returned home and resigned and the accident is the most obvious one.

Back on May 10, 1945, Eisenhower had summoned his victorious generals together for the last time. They were Simpson, Hodges, Patch, and Patton. (Bradley was on leave.) After a celebratory dinner, Eisenhower explained that what he was going to say now was very confidential. Some of them, he said, might well be called before congressional committees in due course. Now, he said, there was an urgent need for continued postwar solidarity, and then, without any form of explanation, he snapped, "Let's agree on the right form of organization."[7]

Patton had realized immediately what Eisenhower had meant, even if the other generals present did not. Eisenhower wanted a cover-up. He wanted them to back him up if there ever was any serious criticism of the strategic blunders he had made during the campaign. His reputation must not be maligned in the postwar era. This was the start of the great "laundering" of anything that might lower Eisenhower's prestige or reflect on his private life.

For example, the key pre-Battle of the Bulge Intelligence summaries, which might have shown just how complacent Eisenhower had been just before his Army was attacked by a quarter of a million German troops, simply vanished.* Patton's own more personal papers went into the vaults of the Patton family and have never been seen since. Captain Butcher, Eisenhower's personal aide, did manage to publish his celebrated *Three Years With Eisenhower*, despite Eisenhower's anger, but the book left a lot out. Even so, Eisenhower had to write scores of letters of apology afterward. Kay Summersby, his *chauffeuse*, wrote her account of life at Eisenhower's side—*Eisenhower Was My Boss*. But it took her another *thirty* years before she dared write the true details of her affair with the Supreme Commander.

Yes, Patton knew a lot about the private and public life of the presidential hopeful. But it is unthinkable that Eisenhower would stoop to having Patton "removed" before he could talk. But the rumors persisted and still persist, just as they do about General Sikorski, the Pole, who was allegedly murdered by Churchill's killers at Gibraltar in 1943; or those that circulate about the attempted murder of de Gaulle by the Western Allies in 1944 because he was getting just too troublesome.

Writing twenty-five years later, Patton's former chief-of-combat, intelligence, Colonel Allen, mentions that he decided to tell his own story of that December because he was "impelled" by "a recent rumor that there was something sinister about Patton's accident."[8]

Fred Ayer, an FBI man, maintains about these rumors, however: "Logic as well as investigative findings dictate that this must have been an accident. One does not hit a car carrying the intended victim of assassination with a truck at low speed and from an angle. Nor does one normally choose a second vehicle as a murder weapon. It is uncertain, and it may be the murderer who is killed, not his target. Also, I was told that the driver of the truck in question felt such deep remorse that he later attempted to commit suicide."[9] Ayer concluded, "No, however tragic, it was not murder; it was fate, one of the fates in which George Patton had always believed had touched him with her bony hand."[10]

*Sir Kenneth Strong, Eisenhower's Chief-of-Intelligence, told the author he had not known of the disappearance of these key documents until twenty-five years later.

But the rumors have persisted, and writing in 1971, Colonel Allen wondered "just where, how and why the rumor got started is as baffling as the tale itself. Inquiries about the source invariably bring vague and ambiguous answers. But there is no ironic relation between the fatal accident and Patton's secret decision to throw up his commission by drastically resigning. . . . General Patton was definitely marked for inactivation in a few months."

Still the rumors persist.*

*One thought is that they were spread later to discredit Eisenhower as a potential candidate for presidency, just as there were rumors that his political opponents tried to buy Kay Summersby's secrets from her.

Twenty-five

As soon as Mrs. Patton heard the news of her husband's accident, she decided to fly to Heidelberg to be near him. Meanwhile the Patton family actually stopped the New Haven train between stations and "virtually kidnapped" the Army neurosurgeon Col. Geoffrey Spurling, who was considered the best doctor for Patton. Together the neurosurgeon and Mrs. Patton flew from Washington in an Army C-34 of the old bucket-seat type.

Meanwhile, in Heidelberg, Patton's doctors issued another bulletin. It stated that the general's condition was still regarded as critical, but the dislocation of the vetebrae was responding satisfactorily to extension. Patton had spent a restful night, sleeping some five hours.

Patton in his awake moments was his usual tough self. When Army nurse Lieutenant Bertha Hohle came into his room to give him a sip of water from a glass tube, he barked in mock irritation, "I won't drink the damned stuff unless it's whiskey!"[1]

On that same day, the Catholic chaplain of the hospital came in to see the sick man. After he had finished reading the ritual for the sick to Patton, he said, "Incidentally, General, your own chaplain has just arrived and will soon be in to see you."

Patton in his somewhat dazed condition thought the Catholic priest was referring to his old Third Army chaplain, the much harassed Colonel O'Neill. "Well," he quipped, "send him in and let him get to work."[2]

With his old-fashioned, simplistic attitude, Patton thought if you managed to get the right prayer, God would come up with the appropriate miracle. Hadn't it worked back in December 1944 when he had summoned O'Neill to his headquarters during the Battle of the Bulge and offered him the

Bronze Star if he could compose a prayer to God to stop the terrible weather that was hampering his counterattack? But this time the hotline to God was dead. Still, as his nephew Fred Ayer wrote later: "Uncle George now called on all his great strength and for the last time. Even with most of his lung capacity paralyzed, he fought back. . . . Both surgeons told my father . . . that in the light of his injuries any man with a less furious will to live would probably have died within the first two or three days."[3]

Mrs. Patton arrived on December 11 and was given a room in the hospital down the corridor from Patton's sick quarters. She went to see him immediately. She found him resting quietly and taking nourishment. His condition had indeed slightly improved, and he was quite cheerful, telling the woman he had often feared more than the Germans, "I am afraid, Bea, this may be the last time we see each other."[4]

In fact, it was now beginning to be thought that Patton would live. He seemed to be getting stronger, and his faithful aide, Colonel Merle-Smith, found him quite cheerful at times, though as Fred Ayer writes, "I doubt that he could have realized that even were he to live, it would be at best as a half-paralyzed man in a wheelchair."[5] That would have been a terrible fate for a man of Patton's vital temperament and pride in his physical prowess.

By the thirteenth Patton's condition had improved so much that his doctors began to think it might be possible to fly him home to the States. Mrs. Patton, in particular, liked the idea, thinking that this would aid her sick husband's recovery, though they thought also that the general would be paralyzed for life now.

Patton himself, apparently, was not so optimistic. In the course of a conversation with his brother-in-law, who had accompanied Mrs. Patton to Heidelberg, he did groan, "This is a hell of a way for a soldier to die!"[6]

On the afternoon of December 19, Patton's doctors issued a statement that the patient was making "very satisfactory progress." One year before, on Tuesday, December 19, 1944, Patton had been the supremely confident star of that famed Verdun conference, where a gloomy, highly nervous Eisenhower had revealed to his generals the full extent of the Bulge debacle. That morning in the freezingly cold conference room of the *Caserne Maginot*, dominated by those barren hills where the greatest battle in history had been fought in 1916, he had turned to Patton and said, "George, I want you to go to Luxembourg and take charge of the battle, making a strong counterattack with at least six divisions. When can you start?"

"As soon as you are through with me," Patton had answered in his usual brash manner.

According to General Strong, "there was some laughter around the table, especially from the British officers present."[7] To them it had seemed a typical Patton reaction, rash and unrealistic. To achieve his aim, Patton would have to swing his Third Army around in a ninety-degree turn, and this would mean moving 133,178 motor vehicles over 1.6 million road miles in the worst winter Europe had experienced in a quarter of a century!

"When can you start?" Eisenhower had persisted.

"The morning of December 22," Patton had answered.

According to Colonel Codman, the reaction to that bold assurance had been "electric." "There was a stir, a shuffling of feet, as those present straightened up in their chairs. In some faces skepticism. But through the room the current of excitement leaped like a flame."[8]

Yes, that had been a great day, with Patton the center of attraction; with Patton bringing hope and renewed belief in success as he had confidently assured Bradley, "Brad, this time the Kraut has stuck his head in a meat grinder . . . *and this time I've got hold of the handle!*"[9]

That had been the year before. Now all that Eisenhower and Bradley were prepared to do for the man who had pulled the chestnuts out of the fire for them in that dark December was to send him a cable. "Bradley has just reminded me," Eisenhower cabled, "that when we three met in Verdun to consider plans, you and your army were given vital missions. Nothing could stop you, including storms, cold, snow-blocked roads and a savagely fighting enemy. We want you to know that in your present battle we are supremely confident that your spirit will again bring victory."[10]

That message was about all that Eisenhower and Bradley contributed to the welfare of the ailing general who had done so much for them during the last campaign. Indeed, Bradley would subsequently state: "It may be a harsh thing to say, but I believe it was better for George Patton and his professional reputation that he died when he did. The war was won; there were no more wars left for him to fight. He was not a good peacetime soldier; he would not have found a happy place in the postwar Army. He would have gone into retirement, hungering for the old limelight, beyond doubt indiscreetly sounding off on any subject any time, any place. In time he probably would have become a boring parody of himself—a decrepit, bitter, pitiful figure, unwittingly debasing the legend.''[11]

At 2 P.M. on the morning of December 20, Patton had an acute attack of breathlessness. His color vanished as the frightening attack went on for about an hour. Now things began to go wrong. His symptoms convinced Colonel Spurling that Patton had suffered a pulmonary embolism. In other words, a blood clot had become loose in his circulatory system and had been carried by the blood stream into his heart. There it had virtually destroyed one lung. As Colonel Spurling explained, ''When a man is older, in bed and paralyzed, he is likely to get such clot in a vein of his leg or arm. It is always a great hazard in the illness of older people.''[12]

As Patton's biographer Ladislas Farago wrote: ''It was strange to think and speak of Patton as an *old* man.''[13]

He recovered reasonably well from the first shock, but then the symptoms of the embolism multiplied. He had already suffered from two embolisms before, in 1937, from which he had naturally recovered, but this time Patton wasn't going to be so lucky. He had about spent that ''gold'' luck that the British General Frederick Allenby had once told him before the war, one only had so much of.

He filled up with mucus. It became ever more difficult for him to expectorate it. His lungs became wetter and wetter. Feverishly his doctors worked to halt the progressive decline. Now Patton was fighting his final battle—the battle for his own survival.

All this time while his lungs continued to let him down, in the manner of old sick people, Patton remained fully conscious. Never once did he lapse into a coma. He kept on talking the whole while in a hoarse, throaty whisper. He could still exchange jokes with Capt. William Duane, a young doctor attending him, and Lt. Margery Rondell, a nurse who kept a constant vigil at his bedside, as he fought to live. And all the while he attempted to reassure his tearful wife, Beatrice.

At two o'clock in the afternoon of December 21, 1945, he fell asleep, and his wife felt she could safely leave her husband's bedside for a while. One hour later Colonel Spurling looked in on him. He was awake and cheerful. He told Spurling that he was feeling better and was more comfortable. Then he lapsed into sleep once more. Spurling saw that he was breathing more heavily, but otherwise there was no sign that Patton was fighting his last battle, for now the long struggle was nearing its end . . .

What thoughts went through his mind that day? Did he recall that hectic December 21 of the previous year when his tanks had rumbled through to Luxembourg heading for the front, its citizens, who expected the thrusting Germans at any moment, crying wildly, *"Patton. . . . Patton Patton . . . !"*

On that day he seemed to be the busiest man in the whole of the Third Army. He had visited every one of his corps and divisional commanders, warning them either to rush into the new battle or face being relieved. All the time he mingled with his soldiers—one pearl-handled revolver strapped outside his coat, the other stuck in his waist—laughing, wisecracking, his usual ebullient, profane self. He was everywhere that snowy December day, dashing from place to place in his jeep, without escort.

Once he had been held up in a traffic jam and his driver, Sergeant Mims, had turned to him and said, "General, the government is wasting a lot of money, hiring a whole general staff. You and me are running the whole Third Army—and doing a better job than they do!"[14]

That night after supper, Patton had announced to Codman, "Be ready for an early start tomorrow. We attack with Third Corps at six."[15]

As supper time approached on *this* December 21, Patton appeared to be sleeping peacefully, but as Lieutenant Rondell looked in on him, suspecting that something had gone wrong, she sensed that her patient was losing this last battle. Hurriedly she called Captain Duane, who ran down the corridor at once to summon Beatrice Patton.

But it was already too late. Even as she reached her husband's bedside he was dead. He had died at ten minutes to six of acute heart failure. Another embolism had struck his left lung and finished him. George S. Patton, who in his time had sent so many young men to their deaths in battle, had died in bed.

Next morning the newspaper headlines read: "GENERAL PATTON DIES QUIETLY IN HIS SLEEP."

Twenty-six

Up to the end of 1945 no American soldier who had been killed in the war had been shipped back to the United States. Now Mrs. Patton, to whom her husband's last words had been "It's too dark . . . I mean too late,"[1] was placed in a quandary. Should an exception be made for General Patton? Then she remembered Patton's words to his children that last night in Washington just before he had returned to Germany for the last time. "I don't know how it is going to happen, but I'm going to die over there. Promise me one thing, let me be buried over there. In God's name don't bring my body home!"

So she decided, in the end, to respect her husband's wishes. But where? Germany he certainly had not freed. France he had, and there were American military cemeteries, some from World War I, all over Northern France, testifying to how much American blood had been shed liberating her. The trouble was that the dead man had hated the "frogs"—with certain exceptions, of course.

Once during his period as governor of Bavaria he had said cynically: "We are turning over to the French several hundred thousand Prisoners of War to be used as slave labor in France. It is amusing to recall that we fought the Revolution in defense of the rights of man and the Civil War to abolish slavery, and have now gone back on both principles."[2]

So France was out of the question. Belgium, too, for although his Third Army had fought in that country during the Battle of the Bulge, its dead had not been buried there, and Patton wished to buried among his own men. In the end Mrs. Patton picked on the tiny country of Luxembourg for her husband's last resting place. It was a fortunate choice. In October 1944, Patton had restored Prince Felix to the throne of that small principality. (It was so tiny that the prince almost couldn't find it and when he did, he complained to Cod-

man, who accompanied him, that the Germans had *not* looted
his palace's furniture, which was very ponderous.)

Luxembourg would take the dead general to its heart. Not
only had he liberated their country in 1944, but he had freed
a large part of it for a second time in January 1945. "Patton
Day" would be an annual event, marked by a public holiday
and official ceremonies. Stamps would be issued to honor
Patton and everywhere throughout that tiny state, with its half
a million population and which can be traversed in an hour
from end to end, there are plaques and signs announcing that
le gènèral Patton slept, fought, or ate there.

For two days Patton lay in state in the *Villa Reiner*, one of
those big white nineteenth-century villas built by rich Hei-
delbergers about the time of Patton's birth five thousand odd
miles away. A seemingly endless procession of ordinary soldiers filed by solemnly to pay their last respects to the great
soldier, who would now never go home like they soon would.
Then, on the evening of the twenty-third, the train set off
from Heidelberg station bearing his body for burial in Hamm
just outside Luxembourg City.

En route through what was the French Zone of Occupation, the solemn train stopped at a score of stations to be
greeted by flower-bearing French guards of honor and bare-
headed Germans paying tribute to their conqueror. At every
stop Mrs. Patton, in deepest black, got out of the train to say
a few words of thanks, while above somewhere in the clouds,
Patton's former Corps Commander Walton Walker, who
hadn't too many years to live himself and would also die as
the result of an automobile accident, followed the train's
progress, unable to land. He had paid for the flight to attend
the funeral of his old boss out of his own pocket.

He, alone, of Patton's old Third Army Corps Commanders
attended the ceremony. Neither Eisenhower nor Bradley attended. Years later when he was President he also forgot to
honor his old comrade—and indeed no American President,
not even President Reagan who was only fifty miles away
from Luxembourg City during his controversial visit to Bitburg in May 1985, has ever honored Patton's grave. The only
senior statesman ever to do so was Winston Churchill, who
laid a wreath on it during a visit to the principality in 1946.

It was four o'clock on the morning of Monday, December

24 when Patton's train arrived at the *Gare de Luxembourg*, directly opposite the Hotel Alpha, where Bradley had had his headquarters for most of that last campaign in Germany. On Christmas Eve one year before, when the Battle of the Bulge had been at its height, Patton had deliberately attended the evening service at the Protestant church in the center of the city, occupying the pew formerly reserved for the kaiser on his official visits to the capital.* It had been a deliberate morale-boosting exercise for the local civilians; for that evening the Germans were only ten miles away. Grimly Patton had stuck it out during the German-spoken service in the freezingly cold, unheated church** in order to calm the excited, nervous civilians, who would soon be subjected to German shelling.

His own mood was glum, too. On the first day of his counterattack toward Bastogne, where the 101st Airborne was surrounded, he had lost three thousand men in dead alone, the Third Army's greatest bloodletting on a single day so far.

That same evening, every one of his hard-pressed Third Army men had received a miniature Christmas card from him, bearing his good wishes on the one side and Chaplain O'Neill's celebrated prayer to God "to restrain these immoderate rains with which we have had to contend" (snow, really) on the other, which had won for him the Bronze Star.

Now they were bringing that bold dashing commander of Christmas Eve 1944 back to Luxembourg once more—to be buried.

The coffin of some silver metal construction was virtually covered with the Stars and Stripes and ringed by flowers as two motionless Third Army men took up the deathwatch; while outside thousands of Luxembourgers who remembered what Patton had done for their little country waited silently in the freezing pre-dawn cold.

At nine o'clock precisely the ceremony commenced. The guard of honor from the Third Army led the procession out

---

*Luxembourg was nominally under Prussian control till 1866.
**Both French and German are spoken in Luxembourg, but the real language of the people is ''letzeburgisch,'' a difficult German dialect with French undertones.

of the station, as other Allied formations presented arms and
the Luxembourg military band played the *"Sonnerie aux
Morts"* with great pomp and solemnity. Patton would have
loved it.

Behind the coffin came Mrs. Patton on the arm of Patton's
old friend General Keyes, followed by a whole clutch of generals, including Truscott, who had succeeded Patton in command of the Third Army, and Eisenhower's "eyes and ears"
General Everett Hughes, that tall, cynical, saturnine man who
knew all about Patton's secret love life. Once Patton had confessed to him in an oddly old-fashioned way about Jean Gordon that "She has been mine for twelve years." One wonders
what he must have been thinking of at that particularly poi-
gnant moment as he emerged into the big square echoing to
the solemn funereal music.

Then the band began to play the American national anthem
and the convoy, led by MP outriders on motorbikes, set off
for Hamm, which was in the hills that lay beyond the tiny
capital. Immediately behind the gun carriage bearing Patton's
coffin came his intimates from his last campaign, Walker,
Gay, and the like, plus Prince Felix of Luxembourg, Generals
Koenig and de Lattre de Tassigny from France, plus a whole
host of Allied generals. Italy, the country against which Patton had fought for over a year before it had changed sides
and become a "co-belligerent," had even sent a full general
to represent it.

After a slow procession through the city, watched by thousands of locals, the little convoy finally reached Hamm Cemetery, where six thousand of Patton's men were buried. Now
the coffin was borne through the gates, followed by Patton's
horse, its saddle and harness covered in black as military
ritual prescribed. Slowly it was carried to where a small,
open tent had been erected, due to the inclement weather,
over the waiting hole. Next to it was the grave of a simple
private soldier, Pfc. John Hrzywarn of Detroit.

Chaplain Carter commenced the little service, and Patton
was sent on his way with the Psalm that David had sung in
the wilderness of Judah: "Oh God, thou art my God; early
will I seek thee; my soul thirsteth for thee, my flesh longeth
for thee in a dry and thirsty land, so I have seen thee in the
sanctuary."

As Patton's biographer Ladislas Farago writes: "It was Patton's own favorite Psalm, devout as well as defiant."[3]

"My soul followeth hard after thee," it went on, "but those that seek my soul to destroy it, shall go into the lower parts of the earth. They shall fall by the sword; they shall be a portion of foxes. But the king shall rejoice in God; every one that sweareth by him shall glory; but the mouth of them that speak lies shall be stopped."

Now it was the turn of Master Sergeant William George Meeks, the tall, dignified, elderly black who had served Patton as an orderly for years and who knew as much about Patton's private life as anyone, though his knowledge has never been recorded. In those days, black soldiers' memories were not noted, and Meeks is long dead. He had landed with Patton back in 1942 when all of Patton's personal gear had been lost overboard from USS *Augusta*, save his precious pistols, which Meeks had. "It was a close shave," Patton had yelled up to him from the landing craft, "the pistols I mean. I hope you have a spare toothbrush with you I can use to clean my foul mouth?"[4]

Now that "foul mouth" was silenced forever, and Meeks was as moved by that sad fact as any one of the top white brass present. As the flag was removed from the coffin and Beatrice Patton stepped forward to place a bouquet of red roses on the lid, Meeks received the flag and waited for the last act.

As the final sad note of "Taps" died away and the Luxembourg Bishop Philippe stepped forward to recite *"De profundis,"* Meeks, his face taut with emotion, tears in his eyes, saluted stiffly and handed the flag to Mrs. Patton for safekeeping. Long-suffering grass widow that she had been these last years, Mrs. Patton would do exactly that, and when in 1953 she, too, died, it was rumored that her ashes were secretly buried in that same grave.

It was all over. Patton was gone, the simple wooden cross* that marked his grave no different from the ordinary dog-

---

*Three years later it was changed to a stone cross, and because of the large number of visitors to it, the grave was moved to the front of Hamm Cemetery, where it remains today, a stone's throw from Luxembourg's International Airport.

faces of his beloved Third Army surrounding it, save for one thing—it bore the four stars of a full general.

On the morrow, the newspapers back in the States would be full of glowing tributes to the "dead hero." He would be compared with Gen. Philip Sheridan. "Patton died as he had lived—bravely," his doctor would be quoted as saying. His flamboyant, swashbuckling act would be lauded over and over again. Veterans of his Third Army from corps commander to humble soldier would be cited. Bombast, sentimentality, and hyperbole would reign. The dead man would have loved it!

Yet Patton himself might well have preferred as his epitaph that piece of doggerel he had written back in the twenties, with his memories of World War I in mind,* which began:

> Dickey, we've trained and fit and died
> Yes, drilled and drunk and bled,
> And shared our chuck and our bunks in life
> Why part us now we're dead.

and ended:

> Fact is, we need no flowers and flags
> For each peasant will tell his son,
> "Them graves on the hill is the graves of Yanks,
> Who died to lick the Hun."
>
> And instead of comin' every spring
> To squeeze a languid tear
> A friendly people's loving care
> Will guard us all the year.

*"*Dead Pals.*"

Twenty-seven

On the morning after Patton's burial that newspaper that had often criticized the general in the past and that, indeed, had indirectly brought about his dismissal from the Third Army, *The New York Times*, published a moving tribute to the dead man. Its lead writer wrote: "History has reached out and embraced General George Patton. His place is secure. He will be ranked in the forefront of America's great military leaders. . . .

"Long before the war ended Patton was a legend. Spectacular, swaggering, pistol-packing, deeply religious and violently profane, easily moved to anger because underneath all his mannered irascibility he had a kind heart, he was a strange mixture, a combination of fire and ice. Hot in battle and ruthless, too, he was icy in his inflexibility of purpose. He was no mere hell-for-leather take commander but a profound and thoughtful military student.

"He has been compared with Jeb Stuart, Nathan Bedford, Forrest and Phil Sheridan, but he fought his battles in a bigger field than any of them. He was not a man of peace. Perhaps he would have preferred to die at the height of his fame, when his men, whom he loved, were following him with devotion. His nation will accord his memory a full measure of that devotion."[1] Fulsome praise indeed from a newspaper that had sometimes taken an anti-Patton stance, probably occasioned by the fact that the war was only recently over and that Patton was still "news."

But as the years began to pass and America turned to other matters, "Patton the legend" started to be forgotten. World War II began to recede into the past, overshadowed and overtaken by new wars and new "heroes." By the time the "swinging Sixties" arrived, who remembered Patton, save portly, middle-aged gentlemen, who when they had drunk too much drink at their local Legion post, boasted they had "fought with Patton"? "Patton the legend" had been relegated to the military history textbooks and boring lectures at West Point on a war that had little significance in the age of the nuclear bomb.

Of course, there had been a few attempts to keep Patton's memory alive, biographies written mostly by amateur writers, with titles such as *Patton: Fighting Man* or others by professionals bearing titles like *General Patton: General in Spurs* or *Patton and His Pistols!* Most of them were exercises in hagiography. For example, general Semmes's effusive characterization of his old comrade (they had been together in World War I) as "the symbol of America . . . great soldier, great sportsman, great friend whose life has ushered in a new day in the affairs of man."[2]

Or else authors attempted to cash in on the more flamboyant side of Patton's character, turning him into that swashbuckling "Ol' Blood and Guts" who roared through Europe in 1944/45 at the head of his all-conquering, unstoppable armored divisions. They were the kind of books read only by old men living in the past and callow teenagers with spots, desperate for some reflected glory.

But at the beginning of that decade of brotherly love and the Beatles, a relative unknown writer chanced upon a certain Joseph Daniel Rosevich—"a distinguished member of the New York City school system," as he called him. Rosevich had not only been Patton's confidential clerk, but he had also kept the general's diaries which Patton had dictated to him almost daily. The writer knew he had made a find! Together with Rosevich, he set to work to research and write a book that would revive the flagging Patton legend dramatically.* The writer was one of those remarkable Hungarians, born at the end of the Austrian monarchy, who seemed able to land on their feet anywhere, effortlessly changing from one language to another, at home anywhere and nowhere: people such as the film magnate Alexander Korda, writer Arthur Koestler, or nuclear scientist Edward Teller, or a host of mi-

---

*Afterward, when these Patton papers were shown to the Patton family, they were so embarrassed that they were locked away and have not been seen again since.

nor artists who left an impoverished Hungary in the mid-twenties to seek their fame and fortune elsewhere.

His name was Ladislas Farago, who first went to Germany, as so many of them did, and then because he was Jewish and the threat of Nazism loomed even larger, moved to England. There, now writing in his third language, English, he became a freelance journalist and finally foreign correspondent for a liberal newspaper, the *Sunday Chronicle*.

When war came, Farago, not one to hide his light under a bushel, claimed special knowledge of the German Army. This took him to Washington and naval intelligence, where he played a role in the development of psychological warfare against the Japanese.

Out of his wartime experiences came his first book on codes and naval intelligence and the start of yet a new career. Farago, soon to become an American citizen, now launched himself as a writer on World War II. By the time he had met Mr. Rosevich, "that distinguished member of the New York City school system," his career had not flourished too well; for World War II had become something of a dead subject.

Now, however, Farago, a man of great imagination (later Mr. Farago would claim to have met Martin Bormann, the Führer's "Gray Eminence," in the heart of the Bolivian jungle some thirty years *after* he had died in Berlin) and sound business sense, realized that he had chanced upon the greatest subject of his writing career. Patton's life story had everything—color, dash, drama, tragedy, and triumph. Indeed, he would subtitle the book, *Patton*, when it finally appeared in 1964, *Ordeal and Triumph*.

In his acknowledgments, Mr. Farago admitted that "He [Patton] was no dreamer of vast human schemes. His aspirations did not extend to the betterment of mankind. . . . If Patton had never lived, the world would not have missed him."[3]

But, according to Farago, Patton was "a complex and justly controversial figure," who survived in "the popular mind, in particular . . . as a great captain of war."[4]

Farago concluded that "it is not easy to draw the portrait of such a man—a mercurial being, haphazard in his thoughts and impulsive in his acts—unless he is written up in a heroic poem. This I never intended to do. Though I realized that, even with my best endeavor, I would be able only to hold a candle to the sun, I set myself the task of developing the Patton story by examining the legend with critical eyes and scrutinizing the man's life with clinical detachment."[5]

The "clinical detachment" with which Farago approached his subject is somewhat suspect, for the portrait of Patton that emerged in his book is more than distorted. After dealing with the first fifty-odd years of his subject's life remarkably swiftly, the author began to treat Patton's war years. Here, immediately, he revealed one of the main themes of his book, a supposed great rivalry and mutual hatred between Patton and the "little fart," Montgomery.

After a first brush in 1942 in North Africa between the two "prima donnas," the rivalry developed apace in the Allied invasion of Sicily. According to Farago, "After the frustrations of Tunisia, Patton was looking forward to the Sicilian campaign, as if it were a championship bout. He was perfectly certain in his own mind that even though he might not destroy Montgomery's image or show him up as something of a fraud, he would establish himself in Monty's league by beating the champ."[6]

Two years later, in January 1945, Farago has Patton threatening to resign if he is placed again under Montgomery's command. "Patton had received word from the United States that 'some Englishmen' were lobbying in Washington to get high-level American support for Montgomery's aspirations (to take over all ground troops in N.W. Europe after the Battle of the Bulge). He immediately went to Bradley and related this prize piece of information to him and was pleased to hear from Bradley that he 'would feel obliged to ask for relief rather than submit Twelfth Army Group to Montgomery's command.' Patton clasped Bradley by the arm and said solemnly, 'If you quit, Brad, I'll be quitting with you.' "[7]

Montgomery, for his part, seems to have been totally unaware of this great rivalry between himself and Patton or the latter's supposed obsession with his actions. In his personal diary he never even *mentions* Patton after July 28, 1943. Indeed, during that Sicilian campaign, where according to Farago, there was a great race between Patton and Montgomery to capture Messina on the far tip of the island first, Montgomery's only concern vis-à-vis his "rival" was to ensure the notorious "slapping incident" didn't come out into the open.

According to the British army newspaper editor, Warwick Charlton, the only time that he was ever rebuked by Montgomery in the long campaign from Alamein to Messina was when he had written an editorial about Patton. "Then this story started coming through from the correspondents—they used to come into the office—about slapping, a lot of rumours. So I talked to people who knew and I published a thing about a report that Patton was being investigated.

"And I got one of only two raps from Monty—that he was very upset—that he didn't think this was right, that Patton was a good man and although it was true that there was this report, that I should have checked back, because he had his responsibilities and it reflected badly on him."[8]

As for the "race for Messina," which Farago details, then it must have been a very one-sided affair; for as Brigadier Williams, Montgomery's chief-of-intelligence acknowledges, "There was old Patton . . . cracking away and occasionally had to be halted to make room for Eighth Army to go through the door—he [Patton] really got his whips out and made a monkey out of us, I reckon . . . had got the campaign sewn up while we were still, you know, clearing our throats. Monty, I think, was left standing by Patton's speed."[9]

Freddie de Guingand, Montgomery's chief-of-staff, an officer who had no reason to be loyal to his old chief,* was more succinct. According to him there was neither race nor rivalry as far as Montgomery was concerned. "No, none. It was all balls that, about who was going to get to Messina first. We were *delighted* when we heard that Patton had got to Messina first—and about that fictitious scene in the film *Patton*—absolute cock. . . . Monty marching at the head of the Highlanders—*all balls*!"[10]

A second major theme in Farago's work was the fact that, in his opinion, Patton felt he was being kept "under wraps" for most of his fighting career in Europe. Both the Supreme Commander, Eisenhower, and his more immediate boss,

---

*An ungrateful Montgomery soon got rid of de Guingand after the war and would not even allow his loyal chief-of-staff to attend the Victory Parade.

Bradley, deliberately attempted to stop him carrying out his war-winning strategies. Indeed *after* Patton's death, according to Farago, "General Bradley frequently claims credit for ideas and plans in the war which Patton on his part represented as his brainstorms and designs . . . In a team set-up like a military command, it is usually difficult, if not impossible, to pinpoint just who thought first of what. Yet the fact remains that Patton's plans and ideas are fully documented in his contemporary papers while Bradley's claims to those same thoughts were published later, in 1951* when Patton was no longer around to contest or reclaim them."[11]

But, in essence, apart from Patton's counterattack from the south into the Bulge, Patton's real—and only—strategic talent was for gaining ground—*and headlines*. As Bradley himself wrote, "Without meaning to detract from his extraordinary achievements, Patton's great and dramatic gains, beginning in Sicily and continuing through Brittany and on across the Seine at Mantes, Melun and Troyes had been made against little or no opposition."[12] For instance, up to the Battle of the Bulge, General "Lightning Joe" Collins's single corps of the Hodges's First Army had suffered more casualties than the *whole* of Patton's Third Army, made up of *three* to *four* corps!

Due to Eisenhower's "broad front" strategy, the problem was not keeping Patton "under wraps," but ensuring he was occupied—yet not to such an extent that his Third Army withdrew supplies and men from the main effort, which was usually being carried out by Hodges's First Army. This was nothing to do with the fighting spirit or quality of the Third Army. It was simply that Hodges's First Army was located in a geographical position where it was calculated that the most strategic gains could be made, i.e., across the Rhine, into the industrial Ruhr, and from there possibly on to Berlin itself. Throughout the campaign in Europe and, in particular, in those last battles in Germany, Patton was constantly attempting to turn what was essentially a flanking action—a side show—into a major push; while, on the other hand, Ei-

---

*This is the date of the publication of Bradley's memoir, *A Soldier's Story*.

senhower and Bradley were trying (albeit rather ineffectively) to stop him from doing exactly that.

Farago's third article of faith was that, profane, vulgar, and dynamic as he was, Patton was a man whose troops loved him, "an instinctively decent human being" who was "modest to the point of prudishness in sexual matters and frowned upon illicit relations."[13]

Of course, Farago was wrong. Patton's profanity and vulgarity often shocked and repelled his younger soldiers, who had been brought up in a civilian environment of the day, where "cuss words" were frowned upon and were replaced by euphemisms such as "gosh," "shucks," "shoot," perhaps even—daringly—"frig." Here was a general—of all people—regaling them with such expletives as "cocksucker," "fuck," "shit," and the like. Even tough young officers like Abe Baum had been shocked speechless by Patton's use of profanity the first time he had heard him speak.

Nor were his soldiers such great admirers of their dashing Commander as Farago maintained they were. The fines and the "bull," which had so exasperated young Bill Mauldin, were anathema to them, as was Patton's ruthless treatment of them. In the movie *Patton*, the general was shown as being wildly cheered by his men after he had made his apology for having slapped the soldiers in Sicily. But as Col. Benjamin "Monk" Dickson, who was there, recalled, "When Patton spoke before the 1st Division to apologize for his conduct during the campaign he ended on a great inspirational note. The massed division, however, remained stonily silent. Not a man applauded and the division was dismissed. It faded away in silence to the great embarrassment of its commander and the total chagrin of Patton."[14] The divisional artillery commander commented that although they "respected Patton for his unquestioned battle brilliance . . . they did not like him personally."[15]

As Patton's public relations officer explained to Sergeant Mauldin, just before that celebrated confrontation between the Army Commander and the twenty-one-year-old noncom, "Patton lives in a little world of his own, a sort of medieval world, where officers are knights and soldiers are dumb peasants."[16]

Naturally Farago knew, too, that Patton was anything but "modest to the point of prudishness."

In those years before the war when he had rounded on his wife "you and your money have ruined my career!"[17] and he had felt he could go no further in the Army, he had taken up with what was called in those days "fast company." He had drunk too much and had indulged in casual affairs. Somewhere about this time he had gone off on a horse-buying trip to a ranch with his niece, Jean Gordon, who was roughly the same age as his own daughter. Jean promptly fell in love with her uncle, and we know she became his mistress, wangling her way to Europe in July 1944. (According to family gossip a note was found on her dead body, after she had killed herself by putting her head in a gas oven, reading, "I will be with Uncle Georgie in heaven and have him all to myself before Beatrice arrives."[18])

But there were others during the course of the campaign both before and after the arrival of Jean Gordon. In North Africa there had been a Mary June Cooper, who was not invited to follow Patton to Britain when he was posted there in 1944. In Knutsford, Cheshire, England where he set his Third Army HQ, Patton got to know some of the local ladies—and it was not just tea and sympathy that they were prepared to offer him.

On one occasion, it was recorded, the duty officer at Peover Hall was astonished to see a beaming commanding general escorting a beautiful Englishwoman down the staircase of headquarters to a waiting staff car—*this at two o'clock in the morning*! And, as was noted before, Patton often boasted to his old crony Hughes about his exploits. It was not exactly modesty "to the point of prudishness."

In the end, Patton emerged from Farago's book as the "most colorful and controversial general of the U.S. Army."[19] He had been a general, fated to fight not only the "Krauts" but his own superiors, Eisenhower and Bradley, plus the evil machinations of the British ally, primarily in the shape of Field Marshal Montgomery. Somehow he had triumphed, in spite of the ordeals he had undergone, and had won the war for America. Vulgar and profane he might well have been, at times cruel, but he had been a red-blooded all-American, whose values had harked back to an older and perhaps better America, and whose first loyalty had been to his American heritage.

Naturally, with its subject and the changing political scene in America (now the country was beginning to become seriously involved in Vietnam), the book was a roaring success. It certainly made a name for Farago. But it did something else, too. It revived the Patton legend once more, picking him out of the obscurity into which all his fellow commanders had now disappeared, even Eisenhower, who had, indeed, become President as Patton had once confidently predicted he would.

The legend was rapidly becoming an "American folk hero." But there was something else yet needed before that took place. After all, there were many millions of Americans who would never read Farago's book. The legend needed to be simplified and visualized so that Patton's life could be depicted to those who never opened a book. The time had come for Patton's wartime years—his ordeal and triumph—to be filmed. There was going to be a movie.

For George S. Patton was going to be accorded the honor, which he would share with only one other commander from that glittering array of generals, both Allied and enemy, who led men into battle in World War II. Like Rommel, whose life had been already filmed with James Mason in the leading role, Hollywood was preparing to make a film of his war years.

Twenty-eight

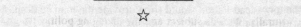

In the same year that Ladislas Farago sold the film rights of his book, five-star General Omar Bradley, a widower now aged seventy-three, surprisingly enough married again. His new bride, Kitty Buhler, a vivacious, twice divorced, forty-four-year-old ash-blonde, had been a Hollywood screenwriter of sorts. Now she encouraged her husband, who was thirty years older than herself, to embark on a grueling two-week visit of the Vietnam battlefront on behalf of *Look* magazine. They came away convinced that Vietnam was "a war at the right place, at the right time and with the right enemy—the Communists."[1]

Now the "GI General," as Ernie Pyle had dubbed him after Capt. Harry Butcher had insisted during the war that the war correspondent must do something to bolster up the retiring commander's public image, started rubbing shoulders with famous movie stars, inviting them to their home in Hollywood. Soon he was hosting at his table people like Bob Hope, Jimmy Stewart, Gregory Peck, and a former actor turned politician—Ronald Reagan. Plain, old, homely Omar Bradley, who as far as we know had not indulged in any amorous liaisons during World War II, as had Eisenhower and Patton, now experienced a kind of rebirth at the side of his pretty, young wife.

Many had thought the general long dead as so many of his contemporaries were. But now with the script of Farago's *Patton* in the planning stage, the movie's producer, Frank McCarthy, who had been one of General Marshall's wartime assistants in Washington, sought the aging general's advice.

But five star generals don't come cheap. Kitty, his wife, persuaded McCarthy to lease Bradley's war memoir, *A Soldier's Story*, as background material for the film and to put Bradley and herself on the payroll as senior advisers. Their contract called for a guaranteed down payment and for a percentage of the movie's profit. Ironically enough, therefore, the long-dead Patton would soon provide the man he despised with a sizable income for the rest of his long life. (Bradley lived to be eighty-eight, dying in 1981.)

The man whom the director, Franklin Schaffner, selected to take the leading role of Patton (old-time actor Karl Malden would play Bradley) looked little like the character he was going to play. George C. Scott had the height, of course, but his face was much heavier, dominated by a huge beak of a nose, and that gravel voice of his no way matched Patton's surprisingly high-pitched one. But Scott did have the presence, the look of brooding authority that Patton had had, and there is no doubt that no other Hollywood actor could have played the role as well as he; though he did confess that he had been unable, in the end, to "get inside" Patton.

Patton: Lust for Glory was a bold attempt to probe in depth and in length—some three hours—Patton's complex character. In spite of a skilled performance by Scott, the man behind the profane, blunt-speaking, blunt-acting general remained elusive. The characterization was not helped by the exaggeration of his rivalry with Montgomery, outrageously characterized by Michael Bates. (One wonders if the field marshal himself ever saw the film.)

Schaffner's control of his material, however, was impressive, and the various campaign scenes and battles were strikingly photographed through an audaciously wide lens. Ironically enough, however, the film's most memorable sequence was Scott's opening speech, a mélange of all Patton's pep talks to his troops going into action for the first time—"no dumb bastard ever won a war by dying for his country," etc., etc.—delivered to the camera against a massive backdrop of the Stars and Stripes.

It was said that when the movie was played to even sophisticated audiences, they rose and clapped and cheered at the end of that long, riveting sequence. The film was a great box-office success and has continued to be shown on television ever since 1970. It turned Patton the legend finally into Patton the folk hero. In the shape of Scott, with his dark scowling face and rasping voice, Patton had now become the essence of America's World War II.

Just like the cowboy hero of the Old West, he had stepped into American mythology. He was a winner, full of spirit and action, ageless (had he lived, he certainly would have become a reactionary anachronism). Now he would live on forever as the symbol of an older, simplistic America, untouched by social change, political doubts, the uncertainties of the seventies and eighties. What would he have made of black mayors, "womens' lib," and all the rest of the socio-sexual baggage of our time? It was said that at the height of the Vietnam War, President Nixon spent hours in front of the movie screen, watching the *Patton* film over and over again!

But was—*is*—Patton the kind of folk hero America needs? He was an autocrat, and his arrogance bordered on contempt. The *real* Patton was no democrat either. Once he boasted he would return to the States after the war either as President— or dictator. One could even conclude that Patton was slightly mad. Neurotics, they say, build castles in the air; paranoics live in them. In those last two years of his life, General Patton seemed to be doing exactly that.

It is now recognized that as a boy Patton suffered from dyslexia. Bright as he was, he couldn't read or write, and he saw the printed page upside down or reversed. The result was a feeling of inadequacy, a limited attention span, and a need to compensate. Throughout his life, thereafter, Patton suffered qualms and doubts, which resulted in shortness of breath, sleeplessness, sweaty palms, intense nervousness— all classic symptoms of a personality disorder.

Accident-prone as he was—he once wrote home he had just suffered his "annual accident"—he seems to have suffered brain damage, which made it difficult for him to stifle his aggression. By the time he had reached his fifties, it appeared, he could no longer control his tendency to flare up into blazing anger.[2]

In 1935 he suffered a severe fall from a polo pony. Thereafter he seemed quite normal until several days later, while out sailing with his wife and children, he asked in sudden surprise, "How in hell did I get here?" He was told he was suffering from concussion. Thereafter, even after only a few drinks, he quickly became very maudlin, sobbing openly as he recited poetry with a slurred voice.

By early 1944, after his near dismissal for the slapping of the soldiers in Sicily, Patton was clearly an emotionally unsettled person. What can only be described as an acute paranoia had appeared. He felt himself completely above the law. He was always unjustly criticized. The press was to blame for everything. Full of self-pity, he wrote to his wife, "One should wear chain mail to avoid the knife thrusts."[3] His moods changed rapidly from euphoria to deepest depression. And his envy of his fellow commanders had become almost pathological. Fearing that they would be promoted before he would be, he literally wished them dead. "I wish something would happen to Clark," he once confided to his diary.[4]

All the time, he felt that "they" were out to stop him, gag him, to deprive him of power and prestige and the applause on which he doted. "They" seemed to include all his fellow American generals, most newspaper correspondents, many of Eisenhower's staff, Congress, the British, the Jews, and so forth. As he wrote to Mrs. Patton, "I have to battle for every yard but it is not the enemy who is trying to stop me, it is 'They.' "[5]

Constantine FitzGibbon, an Anglo-Irish writer, then a captain on Bradley's staff, remembers meeting Patton that summer. It was his job at that time to brief his commander on the enemy's probable intentions. He told Bradley and Patton, who was present at this briefing on the "Falaise Pocket" that, in his opinion, there was no sign of any German withdrawal from the Pocket. As FitzGibbon recalls: "Patton became extremely angry. His outburst, and it stuck in my mind because of the violence of the language, was, when toned down for civilian ears, more or less as follows:

"It's a goddamned lie! I was up there myself this morning, I saw them streaming out. Hell, didn't I kill two thousand of the bastards myself today?"

"Of course, I said nothing. Bradley did not order Patton immediately to strike north and so began 'his' Third Army's spectacular race across an empty France. Three days later the Germans began to pull out of the pocket, thus saving a considerable number of their best combat troops to fight another day."[6]

Some time later FitzGibbon had occasion to meet Patton again, but this was a completely changed Third Army commander. Marshall was visiting France, and there was "more brass about than you could shake a stick at." During his briefing he asked Patton, "General Patton, where is your main railhead?"

"Patton stalled, then got up, went up to the big map of France, began searching about, finally saying in his queer squeaky voice, 'Gee, Sir, it's somewhere just about here, Sir. Always did have trouble with these French names.' [Patton spoke excellent French in reality.] Marshall snorted, 'General Patton, do you or do you not know where you main railhead is?'

"As crestfallen as a housemaid caught with a valuable but not broken teapot in her hand by a strict mistress, Patton replied, 'No, Sir, I don't.'

" 'General Patton,' Marshall snapped acidly, 'you are commanding an American Army overseas. I expect American Army commanders to know the location of their main railhead. You may sit down.' "[7]

Patton sat down.

FitzGibbon commented many years later: "A great many men have been bullied as was I by General Patton. Few can have seen him, apparently cowed and perhaps even frightened by a senior officer."[8] Why this sudden personality change, the lack of moral courage, the dishonesty? Was he just afraid of Marshall? Was it a return of the dyslexia of his youth? We don't know.

By Christmas Eve that year he addressed God in these tones: "Sir, this is Patton talking. The last fourteen days have been straight hell. Rain, snow and more rain, more snow— and I'm beginning to wonder what's going on in Your Headquarters. Whose side are You on, anyway? . . . This, they tell me, is the Crusades all over again except that we're riding tanks instead of chargers. They [his chaplains] insist we are here to annihilate the German Army and the godless Hitler so that religious freedom may return to Europe. Up until now I have gone along with them, for You have given me Your unreserved cooperation. Clear skies and a calm sea in Africa made the landings highly successful and helped us to eliminate Rommel. Sicily was comparatively easy and You supplied excellent weather for our armored dash across France. . . . You have lead German units into traps that made their elimination fairly simple. But now, You've changed horses in midstream. You seem to have given Von Rundstedt every break in the book and frankly, he's beating the hell out of us!''⁹

Patton ended his weird, sacrilegious "prayer" with the demand that God give him "four clear days." "I need these four days to send Von Rundstedt and his godless army to their Valhalla. I am sick of this unnecessary butchery of American youth, and in exchange for four days of fighting weather, I will deliver enough Krauts to keep Your Bookkeepers months behind in their work. AMEN!''¹⁰

By 1945 Patton's values were all hopelessly mixed up. He spoke more and more of the *beauties* of war and the *horrors* of peace. Although he was not noticeably happy on the battlefield (despite the bluster and show, he *was* afraid of shellfire—and after all, he had only spent a couple of days in combat before being wounded in WWI), he now actively sought death. Time and time again he repeated his desire to die in battle—"the last bullet of the last battle." Now he was conducting his operations, such as the Crossing of the Rhine, the Hammelburg Raid, and others, as if the war were being fought for his own personal amusement and advancement. Once he bragged to General H. Arnold of the U.S. Army Air Corps that spring, "Yesterday, guerrillas in a town to my front refused to surrender. So I burnt it down."¹¹ Just like that.

By the end of the war, several of his Third Army intimates had become very worried about him. He seemed increasingly eccentric, emotional, even unstable. Secretly they contacted his old friend and Eisenhower's "eyes and ears," Gen. Everett Hughes and asked if he would come to Bavaria for a few days to divert Patton—they would even send a special plane to Paris for him. On May 11, 1945, Hughes flew to Patton's HQ at Regensburg together with Hughes's current mistress.

Hughes soon learned that Patton had had a scene with Jean Gordon. Perhaps Patton was worrying what would become of her, now that the war was over and Patton was now returning to Beatrice. But that evening, thanks to a huge bottle of champagne provided by a Red Cross girl named Marion Hall, Jean and Patton made up. Later, Patton mystified Hughes by telling him that Jean had handed him "a marked calendar." (Perhaps Jean Gordon was using the old-fashioned Knaus method of days when conception could not take place.) But that was about all that his old friend could get out of Patton. Patton's prime concern seemed simply to be sex—and his prowess as "a cocksman."

The war was over and "now the horrors of peace, pacafism [sic] and unions will have unlimited sway," as he wrote miserably to Mrs. Patton.[12] Now he was seized by fear of the "Mongols" (as he called the Russians). While the rest of the Western world was attempting to pick up the pieces and return to normalcy, he was wishing a new war upon America. His hysteria was fueled by the rapid dismemberment of his Third Army, as soldiers returned to the States for discharge, "while the displaced sons-of-bitches in the various camps are blooming like green trees."[13]

His worries mounted, as he realized there was nowhere for him to go. At nearly sixty, his career was coming to an end—ingloriously. All his contemporaries were being found new jobs. Eisenhower was to become chief-of-staff. Bradley was to take over the Veterans Administration. Clark, whom he hated with a passion, was the American High Commissioner in Austria. Devers, his much despised polo-playing associate, was to take over the Army Field Forces. But there was nothing for him. Nobody seemed to want him.

Again his hysteria rose. He became subject to the delusion that the next war was just around the corner. "I am again in one of those critical periods," he noted. For "the Devil and Moses [have gotten together to plan for an early and certain resumption of hostilities]."[14] His son, George, he wrote to Mrs. Patton, "need not worry about missing a war. The next is on the way." As he saw it. "The noise against me is only the means by which the Jews and Communists are attempting, and with good success, to implement a further dismemberment of Germany."[15] It was the old persecution complex once more. "They" were out to get him again!

In the end, that tragic motoring accident put an end to all the phobias and hysteria. As he quipped to the doctors waiting to receive him at the hospital in Heidelberg: "Relax, gentlemen, I'm in no condition to be a terror now."[16]

He *wasn't*.

American folk hero? I think not. Patton was too complex, too eccentric, too peculiar to fit into that mold. Let us perhaps remember him that day in France, a week after he had started his victorious breakout from the Normandy bridgehead, staring at a "reeking mass of smashed half-tracks, supply trucks, ambulances and blackened German corpses," as Codman described them.

"Encompassing with a sweep of his arm the rubbled farms and bordering fields scarred with grass fires, smoldering ruins and the swollen carcasses of stiff-legged cattle, the General half turned in his seat. 'Just look at that, Codman,' he shouted. 'Could anything be more magnificent?'

"As we passed a clump of bushes, one of our concealed batteries let go with a shattering salvo. The General cupped both hands. I leaned forward to catch his words. 'Compared to war, all other forms of human endeavor shrink to insignificance.' His voice shook with emotion. *'God, how I love it!'* "[17]

Envoi

Today, there is little to be seen of Patton's tumultuous progress through Central Europe in that last year of World War II. There is a plaque commemorating his presence there at his old Luxembourg headquarters in the Pescatore Foundation. But now, where telephones shrilled urgently and self-important staff officers strode back and forth, old men and women wait in numb silence for death. Patton's old HQ has long been an old folks home.

Twenty miles away at Echternacherbruck, where his green, young, black and white soldiers of the U.S. 76th Infantry Division first battled their way across the Sauer River to be surprised by their commander (who they supposed had "swum across"), the shattered houses in the hills still bear traces of that first savage crossing into the "1,000 Year Reich." On the heights, the ruins almost vanished beneath the undergrowth, you can still see the shell holes; and the surviving walls are pocked with bullets and shrapnel like the symptoms of some loathsome skin disease.

Go deeper into those dark-green, remote Eifel forests that stretch virtually to the Rhine itself, and there they are, the rusting traces of their passing, pierced Jerricans, shell cases marked "1945," ration cans that crumble in one's hand, the odd white object that could have been a human bone. Pause in one of those long-abandoned foxhole lines, deep in the forest, and perhaps you might still capture the sounds of those young men of long ago, who are now old or dead these forty-odd years. Is it just imagination, or are those the echoes of their young voices calling out to each other for reassurance, in fear, in their final, pain-racked agony?

Time, progress, and the green earth itself have drawn an almost impenetrable cloak over the scenes of those desperate actions where Patton's young men fought, suffered—and died—four decades ago. So quiet, so innocent are these dark German fir woods, that even the most vivid personal recollections of the murder and mayhem that once took place in them find the mind unwilling to accept the evidence of the map you carry. Could it really have been *here* where that handful of frightened survivors of 5th Infantry Division held out for forty-eight hours; or that terrified "wet-nose" from the 76th Division felt he was "the only Yank in the whole of Germany?"

Germany's cities (how many cities and villages did Patton once boast he had captured—22,000?) have long been rebuilt. Trier, the first great city taken by his Third Army, where he had once amazed his staff by reciting from Caesar, bears no trace of his passing. Those young GIs and airmen from the surrounding American bases who visit the Moselle capital on the weekends have no inkling of how once "Ol' Blood and Guts" sweated out its capture that February; how Colonel Richardson—that "plucky little son-of-a-bitch," who didn't survive the war, risked his life to capture that celebrated bridge across the Moselle. In summer they sit in the pleasant little beer gardens that line the river, drinking the good local beer and ogling the "frowliness," as once their grandfathers had done, unaware of how many of Patton's young men had died in that desperate battle of 1945.

It is no different at the other great German cities that Patton captured. Their shattered ruins have been transformed into the soulless, gleaming architecture of our time, lacking in feeling, lacking in sentiment. Here, among these clinical surroundings, there is no place or time for history. The "hard D-Mark" tolerates no memories!

Nierstein and Oppenheim, where he once ventured across the Rhine and exploded to Bradley, "Brad, tell the world— *we're across*!" are pretty much as they always were: obscure medieval villages, mainly engaged in the production of wine, perched precariously on the edge of the great river. No stone, no plaque, marks Patton's progress here. On into the Franconian countryside, where that tall, rangy, ex-pattern cutter from a Bronx ladies' blouse factory, Abe Baum, had commenced his desperate raid on Hammelburg. There at Schweinheim—"Bazooka Alley," the men of the 4th had called it so long ago—the half-timbered medieval houses are

pockmarked here and there with shellfire and the deeper
gouges made by a *panzerfaust*. Further on, on that winding
country road that Baum took, you can—if you catch the light
at the right angle—see the line of shallow depressions in the
lush, green meadows where a salvo of 75mm fire from Patton's Shermans took the Germans by surprise. And the country inn, where General von Gersdorff narrowly escaped
capture and from whence he warned Hammelburg of the force
coming its way, still stands, hardly changed from what it was
on that March day in 1945.

Hammelburg is once again a German Army camp, alive
with officious, self-important noncoms and red-faced, breath-
less recruits with long hair being chased back and forth. There
is even a museum there, but it is devoted to the glories of the
old German Army. No mention of Patton and his great mistake.

But the old huts that housed Waters and the rest of the
"Kriegies" are there all right—and the old water tower on
which Baum's tankers wasted so much ammunition while their
leader paused, so inexplicably, before rushing the camp. On
one of the old stone buildings there you can still trace the
fading letters in Gothic script, reading *Kommandantura*. It
was here that General von Goeckel organized the defense of
Hammelburg with his "three hundred cripples and congenital
idiots," and put paid to Patton's hopes of rescuing his son-
in-law. Here the train of events was set in motion that paved
the way for Patton's disgrace and downfall.

On and on. Through the last of the great German cities
that he captured, Erlangen, Regensburg, Passau. No sign that
Patton once passed this way. Into that poverty-stricken border
region of Upper Bavaria, where the dirt farmers have been
bypassed by the "economic miracle." Here they still work
barefoot in the fields in the summer and of an evening the
women stand behind their menfolk when they drink their bottle of beer at the kitchen table, happy when they are offered
a sip of the precious liquid.

On and on, a journey that took Patton and his men five
months but that today can be covered in five short hours,
thanks to the modern *autobahn*. But now as you push through
those dark-green forests, where Patton's men once waited for
the green light to commence that drive to "Czechoslovakia

and fraternization,'' you realize that you are on the fringe of another world. For here the signs on the West German side of the border proclaim, *Zonengrenzgebiet* and warn *Achtung, Schiessgefahr!* (''danger of shooting''). The reason for that warning in the midst of this seemingly peaceful countryside is soon clear.

Suddenly—startlingly—there it is, that high, triple-wired fence, with its watchful guards, peering at you through their binoculars, the machine-gun towers, the lethal booby traps. . . . Running through the heart of Germany and down to the Czech frontier for five hundred long miles, that evil monstrosity that separates two worlds, East and West, as it had done now for nearly forty years—*DIE MAUER*! That wall of shame that makes a hollow mockery of all those young men who once sacrificed their lives to achieve freedom in Europe back in 1945. Once Patton's young men had crossed this same frontier to be welcomed with flowers and kisses as ''liberators.'' Today, if their grandsons attempted to do the same, they would be met by bullet and shell.

So, romantic, magnificent anachronism that he was, Patton was perhaps right, after all, when he brooded that last fall of his life about the ''Mongols'' and the new totalitarianism that they had brought with them into Central Europe. Unfortunately for George S. Patton he had been right—*at the wrong time* . . .

Once, back in 1942, after inspecting a bunch of new recruits and mentally comparing them with the tough, keen ''doughboys'' he had commanded in the ''Old War,'' Patton had thrown up his hands in that melodramatic way of his and had exclaimed in apparent disgust, ''We've pampered and confused your youth. . . . Now we've got to try to make them attack and kill! *God help the United States!*''

He need not have feared. For after all, they had not let him down—most of them, at least. They had killed—and had been killed. Now, as he lies there in that lonely, mistenshrouded cemetery above Luxembourg City, surrounded by six thousand of those same young men who paid the supreme sacrifice all those years ago, he can be proud of them. That sea of white crosses, stretching as far as the eye can see, are epitaph enough for George S. Patton.

Appendix

GENERAL PATTON'S PRAYER

Said in the Foundation Pescatore Chapel
in Luxembourg on December 23, 1944

Sir, this is Patton talking. The last fourteen days have been straight hell. Rain, snow, more rain, more snow—and I'm beginning to wonder what's going on in Your headquarters. Whose side are You on, anyway?

For three years my chaplains have been explaining this as a religious war. This, they tell me, is the Crusades all over again except that we're riding tanks instead of chargers. They insist we are here to annihilate the German Army and the godless Hitler so that religious freedom may return to Europe.

Up till now I have gone along with them, for You have given us Your unreserved cooperation. Clear skies and a calm sea in Africa made the landings highly successful and helped us to eliminate Rommel. Sicily was comparatively easy, and You supplied excellent weather for our armored dash across France, the greatest military victory that You have thus far allowed me. You have often given me excellent guidance in difficult command decisions, and You have lead German units into traps that made their elimination fairly simple.

But now, You've changed horses in midstream. You seem to have given Von Rundstedt every break in the book, and, frankly, he's been beating hell out of us. My army is neither trained nor equipped for winter warfare. And as You know, this weather is more suitable for Eskimos than for southern cavalrymen.

But now, Sir, I can't help but feel that I have offended You in some way. That suddenly You have lost all sympathy with our cause. That You are throwing in with Von Rundstedt and his paper-hanging god. You know without me telling You that our situation is desperate. Sure, I can tell my staff that everything is going according to plan, but there's no use telling You that my 101st Airborne is holding out against tremendous odds in Bastogne, and that this continual storm is making it impossible to supply them even from the air. I've sent Hugh Gaffey, one of my ablest generals, with his 4th Armored Division, north toward that all-important road center to relieve the encircled garrison, and he's finding Your weather much more difficult than he is the Krauts.

I don't like to complain unreasonably, but my soldiers from the Meuse to Echternach are suffering the tortures of the damned. Today I visited several hospitals, all full of frostbite cases, and the wounded are dying in the fields because they cannot be brought back for medical care.

But this isn't the worst of the situation. Lack of visibility, continued rains, have completely grounded my air force. My technique of battle calls for close-in fighter-bomber support, and if my planes can't fly, how can I use them as aerial artillery? Not only is this a deplorable situation, but, worse yet, my reconnaissance planes haven't been in the air for fourteen days, and I haven't the faintest idea of what's going on behind the German lines.

Damn it, Sir, I can't fight a shadow. Without Your cooperation from a weather standpoint, I am deprived of an accurate disposition of the German armies, and how in hell can I be intelligent in my attack? All this probably sounds unreasonable to You, but I have lost all patience with Your chaplains who insist that this is a typical Ardennes winter, and that I must have faith.

Faith and patience be damned! You have just got to make up Your mind whose side You're on. You must come to my assistance, so that I may dispatch the entire German Army as a birthday present to Your Prince of Peace.

Sir, I have never been an unreasonable man. I am not going to ask You for the impossible. I do not even insist upon a miracle, for all I request is four days of clear weather.

Give me four clear days so that my planes can fly, so that my fighter-bombers can bomb and strafe, so that my reconnaissance may pick out targets for my magnificent artillery.

Give me four days of sunshine to dry this blasted mud, so that my tanks may roll, so that ammunition and rations may be taken to my hungry, ill-equipped infantry. I need these four days to send Von Rundstedt and his godless army to their Valhalla. I am sick of this unnecessary butchery of American youth, and in exchange for four days of fighting weather, I will deliver You enough Krauts to keep Your Bookkeepers months behind in their work.

Amen

Chapter Notes

PART I: INTO THE REICH

One

1. C. MacDonald. *The Last Offensive*. Washington, D.C.: Office of Chief of Military History, 1973.
2. Edited. *BBC War Report*. London: Collins, 1945.
3. V. Gersdorff. *Soldat im Untergang*. Berlin: Ullstein, 1979.
4. L. Atwell. *Private*. New York: Popular Library, 1958.
5. Ibid.
6. Ibid.
7. J. Giles. *The GI Journal of Sergeant Giles*. Boston: Houghton Mifflin, 1965.
8. Atwell, op. cit.
9. G. Patton. *War As I Knew It*. New York: Pyramid, 1947.
10. Ibid.
11. *Stars and Stripes*. Dec. 19, 1944.
12. Ibid.
13. M. Motley. *The Invisible Soldier*. Detroit: Wayne State University Press, 1977.
14. Letter to author.
15. Letter to author.
16. L. Farago. *Patton*. London: Mayflower, 1969.
17. Ibid.
18. Letter to author.
19. Farago, op. cit.

Two

1. *Esquire* 1944.
2. Farago, op. cit.
3. Ibid.
4. Personal communication to author.

5. D. Irving. *The War Between the Generals*. London: Congdon and Weed, 1983.
6. Ibid.
7. Ibid.
8. Ibid.
9. Personal communication to author.
10. R. Allen. *Lucky Forward*, New York: Manor Book, 1977.
11. Ibid.
12. Ibid.
13. C. Codman. *Drive*. Boston: Little Brown, 1957.
14. Ibid.
15. Allen, op. cit.
16. Farago, op. cit.
17. Ibid.

Three
1. Giles, op. cit.
2. Atwell, op. cit.
3. C. Baker. *Hemingway*. New York: Scribners, 1969.
4. J. Nobusch. *Bis zum bitteren Ende*. Bitburg: Kreis Bitburg, 1982.
5. *History of 76th Division*. Austria, 1945.
6. Patton, op. cit.

Four
1. Patton, op. cit.
2. Allen, op. cit.
3. *History of 76th Div.*, op. cit.
4. Ibid.
5. Ibid.
6. Ibid.
7. Ibid.
8. Patton, op. cit.
9. *Stars and Stripes*, March 1945.
10. C. Whiting, *Sturm zum Rhein*. Trier: Akad. Buchhandel Verlag, 1985.
11. F. Price. *Troy H. Middleton*. Baton Rouge: Louisiana State University Press, 1974.
12. Ibid.

13. Ibid.
14. Allen, op. cit.

Five
1. *History of 76th Div.*, op. cit.
2. Ibid.
3. Giles, op. cit.
4. Ibid.
5. Atwell, op. cit.
6. C. Province. *The Unknown Patton*. New York: Hippocrene Books, 1983.
7. Ibid.
8. Ibid.
9. Ibid.
10. Ibid.
11. Allen, op. cit.
12. Province, op. cit.
13. Allen, op. cit.
14. Ibid.
15. Ibid.
16. Patton, op. cit.
17. *Life*, June 11, 1971.
18. Farago, op. cit.
19. Ibid.
20. Ibid.
21. H. Cole. *The Lorraine Campaign*. Washington, D.C.: Dept. of the Army, 1950.
22. Province, op. cit.
23. Ibid.
24. Codman, op. cit.
25. Ibid.
26. Province, op. cit.

Six
1. H. Trevor-Roper. *The Goebbels Diaries*. London: Secker & Warburg, 1977.
2. Whiting, op. cit.
3. Allen, op. cit.
4. Whiting, op. cit.
5. Ibid.
6. Allen, op. cit.

7. Farago, op. cit.
8. Ayer. *Before the Colors Fade*. Boston: Houghton Mifflin, 1964.
9. Ibid.
10. Ibid.
11. Ibid.
12. Ibid.
13. Ibid.
14. Ibid.
15. Ibid.

PART II: OVER THE RHINE

Seven
1. Personal communication.
2. Allen, op. cit.
3. Personal communication.
4. Ibid.
5. MacDonald. *The Last Offensive*. Washington: Dept. of Defense, 1972.
6. Ibid.
7. Personal communication.
8. Farago, op. cit.
9. *Boston Daily Globe*. March 8, 1945.
10. Whiting, op. cit.
11. Allen, op. cit.
12. Atwell, op. cit.
13. Ibid.
14. Allen, op. cit.
15. Ibid.
16. Ibid.

Eight
1. Allen, op. cit.
2. Ibid.
3. Ibid.
4. Farago, op. cit.
5. Personal communication.
6. Price, op. cit.
7. Atwell, op. cit.
8. Ibid.

9. Personal communication.
10. Ibid.
11. Allen, op. cit.
12. Ibid.
13. Ibid.

Nine
1. Personal communication.
2. Gersdorff, op. cit.
3. Farago, op. cit.
4. A. McKee. *Race for the Rhine Bridges*. London: Souvenir Press, 1971.
5. Price, op. cit.
6. Atwell, op. cit.
7. Ibid.
8. McKee, op. cit.
9. Codman, op. cit.
10. Ibid.
11. Allen, op. cit.
12. Ibid.

Ten
1. Allen, op. cit.
2. Ibid.
3. Ibid.
4. Ibid.
5. Giles, op. cit.
6. McKee, op. cit.
7. Ibid.
8. Farago, op. cit.
9. Ibid.
10. Ibid.
11. Ibid.
12. Ibid.
13. Price, op. cit.

Eleven
1. J. Toland. *The Last One Hundred Days*. New York: Random House, 1966.
2. Ibid.
3. Ibid.

4. C. Whiting. *Bradley.* New York: Ballantine, 1973.
5. *Army Magazine.* June 25, 1965.
6. Farago, op. cit.
7. Personal communication.
8. Toland, op. cit.
9. MacDonald, op. cit.
10. H. Butcher. *Three Years with Eisenhower.* London: Hutchinson, 1946.
11. Personal communication.
12. Ibid.
13. Toland, op. cit.
14. K. Koyen. *The Fourth Armored Division.* Munich: privately printed, 1946.
15. Gersdorff, op. cit.
16. Ibid.
17. Ibid.

Twelve
1. Personal communication.
2. Ibid.
3. Gersdorff, op. cit.
4. Koyen, op. cit.
5. Ibid.
6. Personal communication.
7. Toland, op. cit.
8. Price, op. cit.
9. *Endkampf zwischen Mosel und Inn.* Osnabruck: Munin Verlag, 1976.
10. Whiting. *Bradley*, op. cit.
11. *Time*, October 1945.
12. Personal communication.
13. Price, op. cit.

PART III: THE END RUN

Thirteen

1. Butcher, op. cit.
2. Codman, op. cit.
3. Farago, op. cit.
4. Codman, op. cit.
5. Toland, op. cit.

6. Ibid.
7. Ibid.
8. Farago, op. cit.
9. Butcher, op. cit.
10. Ibid.
11. Ibid.
12. Farago, op. cit.
13. S. Ambrose. *The Supreme Commander.* New York: Doubleday, 1970.
14. Butcher, op. cit.

Fourteen

1. Motley, op. cit.
2. Codman, op. cit.
3. F. Davis. *Across the Rhine.* Alexandria: Time-Life, 1978.
4. Atwell, op. cit.
5. Allen, op. cit.
6. C. Bielenberg. *Als ich noch Deutsche war.* Berlin: Ullstein, 1976.
7. Ibid.
8. Farago, op. cit.
9. Codman, op. cit.
10. Irving, op. cit.
11. Codman, op. cit.
12. Ibid.
13. Irving, op. cit.

Fifteen

1. *Gerichtverfahren gegen Wenzel u.a.* Dusseldorf: 1949.
2. *The New York Times,* March 29, 1945.
3. Personal communication.
4. *Aachener Nachrichten,* April '45.
5. Ibid.
6. Ibid.
7. R. Minott. *The Fortress that Never Was.* London: Longman, 1967.
8. D. Eisenhower. *Crusade in Europe.* New York: Doubleday, 1948.
9. R. Ingersoll. *Top Secret.* London: Collins, 1945.
10. Codman, op. cit.

11. Patton, op. cit.
12. Ibid.
13. Toland, op. cit.

Sixteen
1. *BBC War Report*. London: Collins, 1945.
2. J. Frost. *A Drop too Many.* London: Sphere, 1983.
3. Ibid.
4. Ibid.
5. *BBC War Report*, op. cit.
6. Codman, op. cit.
7. Ibid.
8. Ibid.
9. Ibid.
10. Ibid.
11. Farago, op. cit.
12. Ibid.
13. Province, op. cit.
14. Ibid.
15. Ibid.
16. Toland, op. cit.
17. Ibid.
18. Ibid.
19. Ibid.
20. Patton, op. cit.
21. Ibid.
22. Farago, op. cit.
23. Toland, op. cit.
24. Farago, op. cit.
25. Toland, op. cit.
26. Ibid.
27. Ibid.
28. H. Meyer. *Hitlerjugend Division*. Osnabruck: Munin Verlag, 1985.
29. Ibid.

Seventeen
1. *Der Spiegel*. June 1983.
2. Ibid.
3. Ibid.
4. Ibid.

5. Ibid.
6. Ibid.
7. *History of 76th Div.*, op. cit.
8. Giles, op. cit.
9. MacDonald, op. cit.
10. Ibid.
11. Allen, op. cit.
12. Ibid.
13. Farago, op. cit.
14. Allen, op. cit.
15. Codman, op. cit.
16. Irving, op. cit.
17. Codman, op. cit.
18. Ayer, op. cit.
19. Ibid.
20. Ayer, op. cit.
21. Ibid.
22. Ibid.
23. Irving, op. cit.

Eighteen
1. Ayer, op. cit.
2. Patton, op. cit.
3. Farago, op. cit.
4. Chester Wilmot. *The Struggle for Europe*. London: Collins, 1952.
5. L. Hart. *The Other Side of the Hill*. London: Collins, 1952.
6. Ibid.
7. Ibid.
8. Farago, op. cit.
9. Codman, op. cit.
10. O. Bradley. *A Soldier's Story*. New York: Popular Library, 1964.
11. Hart, op. cit.
12. I Hogg. *Patton*. Greenwich: Bison Books, 1982.
13. Hogg, op. cit.
14. Ibid.
15. Ibid.

Nineteen
1. M. Childs. *Eisenhower: Captive Hero*. New York: Harcourt Brace, 1958.
2. Province, op. cit.
3. Codman, op. cit.
4. Ibid.
5. Ibid.
6. Province, op. cit.
7. Ibid.
8. Farago, op. cit.
9. Ibid.
10. Ibid.
11. Ibid.
12. Ibid.
13. Province, op. cit.
14. R. Murphy. *Diplomat Among Warriors*. New York: Doubleday, 1964.
15. Ibid.
16. Ibid.
17. Farago, op. cit.
18. Murphy, op. cit.
19. *Stars and Stripes*, August 1945.
20. Farago, op. cit.
21. Ibid.
22. Ibid.

PART IV: OCCUPATION

Twenty
1. D. Botting. *In the Ruins of the Reich*. London: Allen & Unwin, 1985.
2. J. McGovern. *Fraulein*. London: Collins, 1957.
3. J. Costello. *Love, Sex and War*. London: Collins, 1985.
4. Ibid.
5. Botting, op. cit.
6. Studs Terkel. *The Good War*. London: Collins, 1985.
7. Botting, op. cit.
8. Ibid.
9. *The Good War*, op. cit.
10. Ibid.
11. G. Kennan. *Memoirs*. London: Collins, 1968.

Twenty-one
1. T. Bower. *Blind Eye to Murder.* London: Deutsch, 1981.
2. Farago, op. cit.
3. J. Gavin. *On to Berlin.* New York: Bantam, 1978.
4. Ibid.
5. Ayer, op. cit.
6. Ibid.
7. *Spiegel*, June 1983.

Twenty-two
1. Ayer, op. cit.
2. Ibid.
3. Ibid.
4. Ibid.
5. Ibid.
6. Ibid.
7. Murphy, op. cit.
8. Bower, op. cit.
9. Ayer, op. cit.
10. Ibid.
11. Province, op. cit.
12. Ibid.
13. Farago, op. cit.
14. Ibid.
15. Irving, op. cit.
16. Farago, op. cit.
17. Ibid.
18. Ayer, op. cit.
19. Ibid.
20. George Forty. *Patton's Third Army at War.* London: Allen, 1978.

Twenty-three
1. Patton, op. cit.
2. Forty, op. cit.
3. Ayer, op. cit.
4. Ibid.
5. Forty, op. cit.
6. Ayer, op. cit.
7. Ibid.
8. Ibid.

9. Ibid.
10. Ibid.
11. Irving, op. cit.
12. R. Allen. *Army Magazine*, June 1971.
13. Ibid.
14. Ibid.
15. Ibid.
16. Ibid.
17. Ibid.
18. Ibid.

Twenty-four
1. Farago, op. cit.
2. Ibid.
3. Ayer, op. cit.
4. Ibid.
5. I. Sayer and D. Botting. *Nazi Gold*. London: Granada, 1984.
6. *Guiness Book of World Records*. New York: Sterling, 1986.
7. Irving, op. cit.
8. *Army Magazine*, op. cit.
9. Ayer, op. cit.
10. Ayer, op. cit.

Twenty-five
1. Farago, op. cit.
2. Ibid.
3. Ayer, op. cit.
4. Ibid.
5. Ibid.
6. Ibid.
7. K. Strong. *Intelligence at the Top*. London: Cassell, 1968.
8. Codman, op. cit.
9. Ibid.
10. Whiting. *Bradley*, op. cit.
11. Ibid.
12. Farago, op. cit.
13. Ibid.

14. Codman, op. cit.
15. Ibid.

Twenty-six
1. Ayer, op. cit.
2. Province, op. cit.
3. Farago, op. cit.
4. Ibid.

Twenty-seven
1. *The New York Times,* December 23, 1945.
2. Farago, op. cit.
3. Ibid.
4. Ibid.
5. Ibid.
6. Ibid.
7. Ibid.
8. N. Hamilton. *Monty.* London: Coronet Books, 1985.
9. Ibid.
10. Ibid.
11. Farago, op. cit.
12. Whiting. *Bradley*, op. cit.
13. Farago, op. cit.
14. Whiting. *Bradley*, op. cit.
15. Ibid.
16. *The New York Times,* December 28, 1985.
17. M. Blumenson. *Patton.* New York: Morrow, 1985.
18. Ibid.
19. Blumenson, op. cit.

Twenty-eight
1. Whiting, op. cit.
2. Blumenson, op. cit.
3. Farago, op. cit.
4. Irving, op. cit.
5. Farago, op. cit.
6. Whiting. *Patton*, op. cit.
7. Ibid.
8. Ibid.
9. ''Patton's Prayer.'' Courtesy M. Milmeister, Luxembourg.

10. Ibid.
11. Irving, op. cit.
12. Whiting, op. cit.
13. Ibid.
14. Ibid.
15. Ibid.
16. Codman, op. cit.
17. Ibid.

Bibliography

Allen, R. *Lucky Forward*. New York: Manor Books, 1977.

Ayer, F. *Before the Colors Fade*. Boston: Houghton Mifflin, 1964.

Blumenson, M. *Patton*. New York: Morrow, 1985.

_____. *Patton Papers*. Boston: Houghton Mifflin, Vol. 1, 1972; Vol. 2, 1974.

Bradley, O. *A General's Life*. New York: Simon and Schuster, 1983.

Essame, H. *Patton: Study in Command*. New York: Scribners, 1974.

Farago, L. *Patton: Ordeal and Triumph*. New York: Obolensky, 1964.

Irving, D. *The War Between the Generals*. New York: Congdon & Weed, 1983.

Patton, G. *War As I Knew It*. New York: Pyramid, 1948.

Whiting, C. *Patton*. New York: Ballantine, 1970.

_____. *Forty-Eight Hours to Hammelburg*. New York: Ballantine, 1972.

Wilmot, C. *The Struggle for Europe*. Westport, Ct.: Greenwood, 1952.

INDEX

TRUE ACCOUNTS OF VIETNAM
from those who returned to tell it all . . .